Management for Professionals

The Springer series *Management for Professionals* comprises high-level business and management books for executives. The authors are experienced business professionals and renowned professors who combine scientific background, best practice, and entrepreneurial vision to provide powerful insights into how to achieve business excellence.

More information about this series at https://link.springer.com/bookseries/10101

Marc Helmold

Performance Excellence in Marketing, Sales and Pricing

Leveraging Change, Lean and Innovation Management

 Springer

Marc Helmold ⓘD
IU, International University of Applied Sciences
Berlin, Germany

ISSN 2192-8096   ISSN 2192-810X   (electronic)
Management for Professionals
ISBN 978-3-031-10096-3   ISBN 978-3-031-10097-0   (eBook)
https://doi.org/10.1007/978-3-031-10097-0

This Springer imprint is published by the registered company Springer Nature Switzerland AG
The registered company address is: Gewerbestrasse 11, 6330 Cham, Switzerland

It takes 20 years to build a reputation and five minutes to ruin it. If you think about that, you'll do things differently.

Warren Buffett

Preface

Megatrends, digitization, the COVID-19 pandemic, new brands and the ongoing globalization has changed the face of many industries. The increasing (especially the digital) interconnection and the unlimited exchange of data and information have led to a maximized transparency of globally offered and sold products and services. This is leading to the question how companies can generate competitive advantages in the long-term. The desires, needs and wants of the consumer are the critical issues today in creating new or offering existing products and services. Companies must therefore develop appropriate marketing, sales and pricing plans to understand and anticipate future customers´ needs.

The book *Performance Excellence in Marketing, Sales and Pricing* is the right answer for applying the appropriate measures and actions in these areas. It outlines successful marketing and sales strategies with a clear focus on practical relevance. Secondly, it is possible to understand the concept, which adds value to products and services from a customer´s point of view. Thus, it will be possible to implement strategies to successfully differentiate the own companies against competitors. Tools like the Marketing Mix or marketing strategies are well explained for practical application in industry. Moreover, the systematic overview and description of *selling, pricing or negotiation concepts* enable the reader to apply the best-case scenario in their company. Each chapter finishes with a case study. Thirdly, the book integrates elements *change, lean or innovation management* as driver for performance excellence. Finally, the book shows how the *marketing, sales and pricing management* will look like in the future.

The book is targeted towards practitioners and academics, who want to apply excellent performance tools in marketing, sales or pricing. The author aims with the book to guide enterprises to performance excellence and the achievement of long-term competitive advantages through best-in-class marketing, sales and pricing activities.

I would like to thank my family and Springer for giving me the chance to publish this book with many USPs.

Berlin, Germany   Marc Helmold
March 2022

Contents

List of Figures

List of Tables

About the Author

Marc Helmold, (MBA) is a professor at IU International University of applied Sciences in Berlin. He teaches in bachelor's, master's and MBA programmes in lean management, procurement, general management, strategic management, leadership and supply chain management.

From 1997 to 2017, he held several posts in top management positions in the automotive and railway industry. Between 1997 and 2010, he worked in several companies like Ford, Ford-Mazda Japan, Porsche and Panasonic Automotive in managerial functions and executed lean workshops throughout the value chain.

From 2013 to 2016, he was the general manager of Alstom Transportation in China and led the sourcing and spare parts marketing and sales activities. He is a professor since 2016 and has his own consultancy. In this capacity, he improves companies' performance.

Acronyms and Abbreviations

A3	Problem-Solving Method
AI	Artificial Intelligence
AM	Additive Manufacturing
AR	Augmented Reality
BDA	Big Data Analysis
BSC	Balanced Score Card
BST	Bombardier Sifang Transportation
BME	Bundesverband Materialwirtschaft, Einkauf und Logistik
BMW	Bayerische Motorenwerke
CRM	Customer Relationship Management
CSR	Corporate Social Responsibility
DSCM	Downstream Supply Chain Management
EDLP	Every Day Low Pricing
ERP	Enterprise Resource Planning
EXW	Ex Works
IMC	Integrated Marketing Concept
IOP	Internet of People
IOT	Internet of Things
IPO	International Procurement Office
ISO	International Standardisation Organisation
IU	International University Bad Honnef
JIT	Just-in-Time
KPI	Key Performance Indicator
LHE	Lean in Higher Education
MBO	Management by Objectives
MPS	Mercedes Benz Production System
OEE	Overall Equipment Effectiveness
OKR	Objectives Key Results
PDCA	Plan, Do, Check, Act
PDSA	Plan, Do, Study, Act
PE	Physical Education
PESTEL	Macro Analysis
PPS	Production Planning System
QR	Quick Response

SCM	Supply Chain Management
SIP	Sales Incentive Plan
SWOT	Strengths, Weaknesses, Opportunities, Threats
TIMWOOD	Seven Types of Waste in Manufacturing
TPS	Toyota Production System
TÜV	Technischer Überwachungsverein
UN	United Nations
USCM	Upstream Supply Chain Management
USP	Unique Selling Propositions
VPS	Volkswagen Production System
VR	Virtual Reality
VW	Volkswagen
3C	3C-Pricing Model: Customers, Competitors, Costs
3M	Muda, Muri, Mura
4P	Marketing Mix: Product, Price, Place, Promotion
7P	Marketing Mix including People, Process, Physical evidence
8P	Marketing Mix including Planet
5R	5 Rights
5S	Seiri, Seiton, Seiso, Seiketsu, Shitsuke
7R	7 Rights

Marketing, Sales and Pricing: Introduction

To me, Marketing is about values.

Steve Jobs

1.1 Definition of Marketing and Sales Management

Marketing is the process of intentionally stimulating demand for and purchases of goods and services; potentially including selection of a target audience; selection of certain attributes or themes to emphasize in advertising; operation of advertising campaigns; attendance at trade shows and public events; design of products and packaging to be more attractive to buyers; selection of the terms of sale, such as price, discounts, warranty and return policy; product placement in media or with people believed to influence the buying habits of others; agreements with retailers, wholesale distributors or resellers; and attempts to create awareness of, loyalty to and positive feelings about a brand (Kotler & Armstrong, 2018). Marketing is typically conducted by the seller, typically a retailer or manufacturer. Sometimes tasks are contracted to a dedicated marketing firm or advertising agency. From a historical point of view, the term marketing denotes the corporate division whose task (function) is to market products and services (offer for sale in such a way that buyers perceive this offer as desirable). From a business point of view, this term has been describing the concept of holistic, market-oriented corporate management to satisfy the needs and expectations of customers and other interest groups (stakeholders) since the beginning of the twenty-first century (Meffert et al., 2008). The understanding of marketing is thus developing from an operational technique for influencing the purchase decision (marketing mix instruments) to a management concept that includes other functions such as procurement, production, administration and personnel. Figure 1.1 shows how marketing, sales, pricing and other aspects are integrated into the value chain as primary function. The marketing function follows the procurement and operations as interface to the customers (Helmold, 2021). Finance, human resources, IT, quality, finance or ethics functions support the value chain processes as secondary

M. Helmold, *Performance Excellence in Marketing, Sales and Pricing*, Management for Professionals, https://doi.org/10.1007/978-3-031-10097-0_1

Fig. 1.1 Concept of marketing, sales and pricing. (Source: Author's source)

function. The corporate management is responsible for the corporate marketing strategy. The corporate strategy, from which the marketing strategy will derive, is a unique plan or framework that is long term in nature, designed with an objective to gain a competitive advantage over other market participants while delivering both on customer, client and stakeholder promises (i.e. shareholder value). Within the appropriate marketing strategy and framework, it is necessary to define the right sales management, the right pricing strategies and the distribution network (Esch et al., 2008). This will be done with innovative tools and processes (Kotler et al., 2017). Sales management is defined as the planning, direction and control of personal selling including recruiting, selecting, equipping, assigning, routing, supervising, paying and motivating as these tasks apply to personal sales force. Sales management specifically contributes to achieve the marketing objectives of a firm. In fact, sales managers set their personal selling objectives and formulate the personal selling policies and strategies (Kotler & Armstrong, 2018).

1.1.1   Early Developments of Marketing

The practice of marketing may have been carried out for millennia, but the modern concept of marketing as a professional practice appears to have emerged the post-industrial corporate world. In addition to the studies of specific cultures or time periods, discussed in the preceding section, some historians of marketing have sought to write more general histories of marketing's evolution in the modern era. A key question that has preoccupied researchers is whether it is possible to identify specific orientations or mindsets that inform key periods in marketing's evolution. Marketers disagree about the way that marketing practice has evolved over time. The study of the history of marketing, as a discipline, is meaningful because t helps to define the baselines upon which change can be recognized and understand how the discipline evolves in response to those changes. The practice of marketing has been known for millennia, but the term "marketing" used to describe commercial activities such as buying and selling products or services came into popular use in the late nineteenth century. The study of the history of marketing as an academic field emerged in the early twentieth century. Marketers tend to distinguish between the history of marketing practice and the history of marketing thought. The history of marketing practice refers to the analysis and investigation into the ways that marketing has been used to define and anticipate needs and demands of customers. The history of marketing has evolved and changed over the past decades and time (Jones & Shaw, 2006). Although the history of marketing thought and the history of marketing practice are distinct fields of study, they intersect at different junctures. Marketing practitioners engage in innovative practices that capture the attention of marketing scholars who codify and disseminate such practices. At the same time, marketing academics often develop new research methods or theories that are subsequently adopted by practitioners. Thus, developments in marketing theory inform marketing practice and vice versa. The history of marketing will remain incomplete if one disassociates academia from practitioners. The publication, in 1960, of Robert J. Keith's article, "The Marketing Revolution", was a pioneering work in the study of the history of marketing practice. In 1976, the publication of Robert Bartel's book, *The History of Marketing Thought*, marked a turning point in the understanding of how marketing theory evolved since it first emerged as a separate discipline around the turn of last century (Keith, 1960).

1.1.2 Needs and Demands as the Trigger for Marketing

Something necessary for people is to live a healthy, stable and safe life. When needs remain unfulfilled, there is a clear adverse outcome: a dysfunction or death. Needs can be objective and physical, such as the need for food, water and shelter, or subjective and psychological, such as the need to belong to a family or social group and the need for self-esteem. Wants are something that is desired, wished for or aspired to. Wants are not essential for basic survival and are often shaped by culture or peer groups. When needs and wants are backed by the ability to pay, they have the potential to become economic demands. Marketing research, conducted for the purpose of new product development or product improvement, is often concerned with identifying the consumer's unmet needs. Customer needs are central to market segmentation which is concerned with dividing markets into distinct groups of buyers on the basis of "distinct needs, characteristics or behaviours which might require separate products or marketing mixes". Needs-based segmentation (also known as benefit segmentation) "places the customers' desires at the forefront of how a company designs and markets products or services". Although needs-based segmentation is difficult to do in practice, it has been proved to be one of the most effective ways to segment a market. In addition, a great deal of advertising and promotion is designed to show how a given product's benefits meet the customer's needs, wants or expectations in a unique way.

1.1.3   Integrated Marketing Concepts (IMC)

Modern marketing concepts integrate marketing, sales and pricing. Integrated marketing communications (IMC) is the use of marketing strategies to optimize the communication of a consistent message of the company's brands to stakeholders. Coupling methods together improves communication as it harnesses the benefits of each channel, which when combined together builds a clearer and vaster impact than if used individually. IMC requires marketers to identify the boundaries around the promotional mix elements and to consider the effectiveness of the campaign's message.

In the mid- to late 1980s, the marketing environment was undergoing profound environmental changes with implications for marketing communications. Media proliferation, audience fragmentation, globalization of markets, the advent of new communications technologies and the widespread use of databases meant that the old methods and practices used in mass marketing were no longer relevant. In particular, the rise of digital and interactive media meant that marketers were relying less on advertising as the dominant form of marketing communications. Amongst practitioners and scholars, there was an increasing recognition that new approaches to marketing communications were required. That new approach would become known as integrated marketing communications. A number of empirical studies, carried out in the early 1990s, found that the new IMC was far from a "short-lived managerial fad", but rather it was a very clear reaction by advertisers and marketers to the changing external environment. Integrated marketing communications is a holistic planning process that focuses on integrating messages across communications disciplines, creative executions, media, timing and stakeholders. An integrated approach has emerged as the dominant approach used by companies to plan and execute their marketing communication programs and has been described as a paradigm shift. IMC unifies and coordinates an organization's marketing communications to promote a consistent brand message. Coordinating a brand's communications makes the brand seem more trustworthy and sound, as it is seen as a "whole" rather than a mixture of different messages being sent out. The IMC perspective looks at the "big picture" in marketing, advertising and promotions. Within the IMC, marketing has developed as depicted in Fig. 1.2.

1.2   Sales Management

Sales management is the planning, direction and control of personal selling including recruiting, selecting, equipping, assigning, routing, supervising, paying and motivating as these tasks apply to the personal sales force. Sales management

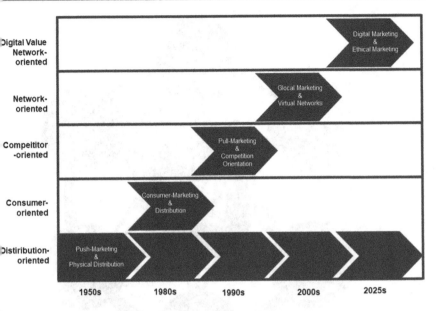

Fig. 1.2. Marketing evolution

focuses on establishing a sales organization and sales processes, which help to ideally coordinate sales operations (Kotler & Armstrong, 2018). Sales management defines appropriate and sustainable sales techniques that allow a company to consistently meet, and even surpass, its sales objectives. Figure 1.3 shows the elements of sales management with the sales organization, sales strategy, sales objectives, sales reporting, sales forecasting, sales execution and controlling.

1.3 Pricing Management

Pricing management determines pricing schemes for a company's products and services. This includes coordinating with production departments to learn how much they cost to make, as well as working with staff in marketing on appropriate campaigns and promotions. Pricing management is the process of integrating all perspectives and information necessary to consistently arrive at optimal pricing decisions (Kraus, 2008). Therefore, strong price management capabilities result in effective management of financial risk and revenue. Pricing concepts and strategies are shown in Fig. 1.4. As companies prepare to roll out new products and services, the pricing management functions have to evaluate pricing opportunities and strategies. Pricing management must set the right policies on pricing in order to achieve its sales targets. These include the base price as well as discounts that may be extended to specific retail partners and dealers (Wilkie & Moore, 2006). The pricing management needs to consider what kind of message the company wants to project with pricing and how the marketing department will handle promotional campaigns.

Fig. 1.3 Sales management elements

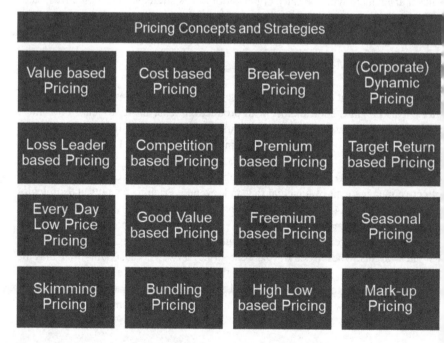

Fig. 1.4 Pricing concepts and strategies. (Source: Author's source)

1.4   Differences Between Marketing and Sales

1.4.1   Introduction to the Differences of Marketing and Sales

Sales and marketing are two business functions within an organization. Both functions impact the strategy of an enterprise and the revenue management. The term, sales, refers to all activities that lead to the selling of goods and services. Also, marketing is the process of getting people interested in the goods and services being sold. Sales is a term used to describe the activities that lead to the selling of goods or services (Düssel, 2006). Salespeople are responsible for managing relationships with potential clients (prospects) and providing a solution for prospects that eventually lead to a sale. Marketing encompasses all activities that help spark interest in your business. Marketers use market research and analysis to understand the interests of potential customers. Marketing departments are responsible for running campaigns to attract people to the business' brand, product or service.

1.4.2   Process of Marketing and Sales

Whether you're writing a marketing or sales plan, both will include details about the history of the company and its overarching goals and initiatives (Tomczak et al., 2018). Then, the plans dive into the aspects of the plan that are specific for each department. The marketing plan lays out what the product is, its price, who it'll be sold to and where it will be sold (Biegel, 2009). This is also known as the 4Ps of marketing: product, price, place and promotion. Goals are set, marketing channels are chosen, and a budget is made for the campaigns the marketing team plans to pursue. Sales plans include details about the sales process, team structure, target market and goals. Plus, the sales plan outlines the action plan, tools and resources that will be used to hit these targets.

1.4.3   Goals of Marketing and Sales

What are the key goals that marketing and sales set? Both departments have the primary focus to generate revenue for the company. The primary goal of marketing is to anticipate and define customer wishes, to look at the big picture and to promote the company, products, services and the brands. Marketing departments are responsible for pricing the products and communicating how the product fills customers' needs and wants. Its goals are often longer term because campaigns can span over the course of many months. For sales, the focus is to hit quotas and sales volume goals – and these tend to be shorter term. Sales goals are often measured month over month (Helmold, 2020). Targets are defined, and sales management calculates how much their department, teams and individual salespeople need to sell to meet the overarching goal (Kotler et al., 2008). Table 1.1 compares the differences between marketing management and sales management.

Table 1.1 Differences between marketing and sales

	Marketing management	Sales management
Focus	Company, SBU, Brands	Consumer/customer
Timeframe	Long term	Short/medium term
Key functions	Image building	Customer acquisition
	Brand building	Customer retention
	Reputation/trust	Customer relation mngt.
	Portfolio management	Sales planning/forecasting
	Consumer insights	
Interfaces/point of contacts	Research and development	Marketing
	Sales	Logistics
	Market research	Purchasing
	Agencies	Controlling
	Purchasing	IT
	Management	Management
Evaluation/measurement	Complex	Transparent
	Research studies	Sales statistics
	High investments	Big data
		Investments in IT/CRM systems

Source: Author's source

1.4.4   Tools and Resources of Marketing and Sales

A CRM database is a tool that can be used by sales, marketing and the company as a whole. The database helps all departments manage relationships with contacts, no matter which stage of the customer lifecycle they are in. Social media can also be leveraged by both business units. For marketing, social media can be used to promote content, and, for sales, it can be used as part of a social selling strategy. Plus, there are tools that are specific to each department.

- Marketing tools
- Conversion rate optimization (CRO)
- Search engine optimization (SEO) tool
- Project management tool
- Data reporting software
- Content creation tool
- Sales tools
- Meetings app
- Documents tool
- Invoicing software
- Email management tool
- Inventory and order management software

The introduction of resources to a marketing or sales strategy is particularly dependent on new technology. For example, AI and live chat are newer tools that marketing and sales can use to develop relationships with leads. This type of personalized communication was not possible until recently, and companies can adopt new software and technology as it is created.

1.5   Case Study: Marketing and Sales Strategy of Louis Vuitton

1.5.1   Introduction to Louis Vuitton

Louis Vuitton is one of the oldest and prominent brands in the fashion industry. It was founded in the year 1854 by Louis Vuitton who was a leather designer. In the twentieth century, it has been a leader in fine leather industry. Dealing with luxurious products, it has expanded its network in 50 countries establishing more than 460 stores. From the year 2006 to 2012, it was named as the world's most valuable in the list of luxury brands. Louis Vuitton offers a perfect blend of handmade as well as machine-made fine leather products for the niche segment of the consumers. As a part of conservation of environment and reduction of the greenhouse gases, Louis Vuitton employed architects and designed the stores that consume the most optimum energy bringing down the energy consumption by 50% between year 1995 and 2010 ensuring the attractive illumination in the stores.

1.5.2   Marketing Mix of Louis Vuitton

The marketing strategy of Louis Vuitton analyses the brand with the marketing mix framework which covers the 4Ps (product, price, place, promotion). There are several marketing strategies like product innovation, pricing approach, promotion planning, etc. These business strategies, based on Louis Vuitton marketing mix, help the brand succeed. Louis Vuitton marketing strategy helps the brand/company to position itself competitively in the market and achieve its business goals and objectives.

1.5.3   Product Strategy of Louis Vuitton

Louis Vuitton is a premium luxury brand that sells finest products. It makes 100% pure consumer luxury leather products and pays utmost care to not let the designs of the product be easily imitable. Louis Vuitton has consciously chosen to only make handmade products and not make machine made. The company hires finest craftsmen and ensures that the product is completely unique. The company registers all its designs and product to avoid imitation. Louis Vuitton makes finest bags, unique dresses, designer shoes, and exquisite watches. They also have other range of products such as wallets, eyewear, jewellery, scarves, briefcases, belts, etc. All these cover the products in the marketing mix of Louis Vuitton. Despite the Covid pandemic, the brand managed to thrive its business globally after an initial setback.

1.5.4 Distribution and Pricing of Louis Vuitton

Louis Vuitton ensures exclusive distribution channel. Their products are not sold at any departmental stores. The company believes in having their own stores. Louis Vuitton has their highly specialized sales persons trained to treat their customers with utmost care. They treat their customers with high warmth and provide personalized attention. They have limited stores, and hence the customer walks up to the store. The limited Louis Vuitton stores reduce costs for the company because the distribution channel is shorter.

1.5.5 Promotion and Advertising Louis Vuitton

Louis Vuitton employs famous musicians, actors and models in their marketing campaigns. Some of the well-known personalities who have been associated with the brand are Jennifer Lopez, Kate Moss, etc. Louis Vuitton is a luxury brand, and therefore the company aims to attract and target the luxury customers and prominent celebrities with their products. It has also employed famous celebrities like Andre Agassi and Steffi Graf in its marketing campaigns. Its primary source of promotion is print media. In cosmopolitan cities, magazines and billboards work the best for the company. The exclusiveness of the brand is portrayed through fashion magazines that the elite class reads. Louis Vuitton does not use television as a medium of promotion primarily because it chooses to remain as a luxury brand and thereby wants to be seen by a certain class of people. Thus, it reaches out at its target audience directly rather than using multiple channels. Hence, this covers the Louis Vuitton marketing mix. Figure 1.5 shows a Louis Vuitton shop in China.

Fig. 1.5 Louis Vuitton store

References

Siegel, B. (2009). The current view and outlook for the future of marketing automation. *Journal of Direct, Data and Digital Marketing Practice, 10*, 201–213.

Düssel, M. (2006). *Handbuch Marketingpraxis – Von der Analyse zur Strategie, Ausarbeitung der Taktik, Steuerung und Umsetzung in der Praxis*. Cornelsen.

Esch, F. R., et al. (2008). *Eine managementorientierte Einführung* (2. Auflage). Vahlen Verlag München.

Helmold, M. (2020). *Total Revenue Management (TRM) case studies, best practices and industry insights*. Springer.

Helmold, M. (2021). *Successful management strategies and tools. Industry insights, case studies and best practices*. Springer.

Jones, B. D. G., & Shaw, E. H. (2006). A history of marketing thought. In B. A. Weitz & R. Wensley (Eds.), *Handbook of marketing*. Sage.

Keith, R. J. (1960). The marketing revolution. *Journal of Marketing, 24*(1), 35–38.

Kotler, P., & Armstrong, G. (2018). *Principles of marketing* (7th ed.).

Kotler, P., et al. (2008). *Grundlagen des marketing* (5th ed.). Pearson Studium München.

Kotler, P., Kartajaya, H., & Setiawan, A. (2017). *Marketing 4.0: Moving from traditional to digital*. Wiley.

Kraus, F. (2008). *Der Transfer der Marktorientierung über Hierarchieebenen – Eine empirische Mehrebenenuntersuchung*. Springer.

Meffert, H., et al. (2008). *Marketing* (10th ed.). Springer.

Tomczak, T., Reinecke, S., & Kuss, A. (2018). *Strategic marketing. Market-oriented corporate and business unit planning*. Springer.

Wilkie, W. L., & Moore, E. S. (2006, December). Macromarketing as a pillar of marketing thought. *Journal of Macromarketing, 26*(2), 224–232.

Marketing Management as Part of the Corporate Strategy

2

> *The essence of strategy is choosing what not to do.*
>
> Michael Porter

2.1 Levels of Strategy

A corporate marketing strategy is a broad marketing plan that creates guidelines to be used throughout the company. Part of this strategy can include company branding and logos. Such a marketing plan is typically designed at the senior management level (Helmold, 2021). The three levels of strategy, developed by Gerry Johnson and Kevan Scholes along with other major managerial thinkers, are a way of defining the different layers of strategy which, in tandem, orient the direction of the organization and define its success (Johnson et al., 2017). The three levels are the following:

1. Corporate strategy level
2. Business and tactical supply chain level
3. Functional or operational supply chain levels

When synchronized and coordinated, successful strategies at each of these levels will contribute to successful overall organizational strategy including the right measures to prevent and avoid inefficiencies in the supply chain and other functions of an enterprise (Khojasteh, 2018). This is the top layer of strategic planning and is often associated with the organization's mission and values, though it is developed in much more significant depth (Helmold, 2021). Corporate strategy is defined by those at the very top of the organization and is an outline of the overall long-term direction and allocation of resources. Questions related to the strategy are normally:

- General, overall strategy and direction in terms of markets, sales and target groups
- Which markets the organization will operate in
- What marketing tools and concepts to apply

© The Author(s), under exclusive license to Springer Nature Switzerland AG 2022
M. Helmold, *Performance Excellence in Marketing, Sales and Pricing*, Management for Professionals, https://doi.org/10.1007/978-3-031-10097-0_2

- Which suppliers and supply chains to procure from
- How the markets will be entered and the general activities of the organization
- How to prevent risks in the upstream or downstream supply chains
- How to apply a supply chain risk management (SCRM) measures

2.1.1   Corporate Strategy

Corporate strategy is crucial as it will define all other decisions that are made within the organization along the line. Smaller, newer organizations which are targeting a very specific niche market, or operate with a small set of unique products/services, will find it far easier to develop a corporate strategy as there are fewer variables to consider. However, larger and more developed organizations will find the process much simpler as they may need to diverge from activities and behaviours which define who they are in order to reach out into new markets and to take new opportunities.

2.1.2   Business Strategy

The business strategy generally emerges and evolves from the overarching corporate strategy which has been set by those at the helm (Tomczak et al., 2018). They are usually far more specific than corporate strategy and will likely be unique to different departments or subdivisions within the broader organization. In general they use corporate strategy as an outline to:

- Define specific tactics and strategies for each market the organization is involved in.
- Define how each business unit will deliver the planned tactics.

Due to their nature, they are more common in larger firms that engage in multiple activities than they are in small businesses. However, they can still be engaged in by smaller organizations who wish to define how they go about each different subsection of their operations, by breaking down the overall scope of the corporate strategy.

2.1.3   Functional Strategy

The functional long-term strategy, also defined as market-level strategy, refers to the day-to-day operation of the company, which will keep it functioning and moving in the correct direction. Whilst many organizations fail because they do not have an overarching corporate strategy, others fail because they have not developed plans for how to engage in everyday activities. Even with an overall direction you wish to head in, without a plan for how to successfully operate, an organization will be unable to progress. These will be numerous and will define very specific aspects and operations within smaller departments, teams, groups and activities. Overall, they define:

- Day-to-day actions which are required to deliver corporate and business strategies
- Relationships needed between units, departments and teams
- How operational goals will be met and how they will be monitored

It is at this level, the lowest in strategic development, that leaders should define how different departments and functions will work together to achieve higher goals. There will be managers that will oversee departments (e.g. manufacturing and HR) that do not perform the same functions but need to be synchronized in order to achieve the goals set out by the corporate and business strategies.

2.1.4 Alignment of Strategies

Though corporate strategy will get all of the attention, it is success at the bottom of the hierarchy – through day-to-day functions – which will truly define where the organization as a whole will succeed. Companies must build from the ground up, in small steps, in order to keep moving forward. If operations break down, so does the organization. As mentioned previously, it is crucially important that each level of strategy is synchronized, both from top-to-bottom and horizontally across the organization. Feedback should down from both corporate strategy to functional strategy, and vice-versa, in order for all three levels to ensure that they are operating in line with one another (Helmold, 2021). Strategy itself will not define organizational success; however, it is a very good place to start. Once sound strategies are in place, an organization can move forward and begin to execute said strategies. They may need some adjustment along the way – and you should be prepared to do so, in response to feedback from different levels and from the external environment – but they should be initially developed in such a way that they will keep the organization in line with its long-term objectives.

2.2 Strategic Triangle

The process of strategic management cycle is a process with three elements as outlined in Fig. 2.1 (strategic triangle or strategic cycle). The three steps are (1) the strategic analysis, (2) the strategic choice and (3) the strategic implementation and will be described in the following sections. The triangle is raising the following questions:

1. Where are we?
2. Where do we want to go?
3. How do we achieve this?

Fig. 2.1 Strategic triangle. (Source: Author's source, adopted from Johnson et al., 2017)

2.3 Strategic Analysis

2.3.1 Analysing Important Factors

The strategic analysis of an organization is about understanding the strategic position of the organization in terms of lean management. This stage requires a profound analysis where the organization stands in terms of Lean Management tools and processes. The existing competencies and resources of the organization need to be assessed to determine if there are any opportunities to be gained from these and to determine if they need to be enhanced in order to pursue strategic objectives and goals. The major stakeholders which influence the organization and the opinions or viewpoints must be taken into account as the purpose of all of the strategic analysis is to define the potential future direction of the organization. The purpose of this phase (strategic analysis) is to create a suitable starting position and to understand the key influences on the present and future state of the organization and what opportunities are afforded by the environment and the competencies of the organization. Assessing the strategic position consists of evaluating the following elements as shown in Table 2.1.

Table 2.1 Tools for the strategic analysis

Tools	Description
PESTEL analysis	Environmental or macro analysis
Industry analysis	Porter's Five Forces (P5F) or micro analysis
SWOT analysis	Internal and external factors
Cultural analysis	Environmental or macro analysis
Benchmarking analysis	Comparing the own company with the best competitor
Stakeholder analysis	Understanding the groups involved

Source: Author's source

Since strategy is concerned with the position a business takes in relation to its environment, an understanding of the environment's effects on an organization is of central importance to the strategic analysis. The historical and environmental effects on the business must be considered, as well as the present effects and the expected changes in environmental variables. The analysis of the environment can be done via the macro and micro analysis (PESTEL, Porters 5 Forces). Additionally, strengths, weaknesses, opportunities and threats complete the assessment of the environment (SWOT). This step is a major task because the range of environmental variables is so great. Another area of the strategic analysis is the evaluation of the strategic capability of an organization and where it is able to achieve a competitive advantage. Considering the resource areas of a business such as its physical plant, its management, its financial structure and its products may identify these strengths and weaknesses. The expectations of stakeholders are important because they will affect what will be seen as acceptable in terms of the strategies advanced by management. Stakeholders can be defined as people or groups inside or outside the organization, who are interested in the activities of the organization. A typical list of stakeholders for a large company would include shareholders, banks, employees, managers, customers, suppliers, government and society. Culture affects the interpretation of the environmental and resource influences (Helmold & Terry, 2021).

2.3.2 Analysing the Environment

A PESTEL analysis or PESTLE analysis is a framework or tool used to analyse and monitor the macro-environmental factors that may have a profound impact on an organization's performance. This tool is especially useful when starting a new business or entering a foreign market. It is often used in collaboration with other analytical business tools such as the SWOT analysis and Porter's Five Forces to give a clear understanding of a situation and related internal and external factors. PESTEL is an acronym that stands for political, economic, social, technological, environmental and legal factors. However, throughout the years, people have expanded the framework with factors such as demographics, intercultural, ethical and ecological resulting in variants such as STEEPLED, DESTEP and SLEPIT. In this article, we will stick simply to PESTEL since it encompasses the most relevant factors in general business. Each element will be elaborated as shown in Fig. 2.2.

2.3.3 Analysing the Industry

Porter is best known for his strategic frameworks and concepts in his paper, which was published in 1980 (Porter, 1980). The five forces model (industry analysis) has five elements that can be utilized to assess the attractiveness and competitive situation of the industry as outlined in Fig. 2.3. The five elements are the following:

1. Rivalry amongst competitors
2. Bargaining power of suppliers
3. Bargaining power of buyers
4. Threat of new market entrants
5. Threat of new substitutes

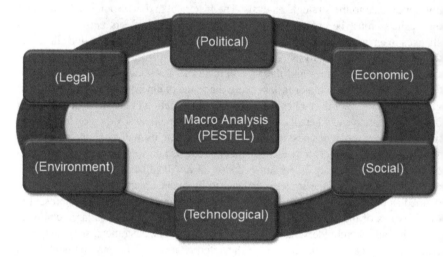

Fig. 2.2 PESTEL analysis. (Source: Author's source)

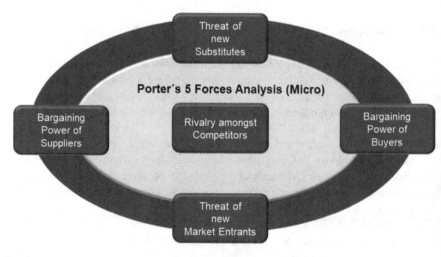

Fig. 2.3 Industry analysis. (Source: Author's source)

The stronger the threat posed by these five competitive forces, the less attractive the industry under consideration and the more difficult it is to achieve a sustainable competitive advantage. Companies should therefore try to be active in an industry with an attractive industry structure and to build up a defensible position in their industry, i.e. a position in which the five competitive forces are as less threatening as possible. Companies can also influence the five forces with the help of appropriate strategic orientation. This can increase the attractiveness of an industry. If, however, companies influence the distribution of competitive forces to the advantage of their own competitive position without being aware of the long-term effects or consciously accepting them, this can also destroy the structure and profitability of an industry.

2.3.4 Analysing the Strengths and Weaknesses

The SWOT (strengths, weaknesses, opportunities and threats) analysis is a framework used to evaluate a company's competitive position and to develop strategic planning. SWOT analysis assesses internal and external factors, as well as current and future potential. This technique, which operates by "peeling back layers of the company", is designed for use in the preliminary stages of decision-making processes and can be used as a tool for evaluation of the strategic position of organizations of many kinds (for-profit enterprises, local and national governments, NGOs, etc.). It is intended to specify the objectives of the business venture or project and identify the internal and external factors that are favourable and unfavourable to achieving those objectives. Users of a SWOT analysis often ask and answer questions to generate meaningful information for each category to make the tool useful and identify their competitive advantage (Fig. 2.4).

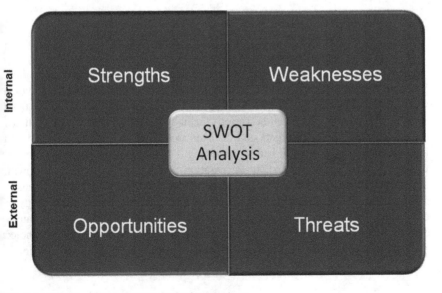

Fig. 2.4 SWOT analysis. (Source: Author's source)

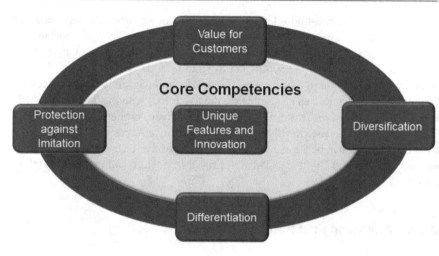

Fig. 2.5 Core competencies. (Source: Author's source)

2.3.5 Analysing the Core Competencies

The core competency concept describes a product, feature, process, skill, brand or activity that a company can perform better than the competition and has thus achieved a competitive advantage. It is determined by the certain characteristics like customer value or benefits, protection against imitation, differentiation, diversification and innovation or unique features as shown in Fig. 2.5. In business, a competitive advantage is the attribute that allows an organization to outperform its competitors.

2.4   Strategic Choice

2.4.1   Generic Strategies

Strategic choice typically follows strategic analysis. Strategic choice involves a whole process through which a decision is taken to choose a particular option from various alternatives. There can be various methods through which the final choice can be selected upon. Managers and decision makers keep both the external and internal environment in mind before narrowing it down to one. It is based upon the following three elements: first, the generation of strategic options, e.g. growth, acquisition, diversification or concentration; second, the evaluation of the options to assess their relative merits and feasibility; and third, the selection of the strategy or option that the organization will pursue. There could be more than one strategy chosen, but there is a chance of an inherent danger or disadvantage to any choice made. Although there are techniques for evaluating specific options, the selection is

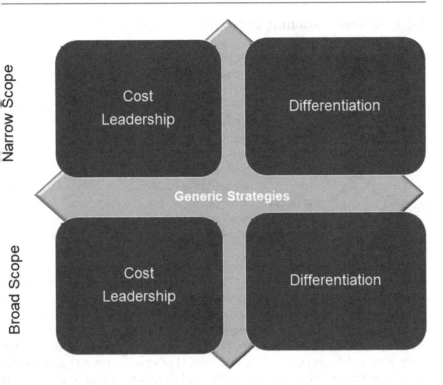

Fig. 2.6   Generic strategies. (Source: Author's own figure, adopted from Porter, 1985)

often subjective and likely to be influenced by the values of managers and other groups with an interest in the organization.

The generic strategies differentiation and cost leadership are a good method to define, in which direction a company should go to increase profitability and to acquire a competitive advantage (Porter, 1980, 1985). Mintzberg provides five definitions of strategy: plan, ploy, pattern, position and perspective (Mintzberg et al., 1995). Firstly, strategy is always a plan. A plan integrates intended action activities based on previous assessment of the situation. Secondly, as plan, a strategy can be a ploy too, really just a specific manoeuvre intended to outwit an opponent or competitor. If strategies can be intended (whether as general plans or specific ploys), they can also be realized. In other words, defining strategy as plan is not sufficient; we also need a definition that encompasses the resulting behaviour. Thirdly, strategy is a pattern. The definitions of strategy as plan and pattern can be quite independent of one another. Plans may go unrealized, whilst patterns may appear without preconception. Plans are intended strategy, whereas patterns are the realized strategy. Fourthly, strategy is a perspective. A perspective is not just of a chosen position but consists of an ingrained way of perceiving the world (Fig. 2.6).

2.4.2 Boston Consulting Matrix (BCG-Matrix)

The BCG matrix is named after the Boston Consulting Group (BCG), whose founder Bruce Henderson developed this matrix in 1970 (Fig. 2.7). This concept should clarify the connection between the product life cycle and the cost experience curve. The matrix is often visualized as a scatter or bubble diagram; the area of a circle then represents the sales of the respective product. The BCG matrix is, put simply, a portfolio management framework that helps companies decide how to prioritize their different businesses and supply chains. It is a table, split into four quadrants, each with its own unique symbol that represents a certain degree of profitability: question marks, stars, dogs and cash cows. By assigning each business to one of these four categories, executives could then decide where to focus their resources and capital to generate the most value, as well as where to cut their losses. The products or business units of a company are assigned to one of the four areas based on their values. Each area embodies a standard strategy. It should give a good recommendation on how to proceed. The life cycle of a typical product runs from the question mark to the star and cash cow to the poor dog. There are also products that do not follow this ideal path. Many product failures and flops do not even reach the star range. An imitating product, on the other hand, may skip the question mark area. The question marks, normally young products, are the newcomers amongst the products. The market has growth potential, but the products only have a small relative market share. Management is faced with the decision of whether to invest or abandon the product. In the case of an investment, the product requires liquid funds, which it cannot generate itself. A typical strategy recommendation is selection and possibly

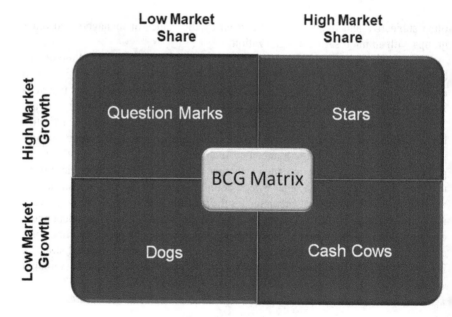

Fig. 2.7 Boston Consulting Group (BCG) matrix. (Source: Author's source)

an offensive penetration strategy to increase market share. The stars are the company's most promising products. You have a high relative market share in a growth market. They already cover the investment needs resulting from market growth with their own cash flow. The strategy recommendation is investment and possibly a skimming strategy to increase profit margins without endangering market share. The cash cows (milking cows) have a high relative market share in an only slightly growing or static market. They produce stable, high cash flows and can be "milked" without further investment. A fixed price strategy or price competition strategy is appropriate. The poor dogs are the discontinued products in the company. They have low market growth, sometimes market contraction, and low relative market share. At the latest as soon as the contribution margin for these products is negative, the portfolio should be adjusted (disinvestment strategy). In addition to assessing the individual products using the standard strategies, the entire portfolio should also be considered. Pay attention to the static financial equalization – the products in the portfolio should support and finance each other. A question mark can only expand if another product and cash cow finances this expansion. Future developments can also be seen. The products should be evenly represented in the individual areas – a company without question marks would have little chance in the future market. The matrix reveals two factors that companies should consider when deciding where to invest, company competitiveness and market attractiveness, with relative market share and growth rate as the underlying drivers of these factors. Each of the four quadrants represents a specific combination of relative market share and growth:

- Low growth, high share. Companies should milk these "cash cows" for cash to reinvest.
- High growth, high share. Companies should significantly invest in these "stars" as they have high future potential.
- High growth, low share. Companies should invest in or discard these "question marks", depending on their chances of becoming stars.
- Low share, low growth. Companies should liquidate, divest or reposition these "dogs".

2.4.3 Ansoff Matrix

The product-market matrix (also Ansoff matrix, after its inventor Harry Igor Ansoff or Z-Matrix) is a tool for the strategic management of companies. It can be used by a management (= company management) who has decided on a growth strategy as an aid for planning this growth. When it comes to market penetration, the focus is on gaining additional market shares with existing products. The company is trying to sell more of its products to existing, new and competitive customers. Existing marketing activities usually have to be adapted to achieve this goal. Although the product portfolio does not change, companies often have to experiment with new advertising concepts in order to further promote product adoption in the existing market.

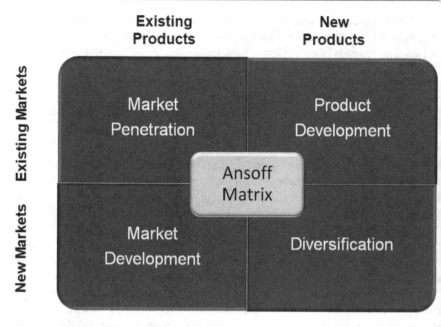

Fig. 2.8 Ansoff matrix. (Source: Author's source)

However, this market penetration can only be successfully implemented up to the point at which the market has not yet been fully saturated. The focus of the market development strategy is on creating new sales markets for existing products. By entering new market segments or opening up further geographical regions, a company puts itself in the position of attracting new target groups for its existing products (Fig. 2.8).

A regionally operating bakery can also offer its own products nationwide, for example, by setting up digital sales channels, and thus generate growth. Of course, the implementation of this strategy is initially offset by considerable investment costs. The chances of success should therefore first be assessed by means of careful planning and a comprehensive risk analysis. If opening up new markets is not an option, it is often worth taking a look at the product development strategy. The existing range is expanded through product innovations or the creation of product variants in the existing market. The resulting added value should encourage consumers to buy. This strategy is particularly attractive for companies in niche markets in which acquiring new customers and upselling would be almost impossible with a pure market penetration strategy. The reluctance to enter new markets is reinforced by high development costs and the risk of failure of the newly developed product. The most risky quadrant of the Ansoff matrix is that of diversification. This requires the development of a new product whilst at the same time opening up a new market. The associated investment costs in terms of product development, business analyses, setting up local subsidiaries, etc. can quickly mean the end of a company if the corresponding ROI is not achieved. The diversification strategy can be broken down into horizontal, vertical and lateral diversification, depending on the degree of risk tolerance of a company:

- Vertical diversification
- Horizontal diversification
- Lateral diversification

Horizontal Diversification

Horizontal diversification describes the development of a new product that is still factually related to the product range previously offered. The existing value chain can continue to be used with minimal adjustments. With horizontal diversification, a company expands its offerings at the same economic level to reach new customers. An example of this type of diversification is the development of the iPad, which with its introduction gradually expanded Apple's existing smartphone and computer portfolio.

Vertical Diversification

With vertical diversification, a company deepens its commitment to sales-oriented activities (forward integration) and/or the actual manufacturing process of its products (backward integration). Diversification does not take place on the same level of the value chain as with horizontal diversification but on the upstream or downstream one. With forward integration, a company takes the sales of its products and services into its own hands, for example, by opening its own branches or an online shop. Backward integration describes the safeguarding of a company's reference markets, for example, by taking over production processes that were previously outsourced to external companies. Whilst horizontal diversification aims to reduce dependency on one product line, vertical diversification focuses on reducing dependence on suppliers and dealers. The acquisition of the necessary skills and know-how for the successful implementation of sales and production processes is in turn associated with high investment costs and thus increased financial risks.

Lateral Diversification

With the lateral diversification strategy, companies expand into completely new markets that have no material connection with the existing business.

The aim and purpose of this alignment is to minimize the dependence on developments in the existing market segment. Google can be mentioned as a good example in this context: In addition to the search engine core business, the company expanded early on into other market segments such as telecommunications (fibre), biotechnology (Calico) or autonomous automotive technology (Waymo). The lateral diversification strategy is used by multinational companies in particular to respond flexibly to changes and trends in the market. The necessary know-how is usually acquired through the acquisition of specialized companies that are already represented in the market of interest. Accordingly, this strategy requires enormous investment costs and harbours not only financial but also immaterial risks, such as a diluted brand image due to product offerings that are too diversified.

Table 2.2   Red ocean and blue ocean strategy

Red ocean strategy	Blue ocean strategy
Compete in existing market spaces	Create uncontested market spaces
Defeat the competition	Make the competition irrelevant
Apply differentiation or cost leadership	Apply differentiation and cost leadership
Achieve a competitive advantage	Achieve value innovations
Segment smartly existing customers	Attract new customers
Exploit existing demand	Create and capture new demands

2.4.4   Blue and Red Ocean Strategies

Blue Ocean Strategy is a method for developing permanently profitable business models from the field of strategic management: The basic idea is that only through the development of innovative and new markets, which really differentiate relevant benefits for the broad mass of customers or non-customers, can "Blue Oceans" offer lasting successes. Amongst other things, this is to be achieved through competition that has become meaningless, new customer acquisitions and optimized cost structures. The concept of the Blue Ocean Strategy was developed by W. Chan Kim and Renée Mauborgne at the Insead Business School, where it was initially referred to as Value Innovation. Based on empirical studies over a period of 15 years and based on the analysis of more than 100 leading companies, examples of companies were found that opened up new, previously unused sub-markets and thus made the previous competition irrelevant. The term ocean describes a market or branch of industry in connection with the blue ocean strategy. "Blue oceans" are understood as untouched markets or branches of industry with little or no competition. Anyone who plunged into the blue ocean would find undiscovered markets or industries. "Red oceans", on the other hand, designate saturated markets, characterized by tough competition, overcrowded with competitors who all offer the same service or the same products. The term "red ocean" is based on the image of bloody fights of predatory fish (the competitors), whilst the "blue ocean" is free from bloody fights. Table 2.2 shows the Red and Blue Ocean Strategy.

2.5   Strategic Implementation

2.5.1   Assessment of Suitability, Acceptability and Feasibility

Strategic implementation is concerned with the translation of the selected strategy into action. The ways in which strategies are implemented are described as the strategic architecture or framework of the organization. Successful implementation of the chosen strategy will be dependent on several factors such as stakeholder's expectations, the employees, the company culture, the will to change and the cooperation within the organization. These elements and how the management and employees work together to adopt the new plan will decide about how successful the strategy implementation is. The available skills and/or the ability to develop new skills when required for the planned change and issues like the structural reorganization and resulting cultural disturbance would also affect success. Resource availability and planning for the utilization of such resources need to be addressed as part of the implementation plan. The entire process necessitates the management of strategic change and will concern handling both hard and soft factors of the organization, i.e. structure and systems and culture and motivation, etc. Implementing a strategy has three elements:

- Organizational structure and layout: Where and how should the organization is split into European, US and Asian divisions? How autonomous should divisions be? What parenting style should be applied?
- Resources: Enabling an organization's resources should support the chosen strategy: What are the appropriate human and non-human resources? What assets need to be acquired?
- Change management: Most strategic planning and implementation will involve change, so managing change, in particular employees' fears and resistance, is crucial.

Johnson and Scholes argue that for a strategy to be successful it must satisfy three criteria. These criteria can be applied to any strategy decision such as the competitive strategies, growth strategies or development strategies:

1. Suitability – whether the options are adequate responses to the firm's assessment of its strategic position
2. Acceptability – considers whether the options meet and are consistent with the firm's objectives and are acceptable to the stakeholders
3. Feasibility – assesses whether the organization has the resources it needs to carry out the strategy

2.5.2   Suitability

Suitability is a useful criterion for screening strategies, asking the following questions about strategic options:

- Does the strategy exploit the company strengths, such as providing work for skilled craftsmen or environmental opportunities, e.g. helping to establish the organization in new growth sectors of the market?
- How far does the strategy overcome the difficulties identified in the analysis? For example, is the strategy likely to improve the organization's competitive position, solve the company's liquidity problems or decrease dependence on a particular supplier?
- Does the option fit in with the organization's purposes? For example, would the strategy achieve profit targets or growth expectations, or would it retain control for an owner-manager?

2.5.3   Acceptability

Acceptability is essentially about assessing risk and return and is strongly related to expectations of stakeholders. The issue of "acceptable to whom?" thus requires the analysis to be thought through carefully. Some of the questions that will help identify the likely consequences of any strategy are as follows:

- How will the strategy impact shareholder wealth? Assessing this could involve calculations relating to profitability, e.g. net present value (NPV).
- How will the organization perform in profitability terms? The parallel in the public sector would be cost/benefit assessment.
- How will the financial risk (e.g. liquidity) change?
- What effect will it have on capital structure (gearing or share ownership)?
- Will the function of any department, group or individual change significantly?
- Will the organization's relationship with outside stakeholders, e.g. suppliers, government, unions, customers, need to change?
- Will the strategy be acceptable in the organization's environment, e.g. higher levels of noise?

2.5.4   Feasibility

This assesses whether the organization has the resources it needs to carry out the strategy. Factors that should be considered can be summarized under the M-word model.

- Machinery. What demands will the strategy make on production? Do we have sufficient spare capacity? Do we need new production systems to give lower cost, better quality, more flexibility, etc.?
- Management. Is existing management sufficiently skilled to carry out the strategy?
- Money. How much finance is needed and when? Can we raise this? Is the cash flow feasible?
- Manpower. What demands will the strategy make on human resources? How many employees are needed, what skills will they need and when do we need them? Do we already have the right people or is there a gap? Can the gap be filled by recruitment, retraining, etc.?
- Markets. Is our existing brand name strong enough for the strategy to work? Will new brand names have to be established? What market share is needed for success – how quickly can this be achieved?
- Materials. What demands will the strategy make on our relationships with suppliers? Are changes in quality needed?
- Make-up. Is the existing organizational structure adequate or will it have to be changed?

2.6   Strategic Pyramid

A useful tool for the translation of the corporate strategy and strategic objectives into negotiations is the strategic pyramid (Johnsons & Scholes, 1997). Strategy in this context is the long-term positioning as well as the decision of the enterprise, which business fields and which strategies to choose. Strategy is therefore "the fundamental, long-term direction of three to five years and organization of a company in order to gain competitive advantages in a changing environment through the use of resources and competences and to realize the long-term goals of the stakeholders" (Fig. 2.9).

2.6.1   Mission and Vision

Enterprises must manifest in their strategy to strive for lean excellence. The mission is the starting point of the strategic pyramid. The mission statement of an enterprise is the long-term purpose of the company and the strategic direction as defined by Johnson and Scholes. The vision or strategic intent describes more specifically what an organization aims to achieve and the long-term aspirations.

Mission example: Become a lean enterprise of excellence on a global basis.
Vision example: Become the world-leading company in lean in the industry in the next 5 years.

Fig. 2.9   Strategic pyramid. (Source: Author's own figure)

2.6.2   Goals and Objectives

The mission and vision are followed by generic goals and specific objectives. Generic goals are not quantified and more general, but specific objectives are quantified and specific. The strategists Johnson and Scholes distinguish in longer-term and generic (English: goals) as well as shorter and quantified objectives (English: objectives) for the company. Quantified goals can include sales, financial, quality, logistics, cost, and alpha goals.

Goal example: Increase and improve quality, reduce cost and provide productivity improvements between 30% and 40% within the next 3 years.
Objectives example: Quantification of the generic aims (goals).

2.6.3   Core Competencies

The next level in the strategic pyramid is the identification of core competencies. Core competencies are those competencies which allow companies to gain a superior or competitive advantage and that are very difficult for your competitors to emulate. These describe the resources, skills, knowledge or any other feature that lead to a competitive advantage. Core competencies must be perceived by customers and clients.

Example: Create lean academy and lean culture.

2.6.4   Strategies

After defining mission, vision, goals and core competencies, the elements must be translated into strategic objectives and key performance indicators (KPI). The long-term implementation of these elements is defined as the formulation of strategic objectives and important for the negotiations. In implementing the strategic goals, negotiations will take place with many stakeholders. Become a lean differentiator by answering customer demands: Reduce operating cost by 25% in 12 months from now, and increase customer satisfaction by 10%.

2.6.5   Strategic Architecture

In addition to buildings, machines, plants, offices, resources or employees, the infrastructure in the sense of strategic management also includes knowledge and innovations of the company that ensure long-term success. This requires facilities, buildings, factories or offices that represent the strategic infrastructure. In addition, however, other success criteria such as resources, knowledge, experts, name recognition, network or innovations are of central importance.

2.6.6   Control and Execution

The final element of the strategic pyramid is the performance control (control and execution) and a target-performance comparison. A suitable tool for this step is the Balance Score Card (BSC) or an action plan. The instrument of the BSC was already developed in 1992 by the professors Norton and Kaplan. The BSC is an instrument in strategic management and includes four categories:

1. Customer satisfaction
2. Financial category
3. Internal processes and improvements
4. Learning organization

In practice, it seems that companies are adapting or expanding the original four dimensions to their specific needs.

2.7   Core Values

2.7.1   Strategies Must Focus on Value Creation

Porter postulated three generic or broad alternative strategies which may be pursued as a response to the competitive pressures. They are termed generic strategies because they are broadly applicable to any industry or business. They are differentiation, cost leadership and focus. A focus strategy may be further defined as cost focus, differentiation focus or cost and differentiation focus. A differentiation strategy may be based on actual unique product features or the perception thereof, conveyed through the use of advertising and marketing tactics, in the eyes of the customers (Werner, 2020). Obviously, the product or service feature must be one with the customer needs or desires. Moreover, such enhanced features and designs or advertising and marketing will increase costs, and customers must be price-insensitive – willing to pay for the differentiated product or service (Kim & Mauborgne, 2015). This willingness to pay for the differentiated product of service is what provides the company relief from competitive pressure, cost pressure specifically. Firms pursuing a cost leadership strategy must make lower production and distribution costs their priority (Helmold & Terry, 2021). By keeping their cost lower than those of their competitors, firms using cost leadership can still price their products up to the level of their competitors and still maintain higher gross profit margins. Alternatively, these firms can price their products lower than those of their competitors in the hope of achieving greater market share and sales volume at the expense of gross profit margins. A focus strategy is based on a particular market, customer, product or geography. A focus strategy is a concentrated, narrowly focused niche strategy. Figure 2.10 shows the example of a Mission Statement of Alstom (formerly Bombardier) Transportation in China International Procurement Office.

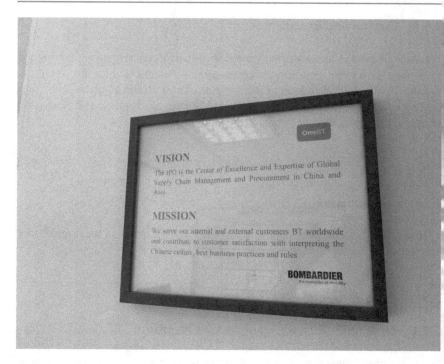

Fig. 2.10 Example of mission statement and vision. (Source: Author's source)

2.8   Case Study: McDonald's Marketing Strategy

2.8.1   Global Player

McDonald's became the leader in the fast-food industry with their strong focus on customer service, response to competition and use of marketing techniques early on in their development. Please note that we are not proposing that the tactics used by McDonald's are the right or wrong way to strategically or ethically achieve growth. This article simply outlines the tactics and history of a company that has grown significantly since its inception (Pafitis, 2020). Initially founded in 1940 at a single location in California, McDonald's quickly became well known locally for its high-quality hamburgers and satisfactory customer service. Eight years later, it became one of the first restaurants to make the transition from traditional sit-down table service to a fast-food business model and added exciting burger variations and milkshakes to its menu. Spurred on by the success of this development, it launched its first franchise agreement in 1952, a decision that would lead to exponential worldwide growth. Indeed, the company now operates almost 40,000 restaurants across the globe and attracted reported international revenues of around $21bn in 2018.

2.8.2   Brand Awareness

The company focused on broad public awareness from the early stages of its development, aiming to create strong brand recognition and market penetration, upon which to promote its growing franchise business further. As its customer base grew, the company investigated its demographics further, to facilitate targeting. McDonald's still maintains this approach, investing in online and offline marketing strategies that promote its clear, brand-centric messaging to broad audiences whilst using other channels such as its dedicated mobile app to reach and retain loyal customers (Pafitis, 2020). As a result of its mass marketing techniques and broad appeal as a fast-serving, affordable eatery, McDonald's has a varied consumer demographic. The chain is most frequented by shoppers under the age of 24, as well as between the ages of 35 and 54. Both male and female buyers typically have low to average incomes, with an affinity for the fast-food industry in general. They are defined as brand-loyal, casual diners, with the average spend per customer estimated at $7.79. A large proportion of these customers are parents to young children, attracted by the brand's family-friendly atmosphere and menu offering. This particular segment was first targeted through the launch of the Happy Meal in 1979, the hugely popular children's meal package that includes a free, themed toy.

2.8.3   Multi-method Advertising

McDonald's uses TV and radio to engender general brand awareness, as well as promote new menu items, meal deals and philanthropic initiatives. Its broadcast channels and timings are chosen specifically for maximum viewership and listenership. In fact, McDonald's is estimated to have spent $52.9m on TV ad airings in the USA during November 2018 – the height of the widely viewed NFL season – offering an indication of the importance the fast-food company places on securing the most prominent broadcast ad spots. The company confirms its objective to secure large-scale awareness, stating that, "the majority of our campaigns are communicated to everyone to ensure they have a broad reach. You may have seen us on TV or heard us on the radio!" Traditional billboard advertisements are also widely used by McDonald's, focusing on the same marketing objectives and content as those that underpin its broadcast ads. Ranging from static to digitally interactive billboards, placed in prominent locations with high footfall and visibility, the company endeavours to maintain positive brand perception and affinity amongst its target audience, as well as associated consumer groups. This is an excellent example of utilizing various promotional techniques that reinforce the same goals, thus encouraging greater overall success, compared to campaigns that are delivered via one method alone. McDonald's also executes creative, captivating outdoor ambient marketing. Ambient advertising is described as placing ad material in extremely unusual or unexpected places and on objects that are not usually utilized for promotional purposes. McDonald's has adopted this subcategory of guerilla marketing to evoke a more significant impact on consumers. The McDonald's Massive McMuffin Breakfast campaign is an example of this. Throughout 2010, the company placed giant paper McDonald's takeaway bags across prominent streets in New Zealand, labelled with the name of its new breakfast menu item. The unmissable, unexpected imagery drew considerable attention from passers-by (supported by the many photos of the spectacle that onlookers shared to social media), successfully raising awareness for the McMuffin breakfast. Other examples include the brand's street markings across pedestrian road crossings, designed to make the typical horizontal crossing lines appear as though they are a portion of fries, protruding out of a McDonald's branded fries' box. The brand uses online advertising to supports its awareness and demand generation goals. The content utilized online remains consistent with McDonald's TV ad and billboard imagery, though both text and graphics are tailored to ensure maximum performance across the particular social media platforms used, including Twitter, Facebook and Instagram. Capitalizing on the increasing consumer trend of food photography, McDonald's encourages customers to share photos of their meals online, with great success. In fact, McDonald's was the second most pictured brand on Twitter, with 4.9 m logo mentions on the social media platform worldwide between September 2018 and February 2019. The company also embarks on search engine optimization (SEO) campaigns, though its organic SEO strategy outweighs paid promotion. As of December 2019, 90.7% of its search traffic to mcdonalds.com was organic, with just 9.3% obtained as a result of paid keywords (Pafitis, 2020).

References

Helmold, M. (2021). *Successful management strategies and tools. Industry insights, case studies and best practices*. Springer.

Helmold, M., & Terry, B. (2021). *Operations and supply management 4.0. Industry insights, case studies and best practices*. Springer.

Johnson, G., et al. (2017). *Exploring strategy* (11th ed.). FT Prentice Hall.

Khojasteh, Y. (2018). *Supply chain risk management. Advanced tools, models, and developments*. Springer.

Kim, C., & Mauborgne, R. A. (2015). *Blue ocean strategy, expanded edition: How to create uncontested market space and make the competition irrelevant*. Harvard Business Press.

Mintzberg, H., Quinn, J. B., & Ghoshal, S. (1995). *The strategy process*. Revised European ed. Prentice Hall.

Pafitis, E. (2020). *Marketing & branding. McDonald's marketing strategy: What your company can learn*. Retrieved December 12, 2021, from https://www.startingbusiness.com/blog/marketing-strategy-mcdonalds.

Porter, M. E. (1980). *Competitive strategy: Techniques for analyzing industries and competitors*. Free Press.

Porter, M. E. (1985). *Competitive advantage. Creating and sustaining superior performance*. Free Press.

Tomczak, T., Reinecke, S., & Kuss, A. (2018). *Strategic marketing. Market-oriented corporate and business unit planning*. Springer.

Werner, H. (2020). *Supply chain management. Grundlagen, Strategien, Instrumente und Controlling*. Springer.

Marketing Concepts

3

*The aim of marketing is to know and understand the customer
so well the product or service fits him and sells itself.*

Peter Drucker

3.1 Marketing Concepts

Marketing is the function and process of building, managing and maintaining an exchange relationship, where you start with attracting the customers, establishing a relationship with them and finally maintaining it by satisfying their needs. That customer can be other businesses or the consumers; therefore, marketing can be business to business or business to consumer depending upon the situation (Kotler et al., 2008). The ultimate function of marketing is the same, and that is to establish a relationship with customers and satisfy their needs by meeting their demands. For instance, telecommunication creates a marketing strategy that first attracts and convinces people to use their calls, messaging and Internet packages. Once people start using, then they ask them to rate their service by giving them stars. The marketing concept is a process when a company plans and implements to maximize profit by increasing sales, satisfying customer's needs and beating competitors (Düssel, 2006; Esch et al., 2008). The purpose is to create a situation that benefits both parties: the customer and the company. The idea of the marketing concept is to anticipate and satisfy the needs and wants of customers better than the competitors. The marketing concepts were originally derived from the book of Adam Smith, *Wealth of Nation*. It remained unknown to the world until the twenty-first century. To fully understand the marketing concept, first, we have to understand needs, wants and demands (Helmold, 2020; Meffert et al., 2008; Kotler & Armstrong, 2018). Table 3.1 shows the description of the three essential elements.

- Needs – it is something necessary for the existence of life; many adverse things can happen without it. The worst-case scenario would be death. Needs comprise of many things, like food, shelter, security, social belonging, self-development, self-esteem and respect.

M. Helmold, *Performance Excellence in Marketing, Sales and Pricing*, Management for Professionals, https://doi.org/10.1007/978-3-031-10097-0_3

Table 3.1 Needs, wants and demands in marketing and sales

Marketing element	Description
Needs	It is something inevitable for the existence of life; many adverse things can occur without it. The worst-case situation would be death. Needs cover many things, like food, shelter, self-development, security, social belonging, self-esteem and respect
Wants	Wants are our desires and wishes in life, our social setup, and culture moulds our wants
Demands	When our desires, needs and wants are backed by our ability to pay, they become demands

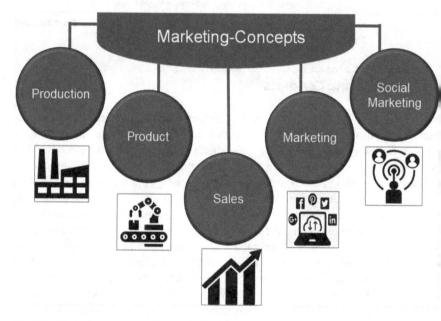

Fig. 3.1 Marketing concepts. (Source: Author's source)

- Wants – wants are our wishes and desires that we want in life, our social setup, and culture shapes our wants.
- Demands – when our wishes, needs and wants are backed by our capability to pay, then they become demands (Fig. 3.1).

3.2   Production-Oriented Marketing Concept

Production-oriented marketing is one of the earliest marketing concepts where the organization concentrates on the ability of its production processes. It is to manufacture the products cheaper to make them ready for the mass population. The centre of the production concept is on the quantity, not the quality of the products.

Table 3.2   Production-related marketing concept

No.	Description
1.	Focus on product availability, competitiveness and affordability
2.	Major goal is the continuous optimization of production and distribution
3.	Profitability through efficient production and optimization
4.	Mass production, mass distribution or mass customization

Fig. 3.2   Production-oriented marketing concept. (Source: Author's source)

Production concept began in the mid 1950s, and it accompanies the Say's Law. It says that supply generates demand in the market. Therefore, according to this law, when a company manufactures a product, it doesn't need to promote its products; it would sell itself. The law became widespread because, at that time, there was no technology and communications, and people used to travel less. The salesman in the store used to be the only retailer, and there were few manufacturers (Kotler et al., 2017). So there used to be a confined variety of products, whatever comes in the market, and then it would have been marketed. For example, McDonald's and fast-food chains in general also aim to ace their operations. Another example is Ford Motor Company. Ford was the first vehicle company; it commenced delivering more vehicles in the market. People purchased it because it was the only product available at the time (Table 3.2 and Fig. 3.2).

3.3   Product-Related Marketing Concept

The core purpose of the product concept is to manufacture cheaper products because the consumers won't pay much price for the products or services. So, the businesses that accompany the product concept manufacture the goods on a mass scale and profit out of the economies of scale.

When manufacturers produce low-cost products, then they follow a broad distribution strategy to reach more audiences. By targeting more people, they can boost their productivity by expanding their market. In the product concept, marketers do not give any importance to the requirements and wants of the customers. Their central focus is to produce more and more goods; quantity matters, not quality. As a result, consumers are usually unsatisfied with the bad quality of the products. The product concept was popular when there were no competitors in the market; whatever you bring in the market, people would take it. For instance, Ford was the first

Table 3.3 Product-related marketing concept

No.	Description
1.	Focus on quality, delivery and other performance criteria or features
2.	Product will sell itself due to specific product features
3.	Emphasis on continuous product improvements
4.	Profitability and growth due product quality and superiority

Fig. 3.3 Product-related marketing concept

vehicle company; it commenced delivering more vehicles in the market. People purchased it because it was the only product available at the time (Table 3.3 and Fig. 3.3).

3.4 Sales-Oriented Marketing Concept

As the name suggests, the idea of selling is to sell the company's product through large-scale marketing and promotional activities (Homburg et al., 2012). It doesn't matter whether they satisfy customers' needs or not. The centre of the management in this method is to finish the transaction of sale; they believe that their job is done once they market their product (Keith, 1960). Therefore, rather than establishing and maintaining a long-term connection with the customer, the customer would come back again. The sale concept is a very precarious strategy because it's based on a very weak notion that the company should sell whatever they're manufacturing instead of meeting customer's demands (Jones & Shaw, 2006). In this approach, marketers believe that if consumers don't like the company's product, they'll buy

Table 3.4 Sales-oriented marketing concept

No.	Description
1.	Sales department and selling function are dominant
2.	The organization sells everything it can sell – idea generation based on sales opportunities
3.	Capacity exceeds demand for sales
4.	Stimulating demand by active sales activities and campaigns

something else and forget about their past shopping experience (Helmold, 2021). So, the whole notion of the sale concept is based on the false presumption that the customers don't remember their past buying experience. For example, blood donations and insurance policies come under the category of sale concept, where the marketer believes that their job is done after making the transaction. Table 3.4 shows the characteristics of a sales-oriented marketing concept.

3.5 Marketing-Oriented Marketing Concept

When it comes to the marketing concept, it is customer-oriented. It places customers in the middle of the marketing process, discovering customers' demands and wants and then meeting those needs better than the competitors. In this method, the marketer assumes that the customer is always right, and his requirements and wants should be their priority. Here, the marketing strategy concentrates on producing a profit by satisfying the needs and wants of customers. It supports a very simple strategy: marketers do not search for the right customers for their product; instead, they build the right product. Thus, marketers seek to bridge the gap between the consumers and the company's products. When you analyse the marketing concept with the sale concept, you may find a huge distinction between both strategies. It won't be wrong if you state that these two strategies are at two opposite extreme poles. The best example of this concept is the Coke vs. Pepsi war (Table 3.5).

Figure 3.4 shows the value chain by Porter (1997) including primary and secondary functions. The value chain represents the stages of production as an orderly sequence of activities. These activities create values, consume resources and are linked in processes. The concept was first published in 1985 by Michael E. Porter in his book *Competitive Advantage*. Every company is a collection of activities that design, manufacture, sell, ship and support its product. All of these activities can be represented in a value chain. The value chain is made up of the individual value activities and the margin. Value activities are activities that are performed to produce a product or service. The margin is the difference between the yield that this product generates and the resources used. The graphic shows the basic model of the Porter value chain. Primary activities are those activities that make a direct, value-adding contribution to the creation of a product or service. In the basic model, these are inbound logistics, production, outbound logistics, marketing and sales and customer service. Support activities are activities that are necessary to carry out the primary activities. They thus make an indirect contribution to the creation of a

Table 3.5 Marketing-oriented marketing concept

No.	Description
1.	Customer-centric approach, in which all departments are aligned with marketing
2.	Customer needs and wants trigger the activities of the enterprise
3.	Marketing as a lead function to coordinate all customer-affected actions
4.	Profitability through centric allocation of customer needs and wants

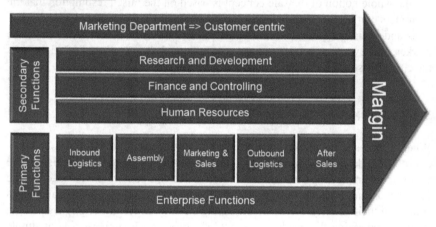

Fig. 3.4 Marketing-oriented concept

product or service. In the basic model, these are company infrastructure, human resources, technology development and procurement.

A company's value chain is linked to the value chains of suppliers and buyers. Together they form the value chain system of an industry. In the marketing-oriented marketing concept, all other functions are coordinated by the overriding aim of customer-centric marketing activities.

3.6   Social Marketing-Oriented Marketing Concept

Societal responsibility of marketing is a marketing concept that holds that a company should make marketing decisions not only by considering consumers' wants and the company's requirements but also the society's long-term interests (Kraus, 2008). The societal marketing concept holds that the organization's task is to determine the needs, wants and interests of a target market and to deliver the desired satisfactions more effectively and efficiently than competitors in a way that preserves or enhances the well-being of both the individual consumer and society in general. Therefore, marketers must endeavour to satisfy the needs and wants of their target markets in ways that preserve and enhance the well-being of consumers and society as a whole. It is closely linked with the principles of corporate social

Table 3.6 Social marketing concept

No.	Description
1.	Society-centric approach based on economy, society and environment
2.	Closely related to corporate social responsibility (CSR)
3.	Pricing and sales must be socially fair
4.	Focus on green and socially responsible value chain activities

responsibility and of sustainable development (Wilkie & Moore, 2006). The idea behind the societal marketing concept is based on the welfare of the entire society because it examines the strategy of the marketing concept. What consumers need doesn't mean that it would be useful for them in the long term. What you need and what is suitable for you and the society as a whole are two entirely different things. For example, we all like sweet, spicy and fast foods. We all desire the same things whenever we go out, but it doesn't imply that it's good for our health and the well-being of the whole society (Tomczak et al., 2018). The goal and aim of the societal marketing concept is to make companies understand that they have a friendly and environmental responsibility, much more important than their short-term sales and profit goals. Businesses should design and operate towards a sustainable future for society; organizations are a part of society and should behave like one. One of the best examples of societal marketing concepts is the Coca Cola Super Bowl Commercial 2014 "America the Beautiful" campaign (Table 3.6).

Societal marketing can be defined as a marketing with a social dimension or marketing that includes non-economic criteria. Societal marketing "concerns for society's long-term interests". It is about "the direct benefits for the organization and secondary benefit for the community". Societal marketing distinguishes between the consumer's immediate satisfaction and longer-term consumer and social benefits. Accordingly, Andreas Kaplan defines societal management as management that takes into account society's overall welfare in addition to mere profitability considerations. It is a three-dimensional concept of marketing – social welfare, individual welfare, organization profit (Fig. 3.5).

3.7   Case Study: PepsiCo's Product-Oriented Marketing

3.7.1   Introduction to PepsiCo

PepsiCo is one of the two leading soda beverages brands in the industry. It was formed after the merger of Pepsi and Frito lay in 1965. The brand continued to perform well even during the economic recession (PepsiCo, 2021). The current CEO of PepsiCo is Indra Nooyi under whose leadership the brand has continued to expand its business and transform its product portfolio. The year 2017 was a year of healthy growth for the brand when PepsiCo achieved a core organic revenue growth of 2.3%. Even after the recession, the soda brands have continued to face difficulties because of the sweeping changes globally throughout the industry. Soda industry is marked by intense competition, and the beverages brands are spending heavily on marketing as well as product innovation in order to achieve

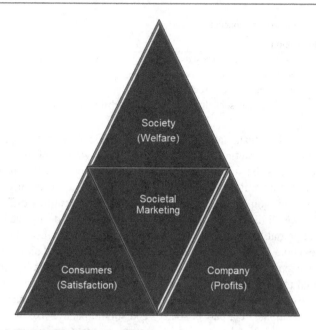

Fig. 3.5 Societal marketing concept

faster growth. Pepsi has been known for creating exciting marketing campaigns. It has 20 billion dollar brands in its portfolio. Its income from food products has kept growing, and in 2017 the brand earned 53% of its revenue from food products and only 47% from the beverages products. The USA is still the largest market for Pepsi from which Pepsi earned 58% of its revenue in 2017. However, the brand is investing in international markets too for faster growth. It has organized its business in six reportable segments. The brand is also investing heavily in technology for superior growth and for marketing. Marketing is one of the primary drivers of business growth for Pepsi. The soda giant invests billions in advertising and promotion. Its nearest competitor is Coca Cola, and both brands are engaged in an intense battle. Each one invests heavily in marketing and product innovation for growth. Pepsi along with its consolidated subsidiaries employs 263,000 people out of which 113,000 were employed in the USA alone.

3.7.2 Positioning and Segmentation

Before moving on to the details of PepsiCo's marketing strategy, take a look upon how it has positioned its brand and products in the market. It has positioned itself as a snacks and beverages brand that includes nutritious and low-calorie choices apart from normal soda products. There are 22 iconic billion dollar brands in its portfolio. Pepsi is positioned as a brand that reflects young energy, and this is also a key theme across its advertising and marketing campaigns. The customers of Pepsi are mainly from the 13 o 35 age group. In other words, you can say it is a brand for the millennials. Pepsi has maintained a pricing strategy that has made it an affordable brand. Its customers are from all income segments including lower middle class to upper class. Now, it has also released smaller options for its several soft drinks to make its products more affordable and accessible. Its customers include teenagers and youth with a modern and fast-moving lifestyle.

3.7.3   Investments in Marketing

PepsiCo has traditionally relied heavily on marketing for driving sales and market growth. Like Coca Cola, it too spends heavily on marketing and promotion. In 2017, its marketing budget was 4.1 billion dollars and that of Coca Cola was 3.9 billion dollars. Pepsi spent 2.4 billion dollars solely on advertising. However, the world of marketing has changed a lot with the rise of the digital technology. A large part of Pepsi's marketing budget goes to digital marketing and advertising. Apart from that, a large sum is also spent on television advertising and other traditional methods of advertising. Any leading brand is investing heavily in digital technology for marketing and better customer experience. Since the rise of social media, brands are connecting with their customers in real time with promotional campaigns. On the one hand, social media has helped the brands with marketing to allow them to connect with millions of customers globally in an instant and without any financial investment. On the other hand, it has also made the brands more conscious regarding product quality and customer service because any comment or news shared on social media reaches millions in a few seconds.

3.7.4   Product Innovations

Pepsi has continued to invest in product quality and packaging to stay the customers' first choice. However, apart from these things, it has continued to diversify its product portfolio bringing new, healthier and more nutritious choices for its customers. Behind its excellent marketing strategy, there is a diverse and rich product portfolio filled with a large variety of flavours and nutritious and tasty choices. Product quality and packaging are very important elements of Pepsi's marketing strategy where it has continued to innovate whether in terms of product quality, variety as well as packaging. Its reward-winning design team has continued to innovate with package design. Regularly updating the package design also helps retain customers and attract new ones. Attractive packages can also drive sales higher, and it is why Pepsi has continued to innovate the packaging style and sizes based on consumer demand and expectations. With time, people's taste and choice of flavours have changed a lot. They are looking for healthier products, and product innovation helps churn demand. However, apart from investing in product quality and design, it is equally important to invest in marketing, and Pepsi promotes its brand through both digital and traditional channels. Figure 3.6 shows the marketing campaign of Pepsi in China.

Fig. 3.6 Pepsi marketing campaign. (Source: Branding in Asia (2020). CHINA, CREATIVE WORK, VMLY&R SPOTLIGHT. Pepsi Launches AR Campaign Calling on China's GenZ to Showcase Their Passions. Retrieved 13.5.2022. https://www.brandinginasia.com/pepsi-launches-ar-campaign-calling-on-chinas-genz-to-showcase-their-passions/)

References

Düssel, M. (2006). *Handbuch Marketingpraxis – Von der Analyse zur Strategie, Ausarbeitung der Taktik, Steuerung und Umsetzung in der Praxis*. Cornelsen.

Esch, F. R., et al. (2008). *Eine managementorientierte Einführung* (2. Auflage). Vahlen Verlag München.

Helmold, M. (2020). *Total Revenue Management (TRM). Case studies, best practices and industry insights*. Springer.

Helmold, M. (2021). *Successful management strategies and tools. Industry insights, case studies and best practices*. Springer.

Homburg, C., Schäfer, H., & Schneider, J. (2012). *Sales excellence. Systematic sales management*. Springer.

Keith, R. J. (1960). The marketing revolution. *Journal of Marketing, 24*(1), 35–38.

Jones, B. D. G., & Shaw, E. H. (2006). A history of marketing thought. In B. A. Weitz & R. Wensley (Eds.), *Handbook of marketing*. Sage.

Kotler, P., et al. (2008). *Grundlagen des marketing* (5th ed.). Pearson Studium München.

Kotler, P., Kartajaya, H., & Setiawan, A. (2017). *Marketing 4.0: Moving from traditional to digital*. Wiley.

Kotler, P., & Armstrong, G. (2018). *Principles of marketing* (17th ed.).

Kraus, F. (2008). *Der Transfer der Marktorientierung über Hierarchieebenen – Eine empirische Mehrebenenuntersuchung*. Springer.

Meffert, H., et al. (2008). *Marketing* (10th ed.). Springer.

Porter. (1997). *Nur Strategie sichert auf Dauer hohe Erträge*. In Havard Manager. Nr. 3, S. 42–58.

PepsiCo. (2021). www.pepsico.com.

Wilkie, W. L., & Moore, E. S. (2006, December). Macromarketing as a pillar of marketing thought. *Journal of Macromarketing, 26*(2), 224–232.

Tomczak, T., Reinecke, S., & Kuss, A. (2018). *Strategic marketing. Market-oriented corporate and business unit planning*. Springer.

B2B and B2C Marketing

4

> *Marketing is about values. It's a complicated and noisy world,*
> *and we're not going to get a chance to get people to remember*
> *much about us. No company is. So we have to be really clear*
> *about what we want them to know about us.*

Steve Jobs

4.1 B2B and BC2 Marketing

4.1.1 B2B Marketing

The two major segments of marketing are business-to-business (B2B) marketing and business-to-consumer (B2C) marketing (Düssel, 2006). B2B (business-to-business) marketing refers to any marketing strategy or content that is geared towards a business or organization (Kotler & Amstron, 2018). Any company that sells products or services to other businesses or organizations (vs. consumers) typically uses B2B marketing strategies. Examples of products sold through B2B marketing include:

- Major equipment
- Accessory equipment
- Raw materials
- Component parts
- Processed materials
- Supplies
- Business services

The four major categories of B2B product purchasers are the following:

- Producers – use products sold by B2B marketing to make their own goods (e.g. Mattel buying plastics to make toys)
- Resellers – buy B2B products to sell through retail or wholesale establishments (e.g. Walmart buying vacuums to sell in stores)

- Governments – buy B2B products for use in government projects (e.g. purchasing contractor services to repair infrastructure)
- Institutions – use B2B products to continue operation (e.g. schools buying printers for office use)

4.1.2   B2C Marketing

Business-to-consumer marketing, or B2C marketing, refers to the tactics and strategies in which a company promotes its products and services to individual people. Traditionally, this could refer to individuals shopping for personal products in a broad sense. More recently, the term B2C refers to the online selling of consumer products (Fig. 4.1).

4.1.3   C2B Marketing

Consumer-to-business marketing or C2B marketing is a business model where the end consumers create products and services which are consumed by businesses and organizations. It is diametrically opposed to the popular concept of B2C or business- to-consumer where the companies make goods and services available to the end consumers.

4.1.4   C2C Marketing

Customer-to-customer marketing or C2C marketing represents a market environment where one customer purchases goods from another customer using a

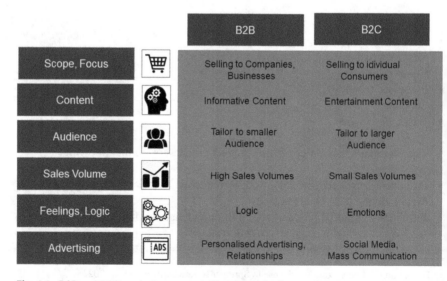

Fig. 4.1 B2B and B2C marketing concept. (Source: Author's source)

third-party business or platform to facilitate the transaction. C2C companies are a new type of model that has emerged with e-commerce technology and the sharing economy.

4.1.5   Differences in B2B and B2C Marketing

The different goals of B2B and B2C marketing lead to differences in the B2B and B2C markets (Esch et al., 2008). The main differences in these markets are demand, purchasing volume, number of customers, customer concentration, distribution, buying nature, buying influences, negotiations, reciprocity, leasing and promotional methods (Kotler et al., 2008, 2017).

- Demand: B2B demand is derived because businesses buy products based on how much demand there is for the final consumer product. Businesses buy products based on customer's wants and needs. B2C demand is primarily because customers buy products based on their own wants and needs.
- Purchasing volume: Businesses buy products in large volumes to distribute to consumers. Consumers buy products in smaller volumes suitable for personal use.
- Number of customers: There are relatively fewer businesses to market to than direct consumers.
- Customer concentration: Businesses that specialize in a particular market tend to be geographically concentrated, while customers that buy products from these businesses are not concentrated.
- Distribution: B2B products pass directly from the producer of the product to the business, while B2C products must additionally go through a wholesaler or retailer.
- Buying nature: B2B purchasing is a formal process done by professional buyers and sellers, while B2C purchasing is informal.
- Buying influences: B2B purchasing is influenced by multiple people in various departments such as quality control, accounting, and logistics, while B2C marketing is only influenced by the person making the purchase and possibly a few others.
- Negotiations: In B2B marketing, negotiating for lower prices or added benefits is commonly accepted, while in B2C marketing (particularly in Western cultures), prices are fixed.
- Reciprocity: Businesses tend to buy from businesses they sell to. For example, a business that sells printer ink is more likely to buy office chairs from a supplier that buys the business's printer ink. In B2C marketing, this does not occur because consumers are not also selling products.
- Leasing: Businesses tend to lease expensive items, while consumers tend to save up to buy expensive items.
- Promotional methods: In B2B marketing, the most common promotional method is personal selling. B2C marketing mostly uses sales promotion, public relations, advertising and social media.

Fig. 4.2   B2B and B2C examples. (Source: Author's source)

Figure 4.2 depicts B2B examples and B2C examples. Companies like HubSpot, IBM and SAP are more oriented towards B2C activities and offer professional business solutions. Disney, Finder or Coca-Cola are oriented towards B2C activities.

4.2   Case Study: Telekom B2B Service

Deutsche Telekom B2B Europe is dedicated to help businesses and public institutions in their digital transformation in Central and Eastern Europe (CEE). The integrated fixed, mobile and ICT solutions we offer are supported by our market-leading mobile and fibre optic networks as well as a data centre footprint that is one of the largest in the region. With activities in 13 European countries, we use our regional presence and dense local access networks to deliver a rich variety of services – from basic fixed or mobile voice and data transmission to complex virtual private networks, clouds, IoT and many other ICT solutions. Our global partners help us to create complete IT ecosystems that organizations can tap into through our one-stop shop, across Europe and beyond.

References

Düssel, M. (2006). *Handbuch Marketingpraxis – Von der Analyse zur Strategie, Ausarbeitung der Taktik, Steuerung und Umsetzung in der Praxis*. Cornelsen.

Esch, F. R., et al. (2008). *Eine managementorientierte Einführung* (2. Auflage). Vahlen Verlag München.

Kotler, P., & Armstrong, G. (2018). *Principles of marketing* (17th ed.). Hoboken.

Kotler, P., et al. (2008). *Grundlagen des marketing* (5th ed.). Pearson Studium.

Kotler, P., Kartajaya, H., & Setiawan, A. (2017). *Marketing 4.0: Moving from traditional to digital*. Wiley.

Sales Management

5

> *Business opportunities are like buses; there's always another one coming.*
>
> Richard Branson

5.1 Definition of Sales Management

The term sales management is a combination of two words – sales and management. Sales is the art of planning in the mind of another, a motive which will induce favourable action. The committee of American Marketing Association has defined it as selling is the personal or impersonal process of assisting and/or persuading a prospective customer to buy a commodity or a service or to act favourably upon an idea that has commercial significance to the seller. Moreover, controlling is any common activity to achieve a per determined goal. Hence, sales management can be defined as the planning, direction and control of selling of business unit including recruiting, selecting, training, equipping, assigning, routing, supervising, paying and motivating as these tasks apply to the personnel of sales force (Kotler & Armstrong). Sales management originally referred exclusively to the direction of the sales force. Later, the term took on broader significance in addition to the management of personal selling. Sales management includes all marketing activities, including advertising, sales promotion, marketing research, physical distribution, pricing and product merchandising.

5.2 Sales Management Process

5.2.1 Introduction to the Sales Management Process

According to the definition of the committee of the American marketing association, sales management meant "the planning, direction and control of personal selling including recruiting, selecting equipping, assigning, routing, supervising, paying and motivating as these tasks apply to the personal sales force".

Sales management is the process of developing a sales force, coordinating sales operations and implementing sales techniques that allow a business to consistently

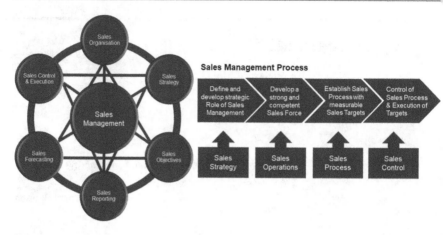

Fig. 5.1   Sales management elements

hit, and even surpass, its sales targets. Sales management is a business discipline which is focused on the practical application of sales techniques and the management of a firm's sales operations. It is an important business function as net sales through the sale of products and services and resulting profit drive most commercial business. These are also typically the goals and performance indicators of sales management. When it comes to boosting sales performance for any size of operation, no matter the industry, the secret to success is always precise sales management processes, which starts with a great sales manager who knows how to inspire and lead a sales department. Besides helping your company reach its sales objectives, the sales management process allows you to stay in tune with your industry as it grows and can be the difference between surviving and flourishing in an increasingly competitive marketplace. Whether you're an experienced or new sales manager, you should be able to evaluate and gain visibility into your current sales force with the following guide to sales management. Once you have a clear picture of what processes to monitor and how to keep track of them, you'll be equipped to pinpoint issues early on, coach people before it's too late and have a better overview of the tasks the team should be doing to increase its sales. There are three "umbrellas" to manage within the sales process (Fig. 5.1):

- Sales strategy
- Sales operations
- Sales process
- Sales control

5.3   Sales Strategy

A sales strategy is a plan to achieve a sales goal and is what directs the selling activities of a start-up business (and in fact any business). Selling is crucial to the success of any business, but it must be orchestrated to deliver success, which is what the

Fig. 5.2 Sales strategy. (Source: Author's source)

sales strategy does (Meffert et al., 2008). A sales strategy is therefore a must for every business; every business needs a sales strategy.

Creating a winning sales strategy means knowing the answers to the key questions:

- Where are we standing in terms of sales management?
- What are the key building blocks of a sales strategy and where do we want to go?
- How do you build a successful sales strategy?

The sales strategy describes how a business will win, retain and develop customers. The sales strategy is closely linked to new product and customer developments and there often referred to as the sales and customer development strategy. The lean start-up is an approach that is different to the traditional approach to starting a business, as the lean start-up favours experimentation over elaborate planning, customer feedback over intuition and iterative design over grand up front design development (Wilkie & Moore, 2006).

There is an important point that I want to make from the outset; that is, a sales strategy is different from marketing strategy. A marketing strategy is the overall approach to marketing products. More specifically, it is how you build a sustainable competitive advantage for the company's products through positioning and differentiation by managing the marketing mix of the 7 Ps (Kraus, 2008; Pelz, 2004). A sales strategy is more about how you win, retain and develop customers. Of course, the marketing strategy goes hand in hand with the sales strategy, as it enables achievement of what is ultimately the most important target: the sales goal (Fig. 5.2).

5.4   Sales Operations

Sales operations refers to the unit, role, activities and processes within a sales organization that support, enable and drive front line sales teams to sell better, faster and more efficiently. Sales operations includes the four elements: sales organization, sales technology, sales rewards (incentives) and sales performance. Through strategically implemented training, software tools and engagement techniques, sales operations leaders enable sales reps to focus more on selling in order to drive business results.

5.5   Sales Organization

Sales organization is the social and hierarchical structure of the sales activities. Sales organization defines the duties, roles and the rights and responsibilities of salespeople engaged in selling activities meant for the effective execution of the sales function (Düssel, 2006; Tomczak et al., 2018). This demands a coherent and unified effort of individuals in the organization in achieving a common goal (Jones & Shaw, 2006). A sales organization is designed to execute functions which go beyond just achieving sales through the department. It is used to attain the qualitative and quantitative objectives of personal selling. These objectives are related to sales volume, profitability and market share. Sales organization is used not only to achieve the present objectives but also to attain a particular future position.

5.6   Sales Technology

The sales operations department aims to support sales managers not only to achieve targets but to optimize the talent pool (i.e. the sales floor) under their care. To do this, a sales operations manager assumes many of the administrative and operational loads required to run a sales organization. This frees up the sales manager to focus on leading sellers in meeting their quotas and making tactical decisions and strategic plans for long-term growth. Depending on the organizational maturity, the sales operations managers can assume responsibility for elements, which create new sales and value. These are (1) generate data-driven insight and forecasts for strategy planning; (2) recruit, on board, and train sales staff; (3) follow content- and knowledge-based management; (4) adhere to customer contract life cycle management; implement compensation and incentives program; (5) enforce processes, methodologies and performance matrices; (6) administer, synchronize and optimize technology stack including CRM. The sales teams harness the power of big data analytics, artificial intelligence and machine learning to improve performance and future proof profitability. However, because tool complexity can distract sellers, sales operations should own the stack. Here's what sales operations leaders should own regarding the tech stack: defragmentation and integration of technology tools, customer relationship management (CRM) platform, business intelligence services, data analytics software, communication and conferencing tools, content sharing and management, contract lifecycle management, email automation, performance management software.

5.7   Sales Incentives

The sales incentive program is a formal scheme used to promote or encourage specific actions or behaviour by sales people during a defined period of time. Hence, programs are primarily used to drive sales, reduce sales costs, increase profitability, develop new territory and enhance margins. Sales incentive programs have the most direct relationship to outcomes. A sales incentive plan (SIP) is a business tool used to motivate and compensate a sales professional or sales agent to meet goals or metrics over a specific period of time, usually broken into a plan for a fiscal quarter or fiscal year. An SIP is very similar to a commission plan; however, an SIP can incorporate sales metrics other than goods sold (or value of goods sold), which is traditionally how a commission plan is derived. Sales metrics used in a SIP are typically in the form of sales quotas (sometimes referred to as point of sale or POS shipments), new business opportunities and/or management by objectives (MBOs) independent action of the sales professional and is usually used in conjunction with a base salary. SIPs are used to incent sales professionals where total sales are not a precise measure of sales productivity. This is usually due to the complexity or length of the sales process or where a sale is completed not by an individual but by a team of people, each contributing unique skills to the sales process. SIPs are used to encourage and compensate each member of the sales team as they contribute to the team's ability to sell. It is not uncommon for the members of such teams to be located in different physical locations and for the product introduction to happen in one location and the purchase of such a product to occur in another location. To achieve growth in this changing and challenging selling environment, many companies have made important changes, like the creation of new digital channels, the addition of specialized roles and the adoption of team-based selling. There is another crucial shift, however, that tends to be overlooked. Fully addressing today's complexities necessitates the development of new, thoughtful compensation models that provide clear motivation for how a salesforce can continue to sell effectively. Salespeople shouldn't be told what to do; they should feel persuaded towards behaviours that will support a company's go-to-market strategy. Adjusting the mix of commissions, quotas, salaries and bonuses for the salesforce can be a driver of growth. Smart revisions of compensation models have been found to have a 50% higher impact on sales than changes in advertising investments.

5.8   Sales Performance

Sales management emerged to improve the sales performance. To achieve that, sales operations people help streamline processes to speed up the sales cycle and enable sellers to close more deals. Preferred metrics vary across teams and organizations. For sales operations, these key metrics provide insight not only on how to improve win rates but also on how the entire process can still be optimized. The following are just a subset of all metrics commonly used by many sales operations units to evaluate past performance and to consistently improve organizational results in the long term: Salesforce Quota Achievement Rate is the percentage of the sales team

Fig. 5.3 Sales operations. (Source: Author's source)

that have achieved 100% of quota during a given period. Average win rate is the ratio of closed-won deals over the total number of won and lost deals. Average sales cycle length is the average length of time it takes to close deals. Average deal size is the average value of deal sizes sellers are managing at any given point in the process. Time spent selling is the actual time sellers spend selling as compared to other tasks such as internal meetings, training and administrative work. Lead response time is the time it takes before leads respond positively to a pitch or call to action. Weighted pipeline value is the estimated value of the pipeline at a given time in the process, used to make profit/loss forecasts. Pipeline efficiency measures how effective sellers are at managing their pipelines. Forecast accuracy computes the rate of error of prior forecasts vs. actual results or performance. Number of Prospect Meetings per Period is a measure of prospecting activity that compares the number of meetings individual sellers were able to set in a given period (Fig. 5.3).

5.9   Benefits of Structured Sales Management

Sales management in practice positively affects everyone involved in the sales cycle. The more mature your sales process is and the more the sales manager adapts and improves it over time, the more likely your team will achieve top performance. In the same way that we've outlined the three aspects of sales management, there are three key stakeholders involved with the sales management process: the sales manager, salesperson and customer.

5.10   Sales Funnel

5.10.1 Purpose of the Sales Funnel

The marketing funnel is a visualization for understanding the process of turning leads into customers, as understood from a marketing (and sales) perspective (Kotler & Armstrong, 2018; Kotler et al., 2008, 2017). The idea is that, like a funnel, marketers cast a broad net to capture as many leads as possible and then slowly nurture prospective customers through the purchasing decision, narrowing down these candidates in each stage of the funnel. Ideally, this marketing funnel would actually be a marketing cylinder, and all of your leads would turn into customers. Though this is not a reality for businesses, it is part of a marketer's job to turn as many leads into customers as possible, thus making the funnel more cylindrical. It's important to note that there is not a single agreed-upon version of the funnel; some have many "stages", while others have few, with different names and actions taken by the business and consumer for each. In the diagram below, we've done our best to pull out the most common and relevant funnel stages, terms and actions, so this information is useful to as many marketers as possible (Helmold, 2021). The sales funnel (also known as a revenue funnel or sales process) refers to the buying process that companies lead customers through when purchasing products. The definition also refers to the process through which a company finds, qualifies and sells its products to customers. A sales funnel provides a clear view of the opportunities available to a sales team, accurately showing the revenue the team is going to make in the months ahead. What is the purpose of a sales funnel? A sales funnel is a model for visualizing every stage in the customer journey, from the time prospective customers learn about a brand to the moment they make a purchase as shown in Fig. 5.5.

5.10.2 Awareness

People and customers have to be aware of the products and services a company is providing. The customers should know about the product features, specifics, quality and the price of the product or service. At this step, enterprises should invest time into content marketing, email outreach, social media campaigns, SEO and online advertisement to achieve brand awareness.

5.10.3 Interest

This step takes awareness to the next level. Once someone's heard of the brand, one needs to capture their interest. Companies need to make them realize that they can provide something they need, even if they did not know they needed it. Drip campaigns, social media campaigns and useful content such as eBooks and videos are key. Many potential customers bail at this step, so it's important to really present your product as a solution to their problems.

5.10.4 Consideration

At this point, the prospect is collecting as much information about a company's solution and its competitors' to decide whether the considered company is the best choice and whether they want to buy from this company. Again, providing videos, how-tos, testimonials, reviews, trials and even webinars will boost the chances of them making it to the next step.

5.10.5 Intent

To get to the intent stage, prospects must demonstrate that they are interested in buying a brand's product. This can happen in a survey, after a product demo or when a product is placed in the shopping cart on an ecommerce website. This is an opportunity for marketers to make a strong case for why their product is the best choice for a buyer.

5.10.6 Evaluation

In the evaluation stage, buyers are making a final decision about whether or not to buy a brand's product or services. Typically, marketing and sales work together closely to nurture the decision-making process and convince the buyer that their brand's product is the best choice.

5.10.7 Purchase

Purchase – You did it! Now give your customer personalized attention, providing helpful emails, good customer service and regular newsletters (a.k.a. nurture them) so that they don't feel abandoned after the sale and continue buying from you. Good customer onboarding will help you not just reduce the churn rate but also improve your customers' CLV by acquiring loyal brand fans (Fig. 5.4).

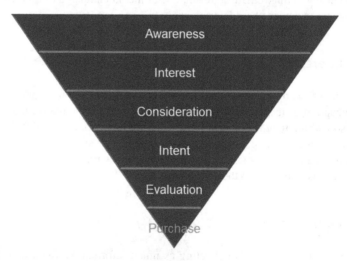

Fig. 5.4 Sales funnel. (Source: Author's source)

5.11   Case Study: Marketing and Sales Strategy in Porsche

5.11.1 Introduction of Porsche

Porsche is a prestigious automobile brand that specializes in high-performance sports cars, SUVs and sedans and has a strong social media presence (Porsche, 2021). Do you want to know how Porsche became so successful in the automotive industry? The reason for this is due to the company's marketing strategy.

Marketing is one of the most important functions of a business that engages in promotion and marketing activities such as market research and advertising for products or services, especially in today's context where marketing innovation has accelerated exponentially and adoption of these techniques can be a make or break factor for the companies. Porsche is a German automotive manufacturer known for producing high-performance sports cars, SUVs and sedans. In 1931, Ferdinand Porsche founded the company. The company's headquarters is in Zuffenhausen, a district of Stuttgart, Germany. Volkswagen AG owns the company, with Porsche Automobil Holding SE owning a controlling stake. Porsche is best known for its powerful, agile sports cars, most notably the iconic 911. Porsche AG owns 29% of Bertrandt AG, a German engineering and design consultancy, and 81.8% of Mieschke Hofmann und Partner. It is still cutting-edge in terms of performance and technology. Its primary goal is to achieve value-generating growth. Every car fan's subconscious is imprinted with the Porsche slogan, "there is no substitute". We've all heard that if you say something often enough, people will believe it, and this is exactly what's happening.

5.11.2 Porsche Marketing Mix

The marketing mix refers to the various areas of emphasis through which a company promotes its brand or product in the market, and they are product, price, promotion and place.

1. *Product Strategy*

Porsche is a well-known company that sells luxury automobiles all over the world. The best luxury cars have technology that is advanced enough to make the passengers feel as if they are in a high-tech hotel suite rather than a car. The 718 Boxster/Cayman, 911, Panamera, Macan, Cayenne and Taycan are currently available from Porsche. The company has expanded its product line-up with vehicles such as an SUV and sedan, as well as the introduction of new sports cars. Porsche luxury cars are appealing because of their touch screen, Bluetooth connection and 3D sound system. When customers purchase a Porsche, they meet their expectations.

2. Price Strategy

Pricing of Porsche ranges from approximately INR.69,98,000 to INR.3,07,83,000. The prices of these automobiles begin at Rs 69.98 lakh for the most affordable model, the Macan, and Rs 1.64 crore for the most expensive model, the 911. When the Porsche Panamera S first hit the market, it was priced around $133,000. However, in order to increase sales, the price was reduced to $120,000 over time. Porsche has been using this technique for quite some time. This is known as price skimming, where you introduce your product at a high price. However, as time passes, the company lowers the prices of its products in order to increase sales. Price skimming is a pricing strategy in which the producer sets a high introductory price to attract buyers who have a strong desire for the product and the resources to purchase it and then gradually lowers the price to attract buyers in the subsequent layers of the market. They also used a psychological pricing strategy. The best part is that if Porsche swaps the prices, there will be little or no change in demand because they have exclusive cars that not everyone can afford. As a result, we can conclude that Porsche does not follow competitor-based pricing.

3. Place Strategy

Porsche has a very simple distribution channel, which gives it a competitive advantage. Zuffenhausen is Porsche's heart, the place where it all started. Porsche's second home is in Leipzig, where the customer centre welcomes 40,000 visitors per year. Although Porsche's origins are in Germany, the fascination with sports cars can be found all over the world. It sells its products all over the world, with the top three countries being China (88,968), United States (57,294) and Germany (26,152). China is the biggest market for Cayenne and Panamera models. Porsche was also able to maintain its growth in all of the major markets.

4. Promotion Strategy

During the 2011 earthquake in Japan, Porsche donated $2.5 million in aid. This improved the brand's image while also allowing it to promote its business by having a better reputation. It advertises on television and other forms of media. They also do offline promotion through magazines, billboards and other means. As a result, they employ both above-the-line and below-the-line marketing strategies.

5.11.3 Porsche Marketing Strategy

Through its marketing strategies, Porsche has set the difficult goal of attracting a younger and more female audience. It aided the company in repositioning its brand without alienating its core customers. Porsche is a successful example of how to effectively segment their target market area and achieve the best marketing results.

Targeting Strategy of Porsche
Porsche caters to privileged and upscale clients. College graduates with a household income of more than $100,000 are among the target audiences, with 85% being males and 15% being females. Its targeted marketing efforts are aimed at increasing the number of female Porsche owners and decreasing the average age of Porsche owners. Porsche hired tennis player Maria Sharapova as a brand ambassador in 2013 in order to reach out to young female audiences. As a result, the percentage of female buyers who purchased the Cayenne SUV and Panamera increased from 8% to 15%.

Porsche Digital Marketing Strategy
Social media is the foundation of the company's digital strategy. It is incorporating social media thinking into its digital marketing to create a strategy that will benefit the company while also interacting socially with customers.

Porsche Advertising Campaign
An advertising strategy is a strategy incorporated for reaching out to and persuading customers to purchase a product or service. It includes campaigns that result in the potential success of the brand. Cramer-Krasselt was the creator of a new multimedia campaign for Porsche's new model, the 911. It created the 30-s spot "Pop Star", which is fast-paced and whimsical. It is part of the larger "Timeless Machine" campaign, which honours the model's impact on pop culture over the last 55 years. Inspired by those fan creations and the culture surrounding Porsche, "Pop Star" depicted the 911 traveling across the screen, transforming into the various objects it has appeared on or as over the years, including a lamp, puzzle, paper clip, Legos and more.

The Power of "Balance" Campaign
To promote the launch of its Cayman model, the brand created a digital campaign, "a series of computer games" called "The Power of Balance". "Advanced engineering. Driving ambition. A perfect fusion of man and machine brought together in true Porsche spirit. This is what makes the new Cayman unique. This is the Power of Balance". This strong model statement and campaign is exactly what enticed the target audience to interact with the brand and play the game. Figure 5.5 shows the Power of Balance advertising campaign.

Fig. 5.5 Porsche advertising campaign

References

Düssel, M. (2006). *Handbuch Marketingpraxis – Von der Analyse zur Strategie, Ausarbeitung der Taktik, Steuerung und Umsetzung in der Praxis*. Cornelsen.

Helmold, M. (2021). *Successful management strategies and tools. Industry insights, case studies and bset practices*. Springer.

Jones, B. D. G., & Shaw, E. H. (2006). A history of marketing thought. In B. A. Weitz & R. Wensley (Eds.), *Handbook of marketing*. Sage.

Kotler, P., & Armstrong, G. (2018). *Principles of marketing* (17th ed.).

Kotler, P., et al. (2008). *Grundlagen des marketing* (5th ed.). Pearson Studium München.

Kotler, P., Kartajaya, H., & Setiawan, A. (2017). *Marketing 4.0: Moving from traditional to digital*. Wiley.

Kraus, F. (2008). *Der Transfer der Marktorientierung über Hierarchieebenen – Eine empirische Mehrebenenuntersuchung*. Springer.

Meffert, H., et al. (2008). *Marketing* (10th ed.). Springer.

Pelz, W. (2004). *Strategisches und operatives marketing*.

Porsche. (2021). *Porsche newsroom*. Retrieved 27 July, 2022. https://newsroom.porsche.com/en/2022/company/porsche-deliveries-2021-worldwide-27003.html.

Tomczak, T., Reinecke, S., & Kuss, A. (2018). *Strategic marketing. Market-oriented corporate and business unit planning*. Springer.

Wilkie, W. L., & Moore, E. S. (2006, December). Macromarketing as a pillar of marketing thought. *Journal of Macromarketing, 26*(2), 224–232.

Economic Pricing, 3C-Pricing and Cost-Estimation Concepts

6

> It's quite fun to do the impossible.

> Walt Disney

6.1 Economic Pricing Model

6.1.1 Introduction: Supply and Demand

In microeconomics, supply and demand is an economic model of price determination in a market. It postulates that, holding all else equal, in a competitive market, the unit price for a particular good, or other traded item such as labour or liquid financial assets, will vary until it settles at a point where the quantity demanded (at the current price) will equal the quantity supplied (at the current price), resulting in an economic equilibrium for price and quantity transacted. It forms the theoretical basis of modern economics. In macroeconomics, as well, the aggregate demand/aggregate supply model has been used to depict how the quantity of total output and the aggregate price level may be determined in equilibrium. The law of supply and demand is a theory that explains the interaction between the sellers of a resource and the buyers for that resource. The theory defines the relationship between the price of a given good or product and the willingness of people to either buy or sell it. Generally, as price increases, people are willing to supply more and demand less and vice versa when the price falls. The theory is based on two separate "laws", the law of demand and the law of supply. The two laws interact to determine the actual market price and volume of goods on the market. The key takeaways are the following:

- The law of demand says that at higher prices, buyers will demand less of an economic goods and products.
- The law of supply says that at higher prices, sellers will supply more of an economic goods and products.

M. Helmold, *Performance Excellence in Marketing, Sales and Pricing*, Management for Professionals, https://doi.org/10.1007/978-3-031-10097-0_6

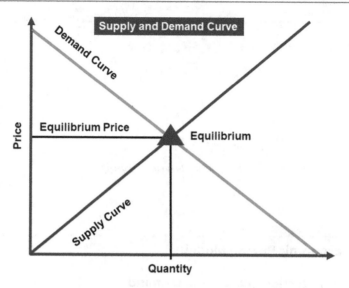

Fig. 6.1 Economic pricing model

- These two laws interact to determine the actual market prices and volume of goods that are traded on a market.
- Several independent factors can affect the shape of market supply and demand, influencing both the prices and quantities that we observe in markets (Fig. 6.1).

6.1.2   Understanding Supply and Demand

The law of supply and demand is one of the most basic economic laws, tied into almost all economic principles somehow. In practice, people's willingness to supply and demand a good determines the market equilibrium price or the price where the quantity of the good that people are willing to supply equals the quantity that people demand.

6.1.3   Demand

The law of demand states that if all other factors remain equal, the higher the price of a good, the fewer people will demand that good. In other words, the higher the price, the lower the quantity demanded. The amount of a good that buyers purchase at a higher price is less because as the price of a good goes up, so does the opportunity cost of buying that good. As a result, people will naturally avoid buying a product that will force them to forgo the consumption of something else they value more. The chart below shows that the curve is a downward slope.

5.1.4   Supply

Like the law of demand, the law of supply demonstrates the quantities sold at a specific price. However, unlike the law of demand, the supply relationship shows an upward slope. This means that the higher the price, the higher the quantity supplied. From the seller's perspective, each additional unit's opportunity cost tends to be higher and higher. Producers supply more at a higher price because the higher selling price justifies the higher opportunity cost of each additional unit sold. It is important for both supply and demand to understand that time is always a dimension on these charts. The quantity demanded or supplied, found along the horizontal axis, is always measured in units of the good over a given time interval. Longer or shorter time intervals can influence the shapes of both the supply and demand curves.

5.1.5   Supply and Demand Curves

At any given point in time, the supply of a good brought to market is fixed. In other words, the supply curve, in this case, is a vertical line, while the demand curve is always downward sloping due to the law of diminishing marginal utility. Sellers can charge no more than the market will bear based on consumer demand at that point in time. Over longer intervals of time, however, suppliers can increase or decrease the quantity they supply to the market based on the price they expect to charge. So over time, the supply curve slopes upward; the more suppliers expect to charge, the more they will be willing to produce and bring to market. For all periods, the demand curve slopes downward because of the law of diminishing marginal utility. The first unit of a good that any buyer demands will always be put to that buyer's highest valued use. For each additional unit, the buyer will use it (or plan to use it) for a successively lower-valued use.

5.1.6   Shifts Versus Movements

For economics, the "movements" and "shifts" in relation to the supply and demand curves represent very different market phenomena. A movement refers to a change along a curve. On the demand curve, a movement denotes a change in both price and quantity demanded from one point to another on the curve. The movement implies that the demand relationship remains consistent. Therefore, a movement along the demand curve will occur when the price of the good changes and the quantity demanded changes per the original demand relationship. In other words, a movement occurs when a change in the quantity demanded is caused only by a change in price and vice versa. Like a movement along the demand curve, the supply curve means that the supply relationship remains consistent. Therefore, a movement along the supply curve will occur when the price of the good changes and the quantity supplied changes by the original supply relationship. In other words, a movement occurs when a change in quantity supplied is caused only by a change in price and vice versa.

Meanwhile, a shift in a demand or supply curve occurs when a good's quantity demanded or supplied changes even though the price remains the same. For instance, if the price for a bottle of beer was $2 and the quantity of beer demanded increased from Q1 to Q2, there would be a shift in the demand for beer. Shifts in the demand curve imply that the original demand relationship has changed, meaning that quantity demand is affected by a factor other than price. A change in the demand relationship would occur if, for instance, beer suddenly became the only type of alcohol available for consumption. Conversely, if the price for a bottle of beer was $2 and the quantity supplied decreased from Q1 to Q2, there would be a shift in the supply of beer. Like a shift in the demand curve, a shift in the supply curve implies that the original supply curve has changed, meaning that the quantity supplied is impacted by a factor other than price. A shift in the supply curve would occur if, for instance, a natural disaster caused a mass shortage of hops; beer manufacturers would be forced to supply less beer for the same price.

6.1.7   Equilibrium Price

Also called a market-clearing price, the equilibrium price is the price at which the producer can sell all the units he wants to produce, and the buyer can buy all the units he wants. With an upward-sloping supply curve and a downward-sloping demand curve, it is easy to visualize that the two will intersect at some point. At this point, the market price is sufficient to induce suppliers to bring to market the same quantity of goods that consumers will be willing to pay for at that price. Supply and demand are balanced or in equilibrium. The exact price and amount where this occurs depend on the shape and position of the respective supply and demand curves, each of which can be influenced by several factors.

6.1.8   Impacts on Supply and Demand

Supply is largely a function of production costs, including:

- Labour and materials (which reflect their opportunity costs of alternative uses to supply consumers with other goods)
- The physical technology available to combine inputs
- The number of sellers and their total productive capacity over the given time frame
- Taxes, regulations or additional institutional costs of production

Consumer preferences among different goods are the most important determinant of demand. The existence and prices of other consumer goods that are substitutes or complementary products can modify demand. Changes in conditions that nfluence consumer preferences can also be significant, such as seasonal changes or he effects of advertising. Changes in incomes can also be important in either ncreasing or decreasing the quantity demanded at any given price.

5.2   3C Pricing Model

5.2.1   Introduction to the 3C Pricing Model

The 3C pricing model is a strategic pricing framework that fundamentally empha->izes the importance of understanding the internal and external business environ-nents. It is based on three factors: customers, competitors and costs. The model aims to encourage companies to bring more value than their competitors at a lower cost to develop and maintain a competitive advantage. It also highlights the trap of being stuck in the middle between companies emphasizing cost and those empha-sizing differentiation. This positioning of not pursuing a clear strategy is often hard to sustain (Helmold, 2020).

- Customers: Comprehensive research providing insight into consumers' wants and needs as well as their perceptions of the value of your brand and products and your competitors' brands and products
- Competitors: Comprehensive and up-to-date analysis of your competitors' prod-ucts, brand and prices as well as where your brand is positioned relative to those competitors
- Costs: Comprehensive understanding of all costs related to offering the product, including development, creative, production, distribution, storage, advertising, manpower and so on

Price signalling is a way for businesses to communicate their pricing strategy to customers and show them that the product offers excellent value for money. High price does not necessarily mean high value and vice versa – manufacturers must hit the sweet spot between profit-making and maximum perceived value to ensure that they get the best from their pricing strategy. That's why pricing strategy has to be a well-defined, clear and transparent part of a business's overall marketing strategy, with the three elements: customers, competitors and costs (Fig. 6.2).

6.2.2   Customer

The customer part of the 3C pricing model focuses on comprehensive research pro-viding insight into consumers' wants and needs as well as their perceptions of the value of your brand and products and your competitors' brands and products (Homburg et al., 2012). How can the perception of customer be used to set price? Customers build internal reference prices in time through exposure to different prices. When they see a new price tag, they compare it to the reference price and form an opinion (Helmold, 2020).

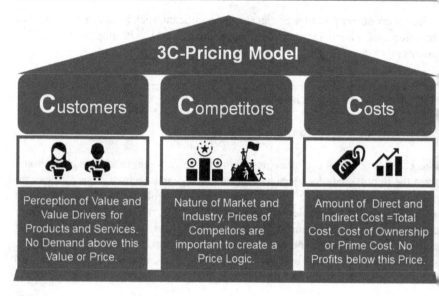

Fig. 6.2 3C pricing model. (Source: Author's source)

6.2.3 Competitors

The element of competitors deals with the comprehensive and up-to-date analysis of your competitors' products, brand and prices as well as where your brand is positioned relative to those competitors. It evaluates the customer's reaction to new prices based on research and historical data, helping retailers and manufacturers map their positions against competitors. Mapping and presenting this data gives a comprehensive picture to businesses regarding their competition – it also helps them plan their pricing and promotions accordingly as they take upstream and downstream suppliers into account. This allows them to price their products optimally to attract buyers who would otherwise pick the competitors. A successful competitor pricing strategy can help businesses increase sales, enhance understanding and cooperation with suppliers and grow revenues. Businesses also undertake competitor pricing strategy analysis because it helps them:

- Highlight their strengths and weaknesses as well as the competitors' capabilities.
- Uncover potential opportunities for the company.
- Inform the value proposition that differentiates them from the competition.

6.2.4 Costs

The element cost in the 3C pricing model refers to the costs incurred to design, create and deliver a product. These costs include direct labour, direct materials, consumable production supplies and factory overhead. Product cost can also be considered the cost of the labour required to deliver a service to a customer. In the latter case, product cost should include all costs related to a service, such as compensation, payroll taxes and employee benefits.

6.3   Cost-Plus Pricing

Cost-plus pricing, also called markup pricing, is the practice by a company of determining the cost of the product to the company and then adding a percentage on top of that price to determine the selling price to the customer. Cost-plus pricing is a very simple cost-based pricing strategy for setting the prices of goods and services. With cost-plus pricing, you first add the direct material cost, the direct labour cost and overhead to determine what it costs the company to offer the product or service. A markup percentage is added to the total cost to determine the selling price. This markup percentage is profit. Thus, you need to start out with a solid and accurate understanding of all the business' costs and where those costs are coming from.

Figure 6.3 depicts an example calculation of the cost-plus calculation method. There are three steps involved in computing cost-plus pricing for a product:

The cost-plus method starts with adding up total material costs (120 Euro), total labour costs (250 Euro) and sales administration and general (50,00 Euro, SGA). The total production cost for one unit amount in this example is 420 Euro. By adding the profit margin and potential discounts, we come to a result and sales price of 554,40 Euro.

Cost Plus Pricing	
	Direct Material Costs	100,00 €
+	Indirect Material Costs	20,00 €
=	Total Material Costs	120,00 €
	Direct Labour Costs	200,00 €
+	Indirect Labour Costs	50,00 €
=	Total LabourCosts	250,00 €
+	Administration Costs	20,00 €
+	Sales & Distribution Costs	30,00 €
=	Sales General Administration (SGA)	50,00 €
=	Production Costs	420,00 €
+	Profit (20%)	84,00 €
=	Net Sales Price	504,00 €
+	Discounts (10%)	50,40 €
=	Sales Price	554,40 €

Fig. 6.3 Cost-plus pricing with direct and indirect costs

Cost Plus Pricing	
Variable Costs per Unit	6,50 €
Estimated Sales Volumes	100000
= Total Variable Costs	650.000,00 €
+ Fixed Costs (Research)	100.000,00 €
+ Fixed Costs (Machine)	30.000,00 €
+ Fixed Costs (Others)	30.000,00 €
= Total Fixed Costs	160.000,00 €
= Production Costs	810.000,00 €
+ Profit (20%)	162.000,00 €
= Target Revenue	972.000,00 €
Estimated Sales Volumes	100000
= Sales Price	9,72 €

Fig. 6.4 Costs-plus pricing with fixed and variable costs

Figure 6.4 shows an alternative method of cost-plus pricing. The steps can be described as follows:

- Step 1: Determine the total cost of the product or service, which is the sum of fixed and variable cost (fixed costs do not vary by the number of units, while variable costs do).
- Step 2: Divide the total cost by the number of units to determine the unit cost.
- Step 3: Multiply the unit cost by the markup percentage to arrive at the selling cost and the profit margin of the product.

In the first step, the variable costs per unit are multiplied with the estimated sales volume (6,50 Euro × 100.000 units = 650.000 Euro as total variable costs). As the next step, the fixed costs must be determined. In the example, the total fixed costs amount to 160,000 Euro. The total production cost amounts to 810,000 Euro, adding variable and fixed cost. A target profit margin with 20% equals 162,000 Euro. Total production cost and profit sum up the target revenue. By dividing the sales volume by the target revenue, we come to a sales price of 9,72 Euro. The sales price per unit is 9,72 Euro.

Figure 6.5 shows the calculation of hourly rates. In the first step, it is necessary to define the contractual agreed days, the presence days and the annual total work hours. The total work hours is the time one worker spends on his job per anno. After deduction of training (40 h per year, 5 days) and general work projects (120 h), we come to the annual productive time in hours. If we multiply this by the number of employees, we will achieve the productive annual time in hours (in our example 7640 h). If we calculate now the calculation basis for hourly rate with labour costs

Hourly Rates Cost Calculation		
	Calandar Days	365
-	Saturdays/Sundays	104
-	Holidays	10
=	Contractual agreed Days p.a.	251
-	Average Absence Time (Sick Leave, Holidays)	40
=	Presence Days	211
x	Average Daily Work Time (Hours)	8
=	Total Work Hours p.a.	1688
-	Training	40
-	General Work and Projects	120
=	Productiveable Availaibility & Time (hrs)	1528
x	Number of Workers (5)	5
=	Productive annual Time (hrs)	7640
+	Labour Costs (5 x 50,000 Euro) p.a.	250.000,00 €
+	Labour Overheads p.a.	40.000,00 €
+	Calculatory Risk Surcharge (10%)	25.000,00 €
=	Calculation Basis for Hourly Rate	315.000,00 €
=	Hourly Rate	41,23 €

Fig. 6.5 Hourly rates calculation

(250,000 Euro), labour overheads (40,000 Euro) and a calculatory risk surcharge (25,000 Euro), we come to a total value of 315,000 Euro. If we divide the 315,000 Euro by the productive annual time (7640 h), we come to the hourly rate of 41,23 Euro.

Figure 6.6 shows the calculation of the machine hourly rate. The method adds all costs (per month) and divides the amounts by the operating time of 150 h per month. The hourly rate for this machine is 55,67 Euro.

6.4 Cost Estimation

A cost estimate is the approximation of the cost of a program, project or operation. The cost estimate is the product of the cost estimating process. The cost estimate has a single total value and may have identifiable component values. A problem with a cost overrun can be avoided with a credible, reliable, and accurate cost estimate. A cost estimator is the professional who prepares cost estimates. There are different types of cost estimators, whose title may be preceded by a modifier, such as building estimator, electrical estimator or chief estimator.

Machine Hourly Rates Cost Calculation	
Fixed Cost (month)	
Reprocurement Costs (+ 20%)	288.000,00 €
Machine = 240.000 Euro	
Operating Time 150 hours/month	
= Caluclatory Depreciation per month	**2.000,00 €**
Procurement Costs 240.000 Euro	240.000,00 €
Calculatory Interest	8,00%
= Caluclatory Interest per month	**800,00 €**
+ Energy Costs	400,00 €
+ Place Costs	3.000,00 €
+ Maintenance & Repair	1.250,00 €
+ Tools & Lubricants	300,00 €
+ Operationg Costs	600,00 €
= Costs per month	**8.350,00 €**
= Hourly Rate	**55,67 €**

Fig. 6.6 Machine hourly rates calculation

6.5   Case Study: Product Strategy and Premium Pricing of Mercedes

6.5.1   Product Strategy of Mercedes

Mercedes Benz is one of the leading premium car brands in the world. One of the strongest points of Mercedes is its products. Mercedes Benz has a wide range of passenger cars, light commercial and heavy equipment vehicles as a part of its marketing mix product strategy. However, the strongest in its product portfolio will be the luxury car segment which consists of sedans, SUVs and sports cars as well. In the new generation segment, it has A-class, B-class and the CLA. In the sedan, it boasts of the E-class, C-class and S-class. Mercedes Benz also has a wide range of cabriolets and roadsters in its product portfolio while it has the GLA, GLE, GLC and GLS in the SUV sector. Also the Mercedes Maybach S class is a true essence of luxury in its own. The Mercedes can boast about its products as not only it has the best of design and luxury but also the best of technology. The 4matic and BlueTEC is one of the best technologies to date. Also apart from dealing with new cars, Mercedes also deals with pre-owned Mercedes through its Mercedes Benz-certified portfolio. By 2022, the company is focusing on investing $11bn for having electric and hybrid cars in the market.

5.5.2   Premium Pricing of Mercedes

Being in the luxury segment, it caters to a niche segment which values quality more than the price, and so the price is always on the higher end. In the overseas market where Mercedes Benz has a huge product variety available, the prices range from $30,000 to $100,000 and above. Primarily, it caters only to the luxury car market, and hence it invests a lot on high-cost materials. Thus, the Mercedes Benz marketing mix pricing strategy is that of premium pricing, based on its features and competition.

References

Helmold, M. (2020). *Total Revenue Management (TRM). Case studies, best practices and industry insights*. Springer.

Homburg, C., Schäfer, H., & Schneider, J. (2012). *Sales excellence. Systematic sales management.* Springer.

Value-Based and Cost-Based Pricing Concepts

7

It's quite fun to do the impossible.

Walt Disney

7.1 Value-Based Pricing

7.1.1 Definition of Value-Based Pricing

Value-based price (also value-optimized pricing and charging what the market will bear) is a pricing strategy which sets prices primarily, but not exclusively, according to the perceived or estimated value of a product or service to the customer rather than according to the cost of the product or historical prices. The approach is most successful when products are sold based on emotions (fashion), in niche markets, in shortages (e.g. drinks at open air festival on a hot summer day) or for complementary products (e.g. printer cartridges, headsets for cell phones) (Anderson & Wynstra, 2010). Goods which are very intensely traded (e.g. oil and other commodities) are often sold using cost-plus pricing. Goods which are sold to highly sophisticated customers in large markets (e.g. automotive industry) have also in the past been sold using cost-plus pricing, but thanks to modern pricing software and pricing systems and the ability to capture and analyse market data, more and more markets are migrating towards market- or value-based pricing. Value-based pricing in its literal sense implies basing pricing on the product benefits perceived by the customer instead of on the exact cost of developing the product (Aspara & Tikkanen, 2013; Homburg et al., 2012). For example, a painting may be priced as much more than the price of canvas and paints: the price in fact depends a lot on who the painter is. Painting prices also reflect factors such as age, cultural significance and, most importantly, how much benefit the buyer is deriving. Owning an original Dalí or Picasso painting elevates the self-esteem of the buyer and hence elevates the perceived benefits of ownership. Where it is successfully used, it will improve profitability through generating higher prices without impacting greatly on sales volumes. Value-based pricing is a strategy of setting prices primarily based on a consumer's perceived value of a product or service as shown in Fig. 7.1.

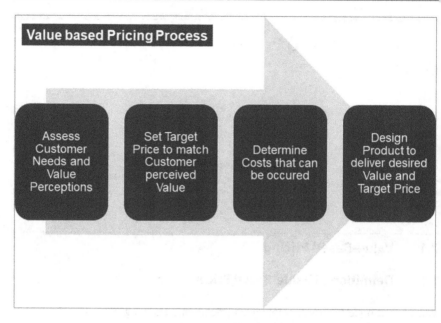

Fig. 7.1 Value-based pricing process. (Source: Author's source)

Value pricing is customer-focused pricing, meaning companies base their pricing on how much the customer believes a product is worth (Macdivitt & Wilkinson, 2012). Value-based pricing is different than "cost-plus" pricing, which factors the costs of production into the pricing calculation. Companies that offer unique or highly valuable features or services are better positioned to take advantage of the value pricing model than companies which chiefly sell commoditized items.

The value-based pricing principle mainly applies to markets where possessing an item enhances a customer's self-image or facilitates unparalleled life experiences. To that end, this perceived value reflects the worth of an item that consumers are willing to assign to it and consequently directly affects the price the consumer ultimately pays.

Although pricing value is an inexact science, the price can be determined with marketing techniques. For example, luxury automakers solicit customer feedback that effectively quantifies customers' perceived value of their experiences driving a particular car model. As a result, sellers can use the value-based pricing approach to establish a vehicle's price, going forward.

7.1.2 Characteristics of Value-Based Pricing

Any company engaged in value pricing must have a product or service that differentiates itself from the competition. The product must be customer focused, meaning any improvements and added features should be based on the customer's wants and needs. Of course, the product or service must be of high quality if the company's executives are looking to have a value-added pricing strategy.

The company must also have open communication channels and strong relation-ships with its customers. In doing so, companies can obtain feedback from its cus-omers regarding the features they're looking for as well as how much they're villing to pay.

7.1.3   Examples of Value-Based Pricing

The fashion industry is one of the most heavily influenced by value-based pricing, where value price determination is standard practice. Typically, popular name-brand designers command higher prices based on consumers' perceptions of how he brand affects their image. Also, if a designer can persuade an A-list celebrity to wear his or her look to a red carpet event, the perceived value of the associated brand can suddenly skyrocket. On the other hand, when a brand's image diminishes for any reason, the pricing strategy tends to re-conform to a cost-based pricing principle.

Other industries subject to value-based pricing models include name-brand phar-maceuticals, cosmetics and personal care.

7.2   Cos-Based Pricing

7.2.1   Definition of Cost-Based Pricing

Cost-based pricing involves setting prices based on the costs for producing, distrib-uting and selling the product. Also, the company normally adds a fair rate of return to compensate for its efforts and risks. To begin with, let's look at some famous examples of companies using cost-based pricing. Firms such as Ryanair and Walmart work to become the low-cost producers in their industries. By constantly reducing costs wherever possible, these companies are able to set lower prices. Certainly, that leads to smaller margins, but greater sales and profits on the other hand, but even companies with higher prices may rely on cost-based pricing. However, these companies usually intentionally generate higher costs so that they can claim higher prices and margins.

Cost-based pricing is the approach which takes the total cost of producing the product or service and adding some amount to allow the business to make a profit. For example, in a retail store, if a merchant buys something for $5, and they sell it for $10 to a customer, this is called cost-based pricing. However, the willingness of the customer to pay is limited by the benefits they can receive: "Benefits are net benefits, where any cost that the customer firm incurs in obtaining the sought ben-efits, apart from purchase price, are included" (Anderson & Wynstra, 2010, 31). Thus, the customer-perceived value is the difference between the net benefit they received and the price the customer paid; the supplier will not make any profit if the products are sold below the cost (Fig. 7.2).

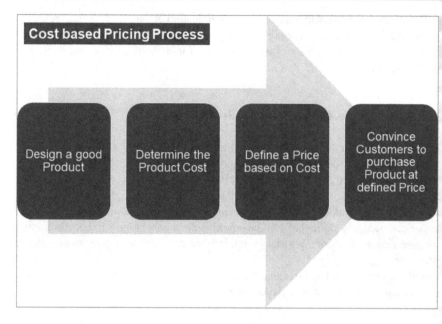

Fig. 7.2 Cost-based pricing process. (Source: Author's source)

Types of Cost-Based Pricing
Generally, there are four types of cost-based pricing. These are the following:

Cost-Plus Pricing
Under this, a company adds a fixed percentage of the total cost as mark-up to come up with the selling price. We can also call it the average cost pricing. The above example of the mobile explains cost-plus pricing. Usually, manufacturing organizations use cost-plus pricing.

Mark-Up Pricing
Under this, the reseller adds a certain amount or percentage of the cost to arrive at the selling price. Most retailers use such pricing. For example, a retailer buys a mobile from the distributor for $500. On $500, the retailer would add a mark-up of $100 to earn a profit.

Break-Even Cost Pricing
Under this, a company aims to cover its fixed cost. Such pricing is mostly used by the industries having high fixed costs, such as the aviation industry. In this, a firm finds the price using a level of sales at which it would break even. Or, we can say it determines the amount that will cover the variable and fixed cost. Then, it sets the selling price above the break-even price using mark-up or cost-plus pricing.

Target Profit Pricing
Under this, a company first sets the target profit that it wants to achieve. Based on the target profit, the company calculates the selling price.

7.2.2   Advantages of Cost-Based Pricing

The following are the benefits or advantages of this pricing method:

- This method ensures that a company always generates profit. However, for this to happen, the mark-up should be sufficient to meet all the expenses. Also, sales should be as per the expectations.
- It is simple to understand and easy to apply.
- This method of costing covers all the production and overhead costs.
- This ensures that a company generates a consistent profit margin even when the cost rises.
- This method is also useful in finding the cost of any customized product.
- If customers are aware of the cost, then they can also understand the reasons behind the product price.
- This method helps companies to bid for large projects.

7.2.3   Drawbacks of Cost-Based Pricing

The following are the drawbacks of cost-based pricing:

- Such a method may result in price to be different from the market rate. Either the price could be much high to discourage buyers or too low to result in a loss.
- This method does not encourage business to make efforts to control the cost. It is because the company simply passes the cost to the buyers under this method.
- It may sometimes ignore the importance of customers.
- This costing method does not take into account the opportunity cost of the investment.
- It does not take into account the demand and competition.
- A company must be aware of all the costs it incurs to set the price. Overlooking any cost may result in underpricing.

7.3   Cost-Based Versus Value-Based Pricing

Several factors affect customer willingness to pay certain prices; for example, the difference of needs between countries, individual customers' needs and wants and the usual customer facing different occasions (actual and present needs) – hence, a plan to suit all time value-based pricing is impossible. An extreme focus on value might leave the customer feeling exploited, leading to negative effects towards the company. In the long term, prices based on value-based pricing are always higher or equal to the prices taken from cost-based pricing – if the prices were any lower, the customer might perceive the actual value to be lower than the cost of producing the good plus a profit margin. Companies will not be interested in producing and selling the product at that price in the long term. Despite being difficult in implementation of both pricing techniques on companies, there should be consideration of values on

Cost based Pricing Process   **Value based Pricing Process**

Fig. 7.3 Examples of cost- and value-based pricing

products and market positioning brought out to the customers in the early stage of product development. Figure 7.3 shows examples of cost-based and value-based pricing concepts.

7.4   Case Study: H&M's Value Proposition Strategy

Being the fast-fashion clothing and accessories for men, children, women and teenagers, H&M became the second-largest global clothing retailer after Zara. The company manages its operation both offline owing more than 5000 stores in 74 countries and online shopping in 33 countries. Erling Persson established H&M exclusively for women's clothing in 1947 in Vasteras, Sweden. Later, the company built subsidiary brands such as Monki, Weekday, Cheap Monday, ARKET, FaBric Scandinavian AB, COS and & Other Stories under the main branch H&M set out worldwide. Besides, the brand also actuated other tyros to start up their careers as designers and did various philanthropic works. You may be wondering how a small clothing store located in Sweden became the second-largest clothing retailer brand in the world. Hereby, H&M followed many marketing strategies that aided the brand to reach heights in the clothing retailer business. H&M always comes up with new products that increase the customer's desire for clothing, that too at an affordable cost. Their only notion is fashion and quality at the best price. They have everything that a person may look for, from normal wear to business suits and sportswear to lingerie sets, all at a reasonable price. They collaborate with other top brands to establish a fresh style. H&M collaborated with Karl Lagerfeld in 2004, Versace in 2011 and Alexander Wang in 2014, and the collaboration with Balmain is the most triumphant to date. They also collaborated with the celebrated Indian designer Sabyasachi in 2021. The collection was named Sabyasachi x H&M. Before releasing the season's collection, they fuel the people's curiosity by promoting it on social media platforms. The brands mostly target the teens; to get their attention, they make sure their brand pops up in every online platform and publicize it by the influencers with a large following. They feature models in different skin colour and sizes, giving the notion that fashion pertains to everyone irrespective of their skin colour or size.

References

Anderson, J. C., & Wynstra, F. (2010). Purchasing higher-value, higher-price offerings in business markets. *Journal of Business-to-Business Marketing, 17*(1), 29–61.

Aspara, J., & Tikkanen, H. (2013). Creating novel consumer value vs. capturing value: Strategic emphases and financial performance implications. *Journal of Business Research, 66*(5), 593–602.

Homburg, C., Schäfer, H., & Schneider, J. (2012). *Sales excellence. Systematic sales management.* Springer.

Macdivitt, & Wilkinson. (2012). *Value-based pricing: Drive sales and boost your bottom line by creating, communicating and capturing customer value.* McGraw-Hill Education.

Service Marketing and Service Sales Management

8

> *Get closer than ever to your customers. So close that you tell*
> *them what they need well before they realize it themselves.*

Steve Jobs

8.1 Importance of Service Sector

The term "service sector" refers to an economic sector that, unlike agriculture and industry, produces no goods but provides a service that satisfies a need. Education, health, finance, government, transportation and trade are service sectors. In 2020, the services sector's share in Germany's gross domestic product amounted to 70.4%, while the secondary and primary sectors generated less than a third of GDP together. The tertiary, or services, sector encompasses all kinds of intangible goods, like consulting and advice, transport or attention. If a country generates its GDP mostly via services, this is often through industries like tourism (including accommodation and hospitality), financial services or telecommunications. Germany is a popular tourist destination and an important financial hub.

Germany is not a "service desert". The services sector in Germany not only generates most of the country's GDP, it also employs the vast majority of the workforce with over 70%. Lately, business confidence in the German services sector has increased significantly, which suggests a stable economy and ideally an increase in production and output in the future. This projection is supported by rising GDP and a stable inflation rate at around 2% (Fig. 8.1).

8.2 Service Marketing and Sales

Service marketing and sales are strategies which promote and showcase the intangible benefits and offerings delivered by a company to drive end customer value. This can be for standalone service offerings or complementary services to tangible products. Service marketing is a concept which focuses mainly on the business of non-physical intangible goods. It is done for company given benefits which cannot

© The Author(s), under exclusive license to Springer Nature Switzerland AG 2022   83
M. Helmold, *Performance Excellence in Marketing, Sales and Pricing*, Management
for Professionals, https://doi.org/10.1007/978-3-031-10097-0_8

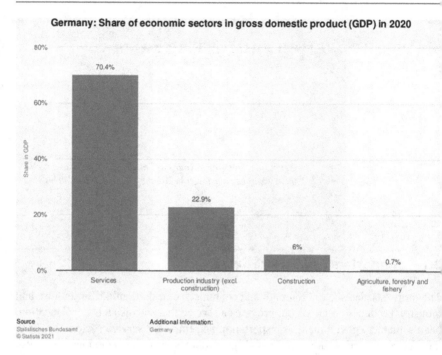

Fig. 8.1 Share of economic sectors in Germany. (Source: Statistical Federal Office 2021)

be seen, touched, felt, etc. These are benefits which are driven mostly by people and process and cannot be kept by a customer. Sectors like hospitality, tourism, financial services, professional services, etc. use service marketing to drive their business. Marketers market different types of entities such as goods, services, events, persons, etc. The marketing of services is known as service marketing. Services are essentially intangible and do not result in the ownership of anything. Its production may or may not be tied to a physical product. Service marketing and sales excellence require excellence in three broad levels: external, internal and interactive marketing. External marketing covers the pricing, distribution and promotion of services to consumers. Internal marketing involves training and motivating employees to serve customers well. Interactive marketing describes the employees' skill in serving the client (Fig. 8.2).

8.3   Characteristics of Services

8.3.1   Characteristics of Services

The American Marketing Association (AMA, 2021) defines services marketing as an organizational function and a set of processes for identifying or creating, communicating and delivering value to customers and for managing customer relationship in a way that benefit the organization and stakeholders. Services are (usually)

ig. 8.2 Characteristics of services. (Source: Author's source)

ntangible economic activities offered by one party to another (Seithamel et al., 2021). Often time based, services performed bring about desired results to recipients, objects or other assets for which purchasers have responsibility. In exchange 'or money, time and effort, service customers expect value from access to goods, abour, professional skills, facilities , networks and systems; but they do not normally take ownership of any of the physical elements involved (Kotler, 2000).

8.3.2 Intangibility

Intangibility is an important consideration that complicates the functional responsibility of a marketing manager, especially while influencing and motivating the prospects/customers. The goods of tangible nature can be displayed, the prospects or buyers can have a view, and they can even test and make a trial before making the buying decisions. The selling processes are thus found easier. We are aware of the fact that services are of intangible nature, and it is intangibility that complicates the task of decision-makers.

While motivating, they find it difficult to perform and display, and the positive or negative opinions regarding the services come up only after the completion of the using process. The customer can't touch the services; they albeit can't smell them. In a true sense, it is not a physical object. It has mental connotations. According to Carman and Uhl, a buyer of products (goods) have an opportunity to see, touch, hear, smell or taste them before they buy.

Of course, we don't find the same thing with the services product. It is the professional excellence of decision-makers that counts here that influences the entire process and that helps them substantially. While selling or promoting services, we need to concentrate on benefits and satisfaction which a buyer can derive after buying. We can hardly emphasize the service itself.

As for example, the banking organizations promote the sale of credit cards by visualizing the conveniences and comforts the holders of the credit cards are likely to get from the same. Services carry with them a combination of intangible perceptions. As for instance, an airline sells the seat from one destination to another.

Here, it is a matter of consumers' perception of the services and their expectations not smelling or tasting the services. They expect safe, fast, decent services. A service by nature is an abstract phenomenon. Thus, it is right to mention that due to intangibility, the selling and marketing of services become much more complicated.

8.3.3   Perishability

Another point complicating the task of a professional is the nature of perishability that we find in the services. The goods if not sold today can be stored, preserved for further selling. Thus, the risk element is here in a different form. However, in the context of services, if we fail to sell the services, it is lost only not for today but even for the future. If a labour stops to work, if a seat in the aircraft remains unsold, if a bedroom in a hotel remains unbooked, a chair in a cinema hall remains vacant, we find the business non-existent, and the opportunities are lost and lost forever. The services can't be stored or preserved. Unutilized or underutilized services are found to be a waste. A building unoccupied, a person unemployed, credit unutilized and vacant beds in a hospital are economic waste. Of course, this is due mainly to its perishability. This makes it essential that decision-makers or the executives by using their professionalism minimize the possibilities of economic waste. The opportunities come and you need to capitalize on the same by using your excellence.

8.3.4   Inseparability

This is also a feature that complicates the task of professionals while marketing the services. The inseparability focuses on the fact that the services are not of separable nature. Generally, services are created and supplied simultaneously by many service providers like dentists, hair dressers or insurance brokers. In other words, the services and their providers are the same. Donald Cowell says, "Goods are produced, sold and then consumed whereas the services are sold and then produced and consumed".

It is inseparability that makes the task of marketing services a bit difficult. The goods are produced at one point and then distributed by others at other points. In the services, we find the selling processes making ways for the generation of services. The professionals while marketing the services thus bear the responsibility of removing or minimizing the gap between the services promised and services offered.

Goods are produced, sold and then consumed, but the services are sold, produced and then used. The inseparability thus makes it essential that the service providers are acting and behaving professionally so that the marketing processes are not to pave the avenues for a degeneration in the quality.

8.3.5 Heterogeneity

Another feature is heterogeneity which makes it difficult to establish standard. The quality of services can't be standardized. The prices charged may be too high or too low. In the case of entertainment and sports, we find the same thing. The same type of services can't be sold to all the customers even if they pay the same price.

The consumers rate the services in a different way. Of course, it is due to the difference in the perception of individuals at the levels of providers and users. The heterogeneity factor makes it difficult to market efficiently. The professionals by using their excellence bear the responsibility of minimizing the problem.

8.3.6 Lack of Ownership

It is also ownership that makes it significant to market the services in a bit different way. The goods sold are transferred from one place to another, the ownership is also transferred, and this provides to the buyers an opportunity to resell. In the case of services, we don't find the same thing. The users have just an access to the service. As, for example, a consumer can use personal care services or Medicare services or can use a hotel room or swimming pool; however, the ownership rests with the providers. An expert opines, "A service is any activity or benefit that one party can offer to another that it is essentially intangible and does not result in the ownership of anything." Here, it is clear that ownership is not affected in the process of selling the services. The issue of ownership has also been clarified by another expert. He says, "Services are those separately identifiable, essentially intangible activities which provide want satisfaction and that are not necessarily tied to use sales of a product or another services. To produce a service may or may not require the use of tangible goods. However, when such use is required, there is no transfer of permanent ownership to these tangible goods". The same theme of not transferring the ownership has also been supported by Batesan. Here, the focus is on the point that transfer of ownership simplifies the task of a marketer since he/she can use it as a motivational tool. In case of services, the professionals experience difficulties because we don't find any scope for the transfer of ownership. The professionals thus need to be more careful while selling or marketing the services.

8.3.7 Variability

Physical goods are produced with a high degree of standardization. They are factory produced or assembled in large numbers with enormous consistency. It is rare to find two cakes of soap like Pears or two pieces of car like Alto different from one another. However, this kind of similarity is near impossible in services. For instance, two visits to a doctor or two lectures of a professor are never exactly same. Two separate stays at a particular hotel are unlikely to be an exact replica of one another. Variability is inherent in services because of their peculiar characteristics including intangibility and inseparability.

There are several reasons that make standardization of services difficult. First, intangibility prevents setting up of precisely defined standards for service product, their conformance and control. The advances in quality like zero defect has been possible due to their tangible character.

Physical goods have tangible dimensions that permit setting up of quality standards, deviations measurement and their minimization. Second, service variability is caused by human involvement and customer-provider interactions. Services are produced and consumed in real time.

Unlike goods, services cannot be produced and then quality checked. The lack of separation between production, physical state and consumption prevents postproduction quality control. A major difference between product marketing and service marketing is that we cannot control the quality of our products, and a P&G control engineer on a production line can control the quality of this product.

When you buy a box of Tide, you can be sure that it will work to get your clothes clean. When you rent a Holiday Inn room, you are sure to some lesser percentage that it will work to give a good night's sleep without any hassle, or people banging on walls and all the bad things that can happen to you in a hotel'. Each service episode tends to be unique in its own right. The interaction between customer and provider cannot be programmed and controlled cent per cent. In spite of a highly regimented service delivery process, each customer brings unique psycho-social aspect to a service encounter. For instance, service encounters are affected by moods and personality combinations between provider and customer. For instance, service provider's mood and emotional state despite high training is difficult to control like a machine. Similarly, one customer is unlikely to have similar mental state in two service episodes. Service inconsistency manifests in different forms. For instance, quality variation can be experienced across different service outlets, for example, two branches of Cafe Coffee Day (CCD) may provide different service experience. Variations in service can also be found across time, too. For instance, the service quality between lunch and dinner services of a restaurant may differ.

8.3.8   Difficulty to Measure Quality of Services

The quality of service requires another tool for measurement. We can't measure it in terms of service level. It is very difficult to rate or quantify the total purchase. As for example, we can quantify the food served in a hotel, but the way a waiter or a carrier serves it or the overall environment or behaviour of other staff can't be ignored while rating the total process (Helmold & Samara, 2019). Hence, we can determine the level of satisfaction at which the users are found satisfied. A firm sells atmosphere, conveniences, consistent quality, status, anxiety, moral, etc.

8.4   Marketing and Sales Strategies for Services

8.4.1   Understanding the Customers' Needs

Services require the right service strategy as shown in Fig. 8.3. With the service economy on the ascension, companies are yearning for mechanisms to connect their service solutions to their customer's problems and have the customer acknowledge that their solution is the best. In order to meet these requirements, the foundations of the model used to deploy such solutions need to be concrete (Wilson et al., 2012). The solution must capture the fundamental nature of the target markets and embody all of the customers' expectations. The attributes require a company to develop a sales strategy that is unique to the service model. There are four essential ingredients for a successful service-based company or solution (Frei & Morriss, 2012). By focusing on these four elements, a company can develop a robust business that is capable of responding appropriately to the unique opportunities and risks that develop when selling services:

- The offering: The service must meet the needs of the target customers, but also the company should provide differentiated excellence in areas where it will be valued by its customers.
- The funding mechanism: The company must identify how the costs of delivering an excellent service will be covered.
- The employee management system: High-quality services require a high-quality workforce for their delivery. Effective management of employee motivation and their ownership of service engagements will be reflected in the reputation of a service business.

Fig. 8.3   Strategies for services

- The customer management system: The customer is part of the value-creation process in service engagements. Accordingly, service companies must develop techniques to manage customers so that their services can be delivered effectively

8.4.2   Applying a Service-Based Strategy

Three service-based strategies can be used to create new services or migrate an existing product to a service offering. They are the "net promoter" strategy, the "hidden assets" strategy and the "applicable processes" strategy. Each requires specific tools to develop the key element of service-oriented arena: customer focus. These strategies encourage customer loyalty, develop customer willingness to promote a company's service and provide a method for analysing customer needs.

8.4.3   Value Creation

A service strategy must always focus to create value for the customers. Value means that the customer is willing to pay for the desired service.

8.4.4   Make Services Tangible

Tangible products are physical; they include cash, inventory, vehicles, equipment, buildings and investments. Intangible services do not exist in physical form and include things like accounts receivable, prepaid expenses and patents and goodwill. Tangibilizing means showing photographs and other graphics, videos, awards and recognitions, testimonials and other elements (e.g. menus) that make the organization's services more real or tangible. Additionally, it is possible to provide customers with supplementary samples.

8.4.5   Establish a Brand Loyalty

Brand loyalty describes a consumer's positive feelings towards a brand and their dedication to purchasing the brand's products and/or services repeatedly, regardless of deficiencies, a competitor's actions or changes in the environment. It can also be demonstrated with other behaviours such as positive word-of-mouth advocacy (Lovelock & Wirtz, 2011). Corporate brand loyalty is where a client buys products from the same manufacturer repeatedly and without wavering, rather than from other suppliers. Loyalty implies dedication and should not be confused with habit with its less-than-emotional engagement and commitment. Businesses whose financial and ethical values (for example, ESG responsibilities) rest in large part on their brand loyalty are said to use the loyalty business model. Brand loyalty, in marketing, consists of a consumer's commitment to repurchase or continue to use the brand. It can be demonstrated by repeated buying of a product, service or other positive behaviours such as word-of-mouth advocacy. This concept of a brand displays imagery and symbolism for a product or range of products. Brands can have the power to engage consumers and make them feel emotionally attached. Consumer's beliefs and attitudes make up brand images, and these affect how they will view brands with which they come into contact.

8.4.6   Personalize Services

Personalization (broadly known as customization) consists of tailoring a service or a product to accommodate specific individuals, sometimes tied to groups or segments of individuals. A wide variety of organizations use personalization to improve customer satisfaction, digital sales conversion, marketing results, branding and website metrics as well as for advertising. Personalization is a key element in social media and recommender systems (Furnham & Milner, 2013). Personalization is affecting every sector of society – work, leisure and citizenship. Personalized service is providing customer the ultimate experiences that are tailored to the consumer's individual needs and preferences. Personalization often makes customers feel more valued, which inspires greater brand loyalty. Companies provide personalized service by documenting customer data and interactions and then leveraging that information to cater to the consumer. Personalized customer service could take the form of communicating with customers through their preferred channels. It could also involve accessing customer data to immediately provide relevant product recommendations or support resolutions.

8.4.7   Set Up a Relationship

Relationship selling is a suitable service sales concept by which a salesperson seeks to build rapport and earn a buyer's trust to win deals, rather than highlighting product features or negotiating the price.

One of the main reasons relationship selling exists is to boost salespeople's personal connection to their customers and clients. Without building a working relationship, customers may feel like they are just a number.

8.5   Lean as a Revenue Driver in the Service Industry

Companies in the service sector are constantly under pressure to deliver excellent customer service, faster response times and valuable support for their customers. Lean can help to optimize all service delivery processes by targeting wastes and either removing them completely or moving to a more effective state as part of a journey of continuous improvement. An IT company, for example, is very different from a manufacturing company; however, it still has many wasteful processes that could be removed or reduced. Lean tools and techniques can improve the customer experience by reducing unnecessary activities such as the number of call transfers and unnecessary IT processes, while also providing solutions to cut down on errors, maximize employee empowerment and become more cost-effective. Financial firms are a prime example of a service sector that cannot afford to be wasteful, due to strong competition, the impact of the recent financial crisis and vulnerability to economic downturns. Yet, it is claimed that at least 40% of costs in the financial sector is spent on wasteful activities that have no added value to the customer. Although they cannot control the fluctuating economy, financial companies can however invest in refining and redefining their own operations to ensure more effective and customer-focused operation.

Lean thinking can provide businesses such as banks, insurance and investment companies with more productive and cost-effective solutions, therefore reducing risk during an economic dip. Lean would also help to improve employee satisfaction, increase customer value and ensure the supporting activities are focused on delivering value.

Marketing companies have so many different processes to their business that, without effective coordination in place, mistakes can easily occur. Every task needs to include a thorough process of planning, writing, designing and proofing to generate a high enough standard of quality for their clients. These ongoing processes are not only extremely time-consuming, but with different tasks being assigned to different departments, project efficiency could also be compromised.

Lean implementation can help marketing companies to streamline their processes by removing tasks that are unnecessary and implementing a much more efficient approach. In doing so, lean also provides a direct improvement on work quality and therefore provides added value for the customer. This allows lean marketing companies to have that added edge over their competitors.

8.6   Case Study: McDonald's Lean Kitchen Area

Lean is defined as a process optimization methodology that focuses on improving the effectiveness and efficiency of a business process by eliminating activities that do not add value to the customers of the organization.

Lean can help service organizations to achieve significant performance improvement. The improvement can be in many dimensions including quality, productivity, cost efficiencies and profitability and customer satisfaction.

Service organizations are struggling with customer demands for better quality service and managerial demands for cost reduction. makes a claim that to date significant improvements have taken place in lean services, yet it is also true that for the majority of the operations departments within lean services potential has hardly been tapped.

Since the early days of Lean, it has been well proven that organizations of any size generally operate with around 90% of process-oriented "waste" leaving a mere 10% of value-added activity delivering services to their customers.

Lean was developed and implemented by the Toyota Manufacturer between 1945 and 1970. Lean was introduced as an alternative approach to mass production techniques. Lean led to raise productivity and quality levels by allowing flexibility of "skilled" production with the volume efficiencies of "mass" manufacturing.

The McDonald brothers, in 1948, closed their restaurant in San Bernardino, California, for three months, reopening it in December as a walk-up hamburger stand that sold hamburgers, potato chips and orange juice and created the "fast-food" concept. This is probably the first lean service implementation in food sector.

Self-Development of Lean Kitchen Area

The McDonald's company has specialists who design the kitchen area themselves, integrating their acquired knowledge into a lean assembly line-style layout that maximized efficiency and output.

Automated Orders from Customers

McDonald's produces food under highly automated and controlled conditions. What is important to understand about this remarkably successful organization is not only that it has created a highly sophisticated piece of technology, but also that it has done this by applying a manufacturing style of thinking to a people-intensive service situation. If machinery is to be viewed as a piece of equipment with the capability of producing a predictably standardized, customer-satisfying output while minimizing the operating discretion of its attendant, that is what a McDonald's retail outlet is. It is a machine that produces, with the help of totally unskilled machine tenders, a highly polished service.

Warming Bins

In the "Made for You" production system, there are no more warming trays. Each sandwich is prepared when the order is received from the customer. Yes, McDonald's sandwiches are more lean. This "Made for You" production system targets under 90 s from order to delivery and that includes 11 s of waiting for the superfast toaster!

Now, the McDonald's invest in front desk automation. Customers place their order at touch screens and then receive a number with a "digital locator", which then notifies staff to where the customer is sitting. Once the order is ready to serve, a McDonald's employee delivers the food to the customer's table.

Lean Processes and Standardized Material

The company uses a standardized and simplified menu and food preparation using assembly flow principles. This allows the company to produce hamburgers on demand and on customer orders. The order-on-demand system is a pull system, in which every requested item is produced individually for each customer. The limited menu helps the company to achieve economies of scale in the upstream business, too. As a result, the process and procurement cost are very low (Fig. 8.4).

Fig. 8.4 McDonald's lean operations. (Source: Author's source)

References

AMA. (2021). *Amer*. American Marketing Association. https://www.ama.org/ociation.

Frei, F., & Morriss, A. (2012). *Uncommon service: How to win by putting customers at the core of your business*. Harvard Business Review Press.

Furnham, A., & Milner, R. (2013). The impact of mood on customer behavior: Staff mood and environmental factors. *Journal of Retail and Consumer Services, 20*, 634.

Helmold, M., & Samara, W. (2019). *Progress in performance management. Industry insights and case studies on principles, application tools, and practice*. Springer.

Kotler, P. (2000). *Marketing management (millennium edition), custom edition for university of phoenix* (p. 9). Prentice Hall.

Lovelock, C., & Wirtz, J. (2011). *Services marketing: People, technology, strategy* (7th ed.). Prentice Hall.

Seithamel, V., et al. (2021). *Services marketing: Integrating customer focus across the firm.* McGraw Hill.

Statistical Federal Office. (2021). *Economic sectors in Germany*.

Wilson, A., Zeithaml, V., Bitner, M. J., & Gremler, D. D. (2012). *Services marketing: Integrating customer focus across the firm*. McGraw Hill.

Marketing Mix

9

The best advertising is done by satisfied customers.

Philip Kotler

9.1 Introduction to the Marketing Mix

Marketing strategy and marketing mix are closely related elements of a complete marketing plan. While marketing strategy is concerned with setting the direction of a company or product line, the marketing mix is primarily tactical in nature and is employed to carry out the overall marketing strategy (Kotler & Armstrong, 2018). The marketing mix refers to the tactics (or marketing activities) that we have to satisfy customer needs and position our offering clearly in the mind of the customer (Opresnik & Hollensen, 2020). It involves the 7Ps in Fig. 9.1; product, price, place and promotion (McCarthy, 1960) and an additional three elements that help us meet the challenges of marketing services, people, process and physical evidence (Booms & Bitner, 1981).

Figure 9.2 depicts the categories of the marketing mix and describes each category in detail.

9.2 Marketing Mix: The 7Ps

9.2.1 Introduction to the 7Ps

Marketers look to the concept of the marketing mix to help them create and present product offerings to.

target markets. Various conceptualizations of the marketing mix can be found in extant literature, from.

the traditional four Ps to seven Ps for the marketing activities and tactics (Helmold, 2020).

Fig. 9.1 Marketing mix. (Source: Author's source)

Marketing Mix						
Product	**Price**	**Place**	**Promotion**	**People**	**Process**	**Physical Evidence**
•Quality	•Positioning	•Distribution	•Communi-	•Qualification	•Customer-	•Appearance
•Image	•Premium	•Trade	cations	•Service Level	focused	•Shop Design
•Branding	•Fremium	Channels	•PR	•Culture	•Lean	•Brand
•Features	•Extras	•Interme-	•Sales Promo-	•Image	•Business-led	Appearance
•Chracteristics	•Free	diaries	tion	•Friendliness	•IT-Support	•Visualisation
•Variants	•Value added	•Channel	•Branding	•Skills	•Design	•Cleanliness
•Mix	Levels	Layers	•Direct or	•Remuneration	Features	•Flow of
•Service	•Service Level	•Segmented	indirect	•Recruitment	•R & D	Operations
•Support	•Price Leader	Channels	Marketing	•Motivation	•Standards	•Packaging
Availability	•Discounts	•Direct or	•Social	•Intrinsic or	•Quality	•Add. Items
•Warranties	•Credit	indirect	Marketing	extrinsic	•Reliability	•Online
	•Payment	Distribution	•Digitisation	Factors	•Flow	Experience
	terms					•Infrastructure

Fig. 9.2 Elements of the marketing mix. (Source: Author's source)

9.2.2 Product

The product category refers to what the company produces (whether it is product or service or a combination of both) and is developed to meet the core need of the customer – for example, the need for transport is met with a car. The challenge is to create the right "bundle of benefits" that meets this need. So what happens as customer needs change, competitors race ahead or new opportunities arise? We have to add to the "bundle of benefits" to improve the offering, create new versions of existing products or launch brand new products (Homburg et al., 2012). When improving the product offering, think beyond the actual product itself – value can be added and differentiation achieved with guarantees, warranties, after-sales or online support, a user-friendly app or digital content like a video that helps the user to make the most out of the product.

9.2.3   Price

This is the only revenue-generating element of the mix – all other marketing activities represent a cost. So it's important to get the price right to not only cover costs but generate profit! Before setting prices, we need to research information on what customers are willing to pay and gain an understanding of the demand for that product/service in the market. As price is also a strong indication of the positioning in the market against competitors (low prices = value brand), prices need to be set with competitors in mind too.

9.2.4   Place

This is the "place" where customers make a purchase. This might be in a physical store, through an app or via a website. Some organizations have the physical space or online presence to take their product/service straight to the customer, whereas others have to work with intermediaries or "middlemen" with the locations, storage and/or sales expertise to help with this distribution.

9.2.5   Promotion

So we have a fantastic product, at an appealing price, available in all the right places, but how do customers know this? Promotion in our marketing mix is about communicating messages to customers, whichever stage they are in the buyer journey, to generate awareness, interest, desire or action.

We have different tools for communication with varying benefits. Advertising is good for raising awareness and reaching new audiences, whereas personal selling using a sales team is great for building relationships with customers and closing a sale. The challenge? To choose the best tool for the job, and select the most effective media to reach our audiences based on what we know about them. If your customer is a regular on Instagram, then that's where you need to be talking to them!

This doesn't just apply to customers. Communicate to other stakeholders too like shareholders and the wider public to build company reputation. The same principles apply; choose the right tools and media that fit with what you are trying to achieve.

9.2.6 People

A company's people are at the forefront when interacting with customers, taking and processing their enquiries, orders and complaints in person, through online chat, on social media or via the call centre. They interact with customers throughout their journey and become the "face" of the organization for the customer. Their knowledge of the company's products and services and how to use them, their ability to access relevant information and their everyday approach and attitude needs to be optimized. People can be inconsistent, but with the right training, empowerment and motivation from the company, they can also represent an opportunity to differentiate an offering in a crowded market and to build valuable relationships with customers.

9.2.7 Process

All companies want to create a smooth, efficient and customer-friendly journey – and this can't be achieved without the right processes behind the scenes to make that happen. Understanding the steps of the customer journey – from making an enquiry online to requesting information and making a purchase – helps us to consider what processes need to be in place to ensure the customer has a positive experience. When a customer makes an enquiry, how long will they have to wait before receiving a response? How long do they wait between booking a meeting with the sales team to the meeting taking place? What happens once they make an order? How do we make sure reviews are generated after a purchase? How can we use technology to make our processes more efficient? All of these considerations help build a positive customer experience.

9.2.8 Physical Evidence

Physical evidence provides tangible cues of the quality of experience that a company is offering. It can be particularly useful when a customer has not bought from the organization before and needs some reassurance or is expected to pay for a service before it is delivered. For a restaurant, physical evidence could be in the form of the surroundings, staff uniform, menus and online reviews to indicate the experience that could be expected. For an agency, the website itself holds valuable physical evidence – from testimonials to case studies, as well as the contracts that companies are given to represent the services they can expect to be delivered.

9.2.9 Planet (8Ps)

Sustainable marketing is the process of creating, communicating and delivering value to customers in such a way that both natural (resources nature provides) and human (resources people provide) capital are preserved or enhanced throughout.

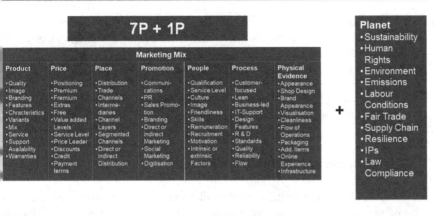

Fig. 9.3 Planet as the eighth element in the marketing mix

Sustainable marketing is the type of marketing that uses products and services that respect the environment and social aspects around. It aims to improve life quality by promoting products, services and ideas that don't harm the environment. The eighth element of the marketing mix can therefore been considered as planet (Fig. 9.3).

9.3 Case Study: Marketing Mix at McDonald's

9.3.1 Marketing Strategy at McDonald's

There are several marketing strategies like product innovation, pricing approach, promotion planning, etc. These business strategies, based on McDonald's marketing mix, help the brand succeed. McDonald's' marketing strategy helps the brand/company to position itself competitively in the market and achieve its business goals and objectives (Schneider, 2018). Marketing strategy of McDonald's analyses the brand with the marketing mix framework which covers the traditional 4Ps (product, price, place, promotion) plus additional 3Ps (people, process, physical evidence). There are several marketing strategies like product innovation, pricing approach, promotion planning, etc. These business strategies, based on McDonald's' marketing mix, help the brand succeed. McDonald's' marketing strategy helps the brand/company to position itself competitively in the market and achieve its business goals and objectives. McDonald's is one of the world's leading fast food chains. McDonald's primarily sells hamburgers, chicken products, cheeseburgers, breakfast items, soft drinks, milkshakes and desserts. McDonald's has also included salads, smoothies, fish wraps and fruits. It is widely known for its hamburgers. All these are the product strategy in its marketing mix. The original restaurant, which was started by McDonald's brothers, sold only hotdogs, hamburgers, cheeseburgers, milkshakes and French fries. The other products sold across the world include Big Mac, Big n Tasty, Double Cheese Burger and McSpicy Burger. In chicken, McDonald's sells McChicken, Premium chicken sandwiches, snack wrap, Chicken Fajita, Chicken McNuggets, Crispy Chicken Deluxe, Grilled chicken deluxe and Artisan grilled chicken. Fish products such as Fish McBites and Filet-O-Fish are known. The brand offers a range of break-fast sandwiches that include bagels, biscuits, Hamdesal, etc. In beverages, Coca Cola is the primary supplier of McDonald's. It also sells hot chocolates and other juices. It adopts the product as per the local taste preference and cultural identity. McDonald's focuses on glocalization strategy and includes snacks or food items which are pre-ferred in that particular country or region. To focus on kids, it also packages "Happy meals" and gives out a toy to attract that segment.

9.3.2 Marketing Mix (7Ps) at McDonald's

McDonald's' 7Ps of marketing comprises elements of the marketing mix that con-sists of product, price, place, promotion, people, process and physical evidence (Petersen, 2016).

Product

McDonald's sells a variety of products to its customers in the UK, namely, burgers, sandwiches, drinks, deserts, etc. McDonald's is an organization that functions in the fast-food industry. Nowadays, taste, preferences, etc. of the customers change fre-quently, as competition is very high in this industry; thus, there may be competitors selling food of a different taste than McDonald's, and customers may develop the taste and thereby sop visiting competitors; thus, McDonald's has to keep its offer-ings in the form of product regularly updated and develop it after heavy research so that customers taste and excitement to go to McDonald's continue. McDonald's sells a wide range of fast-food products such as hamburgers and cheeseburgers, Big Mac, Quarter Pounder with Cheese, Filet-O-Fish, several chicken sandwiches, Chicken McNuggets, wraps and French fries. The company also offers salads, oat-meal, shakes, McFlurry desserts, sundaes, soft serve cones, pies, soft drinks, coffee, McCafé beverages and other beverages (Schneider, 2015). Although, the company has long announced its pledge to increase the nutritional value of its meals, McDonald's' foods widely remain to be perceived as unhealthy.

Price

McDonald's follows cost leadership business strategy and accordingly, and its foods and drinks are offered for competitive prices. The fast-food chain offers customers the possibility to dine for a fraction of costs that are charged by the majority of other restaurants. McDonald's involves various price bundling strategies that offer bun-dling products with meals and other products for customers (Hammad, 2017). They had reduced prices in India by almost 25% so that customers prefer McDonald's as lunch and dining place. Its primary competitors are KFC, Subway, Pizza Hut and Dominos. As part of the promotional pricing strategy, McDonald's offer discounts or bundling on certain products and combination of different menu items as packed together. Their pricing strategy is also adapted to tap the lower middle section of the society. McDonald's' target customers are mostly young teenagers who wish are brand conscious and want convenience. With the growth of home deliveries, there are various discounts offered on the total billed amount as well.

Place

There are 36, 258 McDonald's restaurants in 119 countries (McDonald's, 2016). According to its aggressive expansion business strategy, the company aims to establish its presence in urban, as well as in rural, areas. The company states that 'McDonald's looks for the best locations within the marketplace to provide our customers with convenience. We build quality restaurants in neighbourhoods as well as airports, malls, tollways, and colleges at a value to our customers". Generally, major fast-food restaurants tend to cluster, and in most locations, where there is a McDonald's, there is also a Burger King right across the street. The different types of restaurant formats are McDrive, McCafé, McExpress, McDonald's Next and create your own taste restaurant. Most restaurants allow customers to drive through service with facilities such as indoor and outdoor seating and counter service. McDrive locations are near highways that do not offer seating service. McCafé is an Australian subsidiary creation, and it has increased the sales by 60%. As an open concept design, McDonald's Next used digital ordering and offered free mobile charging and table service. It also banned smoking in its restaurants. McDonald's maintains high-quality standards and stringent hygiene norms.

Promotion

McDonald's has spent huge money on advertising campaign; it makes use of newspaper ads; billboards; signage sponsors; various sporting events like FIFA world cup, Olympic games and Little league; and many more. McDonald's is uses aggressive promotion when it comes to its marketing mix. The TV advertising remains the prime form of advertisement. McDonald's' TV ads show people engaging in popular activities. They have hardly used any negative campaign against their competitors. In India, its burgers do not contain beef, and they have divided its kitchen into vegetarian and non-vegetarian zones. It wanted to focus on volume sales at a low price. Currently, McDonald's uses "I'm Lovin it" branding campaign that was created by Heye and Partner. The brand was the official sponsor of the 1994 FIFA world cup, food partner of NBA and official fast-food restaurant in the Olympics. It had sponsored other events like IndyCar series, Rolex Sports Car series and NASCAR. The famous celebrity spokespeople of McDonald's include Michael Jordan, Kobe Bryant, Venus Williams, Jamie McMurray, Justin Timberlake and several other prominent personalities.

People

McDonald's has a unique way of addressing its customers and also treats its employees very well. The employees working at the company have a dress code to follow, and the company emphasizes on its employees to be customer friendly and cheering and have affection for people. The service delivery of McDonald's is given priority, and customer satisfaction is of utmost importance. Employees are given ratings based on their performance, and they are encouraged to take a large part in decision-making process. Hygiene is of utmost importance followed by quality and service. Each McDonald's outlet has a restaurant manager who has the responsibility to undertake the daily proceedings. Achieving customer satisfaction is the goal of the companies.

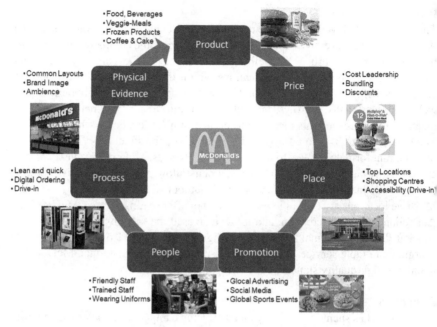

Fig. 9.4 Marketing Mix at McDonald's. (Source: Author's source)

Process

Process is generally the activities undertake to deliver a service to a client or customer. Now for McDonald's, there preparation process is the process which we will talk about here.

The importance of process is also very important for a giant like McDonald's as they have to maintain homogeneity in the process of serving and preparation, and with all this they have to also manage the cultural and legal needs of the UK environment, like usage of oils components, health issue prescribed by the UK government agencies, etc. Thus, McDonald's has to have a homogeneous process though with a small addition of country's needs.

Physical Evidence

Physical evidence means the store ambience, appearance, etc. Taking a visit at McDonald's, one would expect an ambience which is comfortable, fun loving, lively, etc (Fig. 9.4).

References

Booms, B. H. & Bitner, M. J. (1981). Marketing strategies and organization structures for service firms. In: *Marketing of services, American Marketing Association, Chicago* (pp. 47–51).

Hammad, A. (2017). *To examine the marketing communication strategy of McDonald's in UK: Its impact on the buying behaviour of consumers and consideration of factors contributing to the success or failure of the brand.* LAP LAMBERT Academic Publishing.

Helmold, M. (2020). *Total Revenue Management (TRM)*. Springer. Case Studies, Best Practices and Industry InsightsKotler, P. (2019). Kotler: Marketing Management. 4th Ed. Pearson Harlow.

Homburg, C., Schäfer, H., & Schneider, J. (2012). *Sales excellence. Systematic sales management*. Springer.

Kotler, P., & Armstrong, G. (2018). *Principles of marketing* (17th ed.). Amsterdam: Hoboken.

McCarthy, E. J. (1960). *Basic marketing. A managerial approach*. Homewood, IL: Richard D. Irwin.

McDonald's (2016). *Real Estate: McDonald's restaurant development (2016) McDonald's*, Available at: http://www.aboutmcdonalds.com/mcd/franchising/real_estate.html

Opresnik, S., & Hollensen, M. O. (2020). Marketing: Grundlagen und Praxis: Ein managementorientierter Ansatz. 4. Auflage. (Opresnik Management Guides 24). Opresnik Consulting. Kindle.

Peterson, H. (2016) *McDonald's is getting cheaper — and that should terrify Burger King and Wendy's Yahoo! Finance*. Retrieved 5.12.2021. http://finance.yahoo.com/news/mcdonalds-getting-cheaper-terrify-burger-160555106.html

Schneider, W. (2015). *McMarketing: Einblicke in die Marketing-Strategie von McDonald's*. Springer.

Schneider, W. (2018). *McDonald's - ein Lehrstück für strategisches und operatives Marketing*. Books on Demand.

Market Segmentation, Targeting, Differentiation and Positioning

10

> *You need to let the little things that would ordinarily bore you suddenly thrill you.*
>
> Andy Warhol

10.1 Value Proposition

The value proposition is the core of your competitive advantage. It clearly articulates why someone would want to buy from your company instead of a competitor. A value proposition is a concise and compelling description of the core benefit people get from doing business with you. In the case of a special brand, it's the unique value you have to offer that people won't get from elsewhere (Homburg et al., 2022). In the case of products or services, it's the problem they solve or the positive impact they have on people's lives. The value proposition must involve elements like segmentation, targeting, differentiation and positioning as shown in Fig. 10.1.

10.2 Market Segmentation

10.2.1 Definition of Market Segmentation

Market segmentation is described as the process of defining and subdividing a large and homogenous market into clearly identifiable segments having similar needs, wants or demand characteristics. The process of defining and subdividing a large homogenous market into clearly identifiable segments having similar needs, wants or demand characteristics. Its objective is to design a marketing mix that precisely matches the expectations of customers in the targeted segment (Addison & O'Donohue, 2001; Kotler & Armstrong, 2018). The four basic market segmentation strategies are based on behavioural, demographic, psychographic and geographical differences as shown in Fig. 10.2. Few companies are big enough to supply the needs of an entire market; most must break down the total demand into segments and choose those that the company is best equipped to handle. Four basic factors that affect market segmentation are clear identification of the segment:

© The Author(s), under exclusive license to Springer Nature Switzerland AG 2022   105
M. Helmold, *Performance Excellence in Marketing, Sales and Pricing*, Management for Professionals, https://doi.org/10.1007/978-3-031-10097-0_10

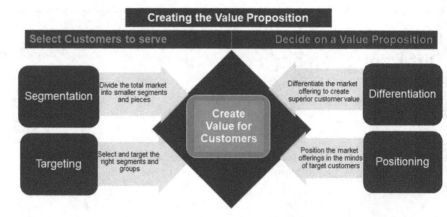

Fig. 10.1 Creating the value proposition

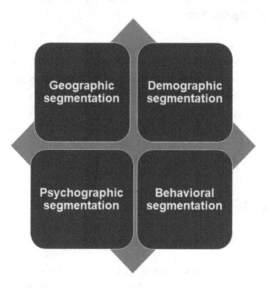

Fig. 10.2 Market segmentation

1. Measurability of its effective size
2. Accessibility through promotional efforts
3. Appropriateness to the policies
4. Resources of the company

10.2.2 Geographic Segmentation

Geographic segmentation divides markets in line with geographic criteria. In practice, markets can be segmented as broadly as continents and as narrowly as neighbourhoods or postal codes. Typical geographic variables include:

- Country Brazil, Canada, China, France, Germany, India, Italy, Japan, UK, USA
- Region north, north-west, mid-west, south, central
- Population density: central business district (CBD), urban, suburban, rural, regional
- City or town size: under 1000; 1000–5000; 5000–10,000 ... 1,000,000–3,000,000 and over 3,000,000
- Climatic zone: Mediterranean, temperate, subtropical, tropical, polar

The geo-cluster approach (also called geodemographic segmentation) combines demographic data with geographic data to create richer, more detailed profiles. Geo-cluster approaches are a consumer classification system designed for market segmentation and consumer profiling purposes (Kotler, 1991). They classify residential regions or postcodes on the basis of census and lifestyle characteristics obtained from a wide range of sources (Gavett, 2014). This allows the segmentation of a population into smaller groups defined by individual characteristics such as demographic, socio-economic or other shared socio-demographic characteristics. Geographic segmentation may be considered the first step in international marketing, where marketers must decide whether to adapt their existing products and marketing programs for the unique needs of distinct geographic markets (Fullerton, 2012). Tourism Marketing Boards often segment international visitors based on their country of origin. A number of proprietary geo-demographic packages are available for commercial use. Geographic segmentation is widely used in direct marketing campaigns to identify areas that are potential candidates for personal selling, letter-box distribution or direct mail. Geo-cluster segmentation is widely used by governments and public sector departments such as urban planning, health authorities, police, criminal justice departments, telecommunications and public utility organizations such as water boards.

10.2.3 Demographic Segmentation

Segmentation according to demography is based on consumer- demographic variables such as age, income, family size, socio-economic status, etc. Demographic segmentation assumes that consumers with similar demographic profiles will exhibit similar purchasing patterns, motivations, interests and lifestyles and that these characteristics will translate into similar product/brand preferences. In practice, demographic segmentation can potentially employ any variable that is used by the nation's census collectors. Typical demographic variables and their descriptors are as follows:

- Age: Under 5, 5–8 years, 9–12 years, 13–17 years, 18–24, 25–29, 30–39, 40–49, 50–59, 60+[46]
- Gender: Male, female
- Occupation: Professional, self-employed, semi-professional, clerical/ admin, sales, trades, mining, primary producer, student, home duties, unemployed, retired
- Socio-economic: A, B, C, D, E or I, II, III, IV or V (normally divided into quintiles)

- Marital status: Single, married, divorced, widowed
- Family life-stage: Young single; young married with no children; young family with children under 5 years; older married with children; older married with no children living at home, older living alone
- Family size/number of dependants: 0, 1–2, 3–4, 5+
- Income: Under $10,000; 10,000–20,000; 20,001–30,000; 30,001–40,000, 40,001–50,000, etc.
- Educational attainment: Primary school; some secondary, completed secondary, some university, degree; postgraduate or higher degree
- Home ownership: Renting, own home with mortgage, home-owned outright
- Ethnicity: Asian, African, Aboriginal, Polynesian, Melanesian, Latin-American, African-American, American Indian, etc.
- Religion: Catholic, Protestant, Muslim, Jewish, Buddhist, Hindu, other

In practice, most demographic segmentation utilizes a combination of demographic variables. Visualization of two approaches to demographic segmentation using one and two variables. On the left, a single variable (age) is used. On the right, two variables (income and occupation) are used to form the segments. The use of multiple segmentation variables normally requires analysis of databases using sophisticated statistical techniques such as cluster analysis or principal components analysis. These types of analysis require very large sample sizes. However, data collection is expensive for individual firms. For this reason, many companies purchase data from commercial market research firms, many of whom develop proprietary software to interrogate the data. The labels applied to some of the more popular demographic segments began to enter the popular lexicon in the 1980s. These include the following:

- DINK: Double (or dual) income, no kids, describes one member of a couple with above-average household income and no dependent children, tend to exhibit discretionary expenditure on luxury goods and entertainment and dining out
- GLAM: Greying, leisured and moneyed. Retired older persons, asset rich and high income. Tend to exhibit higher spending on recreation, travel and entertainment
- GUPPY: (a.k.a. GUPPIE) gay, upwardly mobile, prosperous, professional; blend of gay and YUPPY (can also refer to the London-based equivalent of YUPPY)
- MUPPY: (a.k.a. MUPPIE) mid-aged, upwardly mobile, prosperous, professional
- Preppy: (American) well educated, well-off, upper-class young persons, a graduate of an expensive school. Often distinguished by a style of dress
- SITKOM: Single income, two kids, oppressive mortgage. Tend to have very little discretionary income, struggle to make ends meet
- Tween: Young person who is approaching puberty, aged approximately 9–12 years; too old to be considered a child, but too young to be a teenager; they are "in between"

- WASP: (American) White, Anglo-Saxon Protestant. Tend to be high-status and influential white Americans of English Protestant ancestry
- YUPPY: (a.k.a. yuppie) young, urban/upwardly mobile, prosperous, professional. Tend to be well-educated, career-minded, ambitious, affluent and free spenders

10.2.4 Psychographic Segmentation

Psychographic segmentation, which is sometimes called psychometric or lifestyle segmentation, is measured by studying the activities, interests and opinions (AIOs) of customers. It considers how people spend their leisure and which external influences they are most responsive to and influenced by. Psychographics is a very widely used basis for segmentation, because it enables marketers to identify tightly defined market segments and better understand consumer motivations for product or brand choice.

While many of these proprietary psychographic segmentation analyses are well-known, the majority of studies based on psychographics are custom designed. That is, the segments are developed for individual products at a specific time. One common thread among psychographic segmentation studies is that they use quirky names to describe the segments

10.2.5 Behavioural Segmentation

Behavioural segmentation divides consumers into groups according to their observed behaviours. Many marketers believe that behavioural variables are superior to demographics and geographics for building market segments, and some analysts have suggested that behavioural segmentation is killing off demographics. Typical behavioural variables and their descriptors include:

- Purchase/usage occasion: Regular occasion, special occasion, festive occasion, gift-giving.
- Benefit-sought: Economy, quality, service level, convenience, access.
- User status: First-time user, regular user, non-user.
- Usage rate/purchase frequency: Light user, heavy user, moderate user.
- Loyalty status: Loyal, switcher, non-loyal, lapsed.
- Buyer readiness: Unaware, aware, intention to buy.
- Attitude to product or service: Enthusiast, indifferent, hostile; price conscious, quality conscious.
- Adopter status: Early adopter, late adopter, laggard.
- Scanner data from supermarket or credit card information data.
- Note that these descriptors are merely commonly used examples. Marketers customize the variable and descriptors for both local conditions and for specific applications. For example, in the health industry, planners often segment broad markets according to "health consciousness" and identify low, moderate and

highly health conscious segments. This is an applied example of behavioural segmentation, using attitude to product or service as a key descriptor or variable which has been customized for the specific application.

10.3   Other Segmentation Concepts

10.3.1 Attitudinal Segmentation

Attitudinal segmentation provides insight into the mindset of customers, especially the attitudes and beliefs that drive consumer decision-making and behaviour. An example of attitudinal segmentation comes from the UK's Department of Environment which segmented the British population into six segments, based on attitudes that drive behaviour relating to environmental protection:

- Greens: Driven by the belief that protecting the environment is critical; try to conserve whenever they can.
- Conscious with a conscience: Aspire to be green; primarily concerned with wastage; lack awareness of other behaviours associated with broader environmental issues such as climate change.
- Currently constrained: Aspire to be green but feel they cannot afford to purchase organic products; pragmatic realists.
- Basic contributors: Sceptical about the need for behaviour change; aspire to conform to social norms; lack awareness of social and environmental issues.
- Long-term resistance: Have serious life priorities that take precedence before a behavioural change is a consideration; their everyday behaviours often have a low impact on the environment but for other reasons than conservation.
- Disinterested: View greenies as an eccentric minority; exhibit no interest in changing their behaviour; may be aware of climate change but have not internalized it to the extent that it enters their decision-making process.

10.3.2 Generational Segmentation

A generation is defined as "a cohort of people born within a similar span of time" (15 years at the upper end) who share a comparable age and life stage and who were shaped by a particular span of time (events, trends and developments) (Locker & Flint, 2007). Generational segmentation refers to the process of dividing and analysing a population into cohorts based on their birth date (Wedel & Kamakura, 2010). Generational segmentation assumes that people's values and attitudes are shaped by the key events that occurred during their lives and that these attitudes translate into product and brand preferences (Homburg et al., 2022). Demographers, studying population change, disagree about precise dates for each generation Dating is normally achieved by identifying population peaks or troughs, which can occur at different times in each country. For example, in Australia the post-war population boom peaked in 1960, while the peak occurred somewhat later in the USA and Europe, with most estimates converging on

1964. Accordingly, Australian Boomers are normally defined as those born between 1945 and the 1960s, while American and European Boomers are normally defined as those born between 1946 and 1964. Thus, the generational segments and their dates discussed here must be taken as approximations only. The primary generational segments identified by marketers are as follows:

- Builders: Born 1920–1945
- Baby Boomers: Born about 1946–1964
- Generation X: Born about 1965–1980
- Generation Y, also known as Millennials: Born about 1981–1996
- Generation Z, also known as Zoomers: Born 1997–2012

10.4   Targeting

Market targeting is a process of selecting the target market from the entire market. Target market consists of group/groups of buyers to whom the company wants to satisfy or for whom product is manufactured, price is set, promotion efforts are made, and distribution network is prepared.

10.5   Positioning

In marketing and business strategy, market position refers to the consumer's perception of a brand or product in relation to competing brands or products. Market positioning refers to the process of establishing the image or identity of a brand or product so that consumers perceive it in a certain way. According to advertising guru, David Ogilvy, "Positioning is the act of designing the company's offering and image to occupy a distinctive place in the minds of the target market". The goal is to locate the brand in the minds of consumers to maximize the potential benefit to the firm. A good brand positioning helps guide marketing strategy by clarifying the brand's essence, what goals it helps the consumer achieve and how it does so in a unique way. The technique known as perceptual mapping is often used to understand consumers' mental representations of brands within a given category. Traditionally, two variables (often, but not necessarily, price and quality) are used to construct the map. A sample of people in the target market is asked to explain where they would place various brands in terms of the selected variables. Results are averaged across all respondents, and results are plotted on a graph, as illustrated in the figure. The final map indicates how the *average* member of the population views the brand that makes up a category and how each of the brands relates to other brands within the same category. While perceptual maps with two dimensions are common, multidimensional maps are also used. There are a number of different approaches to positioning:

1. Against a competitor
2. Within a category
3. According to product benefit

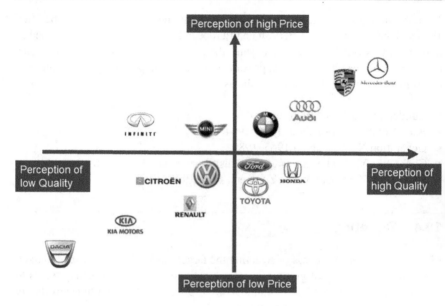

Fig. 10.3 Positioning. (Source: Author's source)

4. According to product attribute
5. For usage occasion
6. Along price lines, e.g. a luxury brand or premium brand
7. For a user
8. Cultural symbols, e.g. Australia's Easter Bilby (as a culturally appropriate alternative to the Easter Bunny)

Figure 10.3 depicts an example of potentially perceived quality and price in the automotive industry. The perceptual positioning map is an ideal tool to map the position of brands with a market or industry.

10.6   Differentiation

10.6.1 Definition of Differentiation

Differentiation (or simply differentiation) is defined as the process of distinguishing a product or service from others. The goal is to make a product, service or specific feature more attractive to a particular target market. The process of differentiation involves differentiating it from competitors' products as well as a firm's own products. Differentiation in marketing means creating specialized products that gain competitive advantage with a particular segment of the market. Differentiation enables long-term sustainable competitive advantages and integrates unique features; elements are processes, which are difficult to copy. Figure 10.4 depicts the differentiation options into product, service, channel, people or image differentiation.

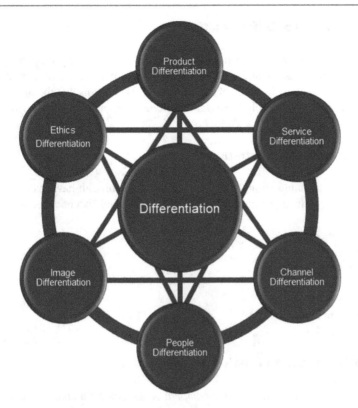

Fig. 10.4   Market differentiation. (Source: Author's source)

10.6.2 Product Differentiation

Product differentiation is a marketing strategy designed to distinguish a company's products or services from the competition. Successful product differentiation involves identifying and communicating the unique qualities of a product or company while highlighting the distinct differences between that product or company and its competitors. Product differentiation goes hand in hand with developing a strong value proposition so that a product or service is attractive to a target market or audience.

10.6.3 Service Differentiation

A common rationale involves using service differentiation to take advantage of strategic, financial and marketing opportunities. The fact that services are less visible and more labour-dependent makes them a strategic opportunity and a sustainable source of competitive advantage. Companies that succeed in service differentiation typically have *well-trained service employees* who follow basic steps to listen to customer problems, work toward a satisfactory resolution and follow up to ensure the customer is happy with the outcome.

10.6.4 Channel of Differentiation

Companies can achieve competitive advantage through the way they design their distribution channels' coverage, expertise and performance. A firm can also gain competitive advantage by channel differentiation. This means that the firm *differentiates itself by differentiating their channel's coverage, expertise and performance.*

10.6.5 People Differentiation

Companies can gain a strong competitive advantage through having better-trained people. Better trained personnel should exhibit following six characteristics:

- Competence
- Courtesy
- Credibility
- Reliability
- Responsiveness
- Communication

10.6.6 Image Differentiation

Image differentiation is *a source of competitive advantage*; a company may differentiate itself from its competitors by image; the particular image or "personality" it acquires is created by its logo and other symbols, its advertising, its atmosphere, its events and personalities.

10.6.7 Ethics Differentiation

Companies are trying to differentiate by applying social and ethical standards throughout their activities. Ethical standards are promoted to stakeholders and customers.

10.7   Case Study: Image Differentiation of Hennessy Cognac

Jas Hennessy & Co., commonly known simply as Hennessy (French pronunciation: [ɛnɛsi]), is a French cognac distiller with its headquarters located in Cognac, France. Jas Hennessy & Co. sells about 50 million bottles a year worldwide, making it the largest cognac producer, supplying more than 40% of the world's cognac, a variety of brandy. The company is owned by Moët Hennessy, which is in turn owned by LVMH (66%) and Diageo (34%). The Hennessy cognac distillery was founded by Irish Jacobite military officer Richard Hennessy in 1765. His son James Hennessy gave the company its name Jas Hennessy & Co in 1813. During the 1970s, Kilian Hennessy, a fifth-generation direct descendant of Hennessy, became the CEO of Hennessy, succeeding his first cousin Maurice-Richard. Kilian Hennessy spearheaded the company's 1971 merger with Moët et Chandon, which created Moët Hennessy.

Moët Hennessy merged with Louis Vuitton in 1987, creating one of the world's largest luxury brand conglomerates, Louis Vuitton • Moët-Hennessy or LVMH. In 1988, a management crisis led to the group's takeover by Bernard Arnault, owner of the haute couture house Christian Dior, with the support of Guinness. Figure 10.5 shows the prime product with Hennessy Cognac. Recently, Hennessy has tried to broaden the appeal of the drink beyond its traditional base of older drinkers by introducing new products such as "Pure White", "Hennessy Black" and "Fine de Cognac" and marketing them accordingly. Increasing trial and frequency of consumption of Hennessy Fine de Cognac was not an easy task. Hennessy has traditionally eschewed major above-the-line campaigns. It is perceived as a "special" drink for "special" occasions, and, as a result, Hennessy has had a low share of the cognac market, so that the company started an advertising campaign with the goal to differentiate and to gain more market share. The differentiation and advertising campaign objectives were to increase awareness of the brand and attract a new audience to Hennessy without alienating existing customers. To increase awareness, with the limited

Fig. 10.5   Market differentiation of Hennessy Cognac. (Source: Author's source)

budget, a press campaign targeted publications that revealed high concentrations of Hennessy customer profiles. To bring new people to the brand, Archibald Ingall Stretton used responsive media around these consumers to recruit prospective customers. Once they were uncovered, interacting with them began with a prestigious call to action. A traditional sales promotion method for gathering names did not sit well with the premium credentials of the brand. Research showed that the target audience defined "richness" more in how they lived their lives than in materialistic terms, and they sought out luxury brands that reflected this attitude. The campaign, therefore, concentrated on recognizing the human moments that enrich life – the small moments that make life worth living. Through the creative executions, the campaign asked its audience both to notice and celebrate these enriching moments in their lives, with the theme "enjoy the moment". This was brought to life across a range of media by inviting the audience to describe their perfect moment, with a £10,000 incentive to "make it happen".

The multimedia campaign used press advertising, press inserts, direct mail, e-mail, online advertising and a dedicated microsite. Press ads were placed in specialist titles driving sales with specific retailers. Press inserts defied the usual creative conventions and were made to look like jewellery bags and record sleeves. These were placed in The Daily Telegraph and specialist press whose readership showed a high match rate to the Hennessy customer profile. The campaign finishes at the end of January, and a number of elements are still in play. However, results to date show more than 6000 responders have been added to a new database for ongoing dialogue. Approximately 80% of these fell within the younger audience profile. There were a huge number of hits to the website, and the direct-mail response rate was four times higher than the industry standard. Most importantly, sales of Fine de Cognac experienced very strong growth in relevant stores throughout the promotion.

References

Addison, T., & O'Donohue, M., (2001). *Understanding the customer's relationship with a brand: The role of market segmentation in building stronger brands.* In Market research society conference, London.

Fullerton, R. (2012). Segmentation in practice: An overview of the eighteenth and nineteenth centuries. In C. Homburg, H. Schäfer, & J. Schneider (Eds.), *Sales excellence. Systematic sales management.* Springer.

Gavett, G. (2014, July 9). What you need to know about segmentation. *Harvard Business Review.*

Homburg, C., Klarmann, M., & Vomberg, A. (2022). *Handbook of market research.* Springer.

Kotler, P. (1991). *Marketing management: Planning, analysis, implementation and control* (9th ed.). Pearson.

Kotler, P., & Armstrong, G. (2018). *Principles of marketing* (17th ed.). Amsterdam: Hoboken.

Locker, C. P., & Flint, D. J. (2007). Customer segments as moving targets: Integrating customer value dynamism into segment instability logic. *Industrial Market Management, 36*(6), 810–822.

Wedel, M., & Kamakura, W. A. (2010). *Market segmentation: Conceptual and methodological foundations* (pp. 8–9). Springer.

Direct and Indirect Marketing, Sales Promotion and Public Relations

11

Where there is no Standard there can be no Kaizen.

Taiichi Ohno

11.1 Promotion Tools and Concepts (Fig. 11.1)

11.2 Direct and Indirect Marketing

11.2.1 Direct Marketing

Direct marketing is a form of communicating an offer, where organizations communicate directly to a pre-selected customer and supply a method for a direct response. Among practitioners, it is also known as direct response marketing. Direct marketing includes a number of traditional marketing strategies that everyone is familiar with. For example, TV commercials are a form of direct marketing. So are billboards, magazine ads, radio ads and telemarketing. That's not to say that digital marketing can't be direct. For example, email marketing and PPC advertising are also forms of direct marketing. You're essentially trying to find and address a specific audience – and you're trying to get them to take action right away. The following are some of the advantages to such a strategy.

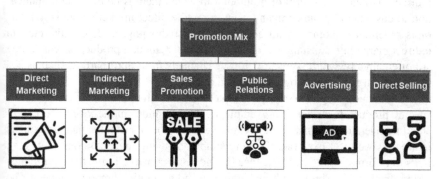

Fig. 11.1 Promotion mix. (Source: Author's source)

M. Helmold, *Performance Excellence in Marketing, Sales and Pricing*, Management for Professionals, https://doi.org/10.1007/978-3-031-10097-0_11

11.2.2 Advantages of Direct Marketing

You can identify specific audience segments, thereby allowing you to connect with people who are likely interested in your product or service already. For example, if you run a TV commercial, you can choose a time slot on a channel that you know your audience is watching.

If you know the audience you're addressing, then you can personalize your messages, thereby allowing you to nurture leads and build stronger relationships. For example, using the data you have to segment your email list allows you to send more relevant content to your recipients.

The data you collect from your direct marketing efforts is more measurable. For example, you can track your email response rate to determine how effective your direct marketing strategy is and to make adjustments accordingly.

While there are plenty of advantages to implementing certain direct marketing techniques, there are some potential drawbacks as well. These can include the following:

11.2.3 Disadvantages of Direct Marketing

If you're too overzealous, your direct marketing efforts may cross privacy boundaries and may even come off as spam, which will hurt your brand reputation.

You have to have an understanding of who your audience is and where you can find them. Otherwise, you may be advertising to people who aren't interested in your brand, which is a waste of time and money.

Your overall reach won't be as widespread since direct marketing requires you to focus on a specific audience to be effective.

11.2.4 Indirect Marketing

Indirect marketing is a form of promotion in which there is no direct communication to customers by the company using it. While direct marketing actively interrupts potential customers with advertisements, radio jingles, cold calls, etc., in indirect marketing, consumers are merely reminded about a product of which they are often already aware. Typically, it uses channels from third parties, such as TV shows, social networks, blogs, videos and e-books.

Indirect marketing is essentially marketing in which you're not trying to sell a specific product or service. For example, content creations in the form of a blog or email newsletter are forms of indirect marketing. A lot of social media marketing is indirect as well, for example, if you're simply engaging in discussions or posting links to informative articles. The idea behind indirect marketing is that you're nurturing relationships, building brand authority and generating brand awareness. The following are some of the advantages of indirect marketing:

Direct Marketing	Indirect Marketing
Paid Advertising	Search Engine Optimisation
Email Marketing	News Articles and Press
Direct Mail	Sponsorships
Sales Calls	Useful Blog Posts
Advertising on Social Media	Social Media Fan Pages
Advertising with billboards	Referrals
Television ads	Influencers
and sometimes newspaper ads	Online Reviews

Fig. 11.2 Direct and indirect marketing. (Source: Author's source)

11.2.5 Advantages of Indirect Marketing

You provide value to your customers without coming off as self-serving, which helps to build your brand reputation and increase brand trust.

Indirect marketing is typically much less expensive than direct marketing.

Indirect marketing is a long-term strategy, which means that your efforts will continue to have an impact throughout the future. For example, you might write a blog post that someone reads years later.

As beneficial as indirect marketing is, there are a couple of disadvantages when compared to direct marketing. These disadvantages include the following:

11.2.6 Disadvantages of Indirect Marketing

Tracking performance is more difficult. This is because you're not honing in on specific customers – you're casting a wider net.

Indirect marketing efforts may not have an instant impact – it may take some time before they begin drawing in new customers. As such, it can be frustrating not to see an immediate impact on sales.

Because it's a long-term strategy, indirect marketing requires constant attention. Whereas direct marketing tactics can work on their own, indirect marketing functions as a whole. This means that you need to be constantly working at it. There's basically no end in sight (Fig. 11.2).

11.3 Sales Promotion

Sales promotion is a set of marketing technologies aimed to stimulate the demand in particular products and increase brand awareness. Limited in time, it creates a feeling of time-sensitiveness, generates new leads and keeps existing customers engaged (Homburg et al., 2012). Sales promotion is one of the elements of the promotional mix. The primary elements in the promotional mix are advertising, personal selling, direct marketing and publicity/public relations. Sales promotion uses both media and non-media marketing communications for a pre-determined, limited time to increase consumer demand, stimulate market demand or improve product availability. Examples include contests, coupons, freebies, loss leaders, point of purchase displays, premiums, prizes, product samples and rebates. The advantages of sales promotion are the following:

Sales promotions can be directed at either the customer, sales staff or distribution channel members (such as retailers). Sales promotions targeted at the consumer are called consumer sales promotions. Sales promotions targeted at retailers and wholesale are called trade sales promotions.

- It helps to generate new leads. Sales promotion can boost your product image since it encourages sharing information about it within social groups related to your business. If you sell training football shoes, people keen on playing football will share the message.
- Allows re-engaging with your existing audience. Once a person subscribed to a brand's email newsletters, they will receive regular sales promotions. It is a way to keep the audience engaged and maintain a close connection with the company, which is crucial for building loyalty.
- Skyrockets revenue. Sales promotions help companies to increase the number of sold goods, even though they need to lower the price to achieve that goal. Of course, merely reducing the price is not enough; people should need your product, while the discount is only another reason to make a purchase.
- Increases brand awareness. Sales promotion is a way to make a name for your brand because people are more likely to talk about a company that proposes benefits and saves their money. That's what sales promotion does (Fig. 11.3).

Although the main goal of sales promotion is to increase demand in a particular product, you can reach several important goals. Understanding them will help you create an effective promotion strategy.

- Launch a new product. If you're going to expand and turn your small coffee shop into a bakery, you need to reach new market segments. You can attract new customers by offering a free cookie with each cup of coffee or suggest visitors set their own price once in a while.
- Attract new clients. This objective should be your long-term goal since it allows your business to grow. Your potential clients are likely your competitors' customers, so, analysing their product and benefits, you can offer something more valuable.
- Stay competitive. Researching and analysing your competitors will not only help you attract new clients but constantly improve your product and customer service.
- Make existing customers buy more. It's always easier to make an existing customer buy more than attract new clients. Provide each client with a personalized

Fig. 11.3   Sales promotion. (Source: Author's source)

approach – it will help you build customer loyalty. As a result, clients will promote your brand organically.

- Sell during the off-season. Goods like swimwear, boats, tents, air conditioners and refrigerators are definitely more popular in summer but you should consider special strategies to sell them throughout the year. Offer time-limited discounts, "1 + 1 = 3" campaigns and other marketing tricks.
- Run clearance campaigns. They're especially popular before summer and winter. As dealers need to make room for a new collection, they often run total clearance campaigns when users can buy goods from old collections at extremely reduced prices.

There is a variety of ways to run a successful sales promotion, but let's focus on some most frequently used ones, using a cup of coffee as an example.

- Price deal. It is a temporary cost reduction, for instance, 20% off for a coffee for a week.
- Loyalty reward program. This means that customers collect points or credits when they buy coffee. If they get 10 points, for example, they will have one coffee for free.
- Bonus-pack deal. It means that a customer can get more products paying the original price. For instance, they pay a dollar for one cup of coffee and get free

candy, which gives some positive emotions and makes them come back in the future.

- Giveaways. These tactics aim to increase brand awareness. It means giving some items for free in exchange for personal information to use in further marketing. For example, offer a free cup of coffee in exchange for a phone number, which you can use for many purposes: promoting new sales, sharing updates and news with short text messages, etc.
- Coupons. You can sell coffee for the original price and give a coupon, which will make the next purchase 5% cheaper.
- Mobile couponing. It stands for coupons received on mobile phones via SMS. To get a discount, a customer needs to show the coupon on their smartphone.
- Sampling. Choosing this promotion type, companies give a sample of the product, for instance, the first cup of coffee to promote a new taste.

11.4   Public Relations

Public relations is **a strategic communication process that builds mutually beneficial relationships between organizations and their publics**. Public relations can also be defined as the practice of managing communication between an organization and its publics.

11.5   Case Study: Public Relations in Siemens

Werner von Siemens paid great attention to the positive image of his company throughout his life. However, first and foremost, he saw himself as an inventor who refused to present his products in a media-effective way using "reclame". He was of the opinion that "the really useful things will find their way and recognition anyway". His products should be characterized by performance and ease of everyday life. Nevertheless, Werner von Siemens always knew how to put the services and products of his company in the right light, as long as the measures that could be used corresponded to his idea of a serious, publicly effective appearance. Even in the early years of the development of public relations, which at that time was still called advertising or propaganda, Werner von Siemens used a number of means to inspire every class of society with his products and to win over financiers. It was part of the company's PR repertoire to combine the effect of the demonstration with that of cultivating relationships. Siemens implemented this by inviting important representatives from politics and business to present new products. Through his career as an officer, Werner von Siemens was also able to establish good contacts with the imperial court. These relationships were intended to increase the company's prestige, and, at the same time, Siemens recommended itself as a competent contact in the field of electrotechnical energy. For example, he equipped the imperial court with electric lighting for festive balls. The Empress also regularly asked him to demonstrate technical innovations at her charity events. In addition, innovation and marketing events were held in-house, where technical innovations in the field of medicine were presented and demonstrated. Siemens invited doctors and other specialist audiences to attend. The digitization of social communication and the associated changes in the structure and production of the public have led to major changes in corporate communication being observed since the 2000s. In the course of a focus and stronger integration of corporate communication; this also includes the organizational abolition of external and internal communication and the development of newsrooms since around 2015. At Siemens, a focus, an individualization and an increase in the speed of corporate communication, at the same time greater flexibility (the agile communication department in a more agile company), went hand in hand with this development. Clarissa Haller, the current head of Siemens communications, highlights the major changes to the Siemens newsroom in 2019 as the greater diversity and greater internationalization of Siemens corporate communications. At the same time, the development of the instruments (e.g. "Trello" as a tool) leads to better and more flexible use of such instruments in strategic planning but also in controlling. "Real-time controlling" could be the keyword for this.

Reference

Homburg, C., Schäfer, H., & Schneider, J. (2012). *Sales excellence: Systematic sales management.* Springer.

12

> *For every sale you miss because you're too enthusiastic, you
> will miss a hundred because you're not enthusiastic enough.*
>
> Zig Ziglar

12.1 Selling Concepts

12.1.1 Introduction to Selling Concepts

The selling concept is a part of marketing management and one of several concepts
that make up a marketing strategy. A sales concept analyses buying and selling
effects to place the focus primarily on generating sales transactions (Czinkota et al.,
2021). Selling concepts place emphasis on goods the consumer may not ordinarily
buy or necessarily need. The selling concept came into practice following the Great
Depression era when goods were not in great supply. Once the depression ended,
companies with an abundance of products needed to move their inventories, and the
selling concept followed shortly thereafter. Today's selling concept has evolved to
assume the customer will buy the product without regret, or, if they do, their feelings won't linger, and the customer will buy the product again at a future date
(Homburg et al., 2012). Figure 12.1 shows the most common selling concepts and
examples. The most common selling concepts are social selling, cross-selling,
upselling, deep selling, consultative selling and virtual or visual selling.

12.1.2 Characteristics of Selling Concepts

Selling concepts are based on the assumption and premise that the customers will not
buy goods or services of a specific brand unless the company performs targeted sales
and promotional activities at a large scale in order to convince the customers to purchase
products and services (Borthwick, 2020). Therefore, businesses and companies should
carry out promotional and targeted sales activities to accelerate their product sales in the
market (Zentes et al., 2019). Customers have inner needs, and your job is to convert
their inner needs into buying your product through motivation and persuasion. The

Selling Concepts and Focus			
Type of Selling	**Focus + Product**	**Example**	
Social Selling	Personalised Selling	LinkedIn	Linked in
Cross Selling	Additional Products	McDonalds	zalando
Up Selling	Better Products	Apple	
Deep Selling	More Products	Example	Mcdonald's
Consultative Selling	Advisory and Expertise	McKinsey	McKinsey & Company
Virtual Selling	Online	Alibaba	Alibaba Group
Visual Selling	Attention, Posters	OmniMedia	OMNI-MEDIA

Fig. 12.1. Selling concepts. (Source: Author's source)

selling concept is very useful for selling unsought goods, i.e. insurance, where a company finds the target segment of the market first, and then it persuades the customers by explaining the benefits of the product. The final goal of selling concepts is to sell many products to increase the net profit. Selling concepts have the following characteristics:

- It focuses on the needs of the inner of businesses and companies.
- Goods and services define their business in the selling concept. It focuses on everyone, whether they're kids or adults, as long as they can buy goods and services.
- As the sale of your business increases, the profitability would increase.
- If the business environment is competitive, then this marketing concept would be less favourable.
- The concept is applicable where you price your product based on the cost. They are short-term oriented.
- Encyclopaedia, door to door selling, insurance and online shopping are some of the main examples of selling concepts.

12.2 Social Selling

12.2.1 Introduction to Social Selling

The term social selling (English for social selling, also called social commerce) describes the establishment and expansion of a customer relationship as part of the sales process. The goal is to use active social media behaviour (posting pictures, etc.) to strengthen customer relationships with other members and thereby generate leads. The definition highlights that social selling is seen as a distinct sales approach that focuses on using social and digital channels to build customer relationships. In contrast to social media marketing, the customer can be directly involved and specifically address his needs. In a dialogue, the company representative approaches the individual potential customer, comes into contact and creates a trusting relationship. In this way, you get closer to the customer than classic online trading allows. In a study, companies were asked what role social selling plays in the company. For 55 per cent of all companies surveyed, social selling did not play a role in the company. Only 14 per cent of the participants stated that social selling is of great importance. There are four categories for successful social selling:

12.2.2 Establishing a Personal Brand

This component depends on how well the profile is designed. All profile sections should be filled in with detailed information. Personal branding also involves posting content and interacting with content uploaded by others with likes and comments. Sharing posts that provide valuable information underpins your role as an expert in the field.

12.2.3 Finding the Right People

It should be ensured that the right decision-makers are found. In addition, the connection to connections of the second degree should also be established (persons with whom there is no direct connection but the connections of the connections).

12.2.4 Dealing with Knowledge

This metric is based on the content that has been shared and consumed. An easy way to increase this number is to share relevant information to promote yourself as a reliable source of information.

12.2.5 Building Relationships

Additional connections can be established to increase the range of the network. An attempt is made to establish a connection with people who make purchasing decisions.

12.3   Cross-Selling

Cross-selling is a sales technique used to get a customer to spend more by purchasing a product that's related to what's being bought already. Amazon reportedly earns around 35 per cent of its sales by cross-selling. That approach allows a retailer to prompt a shopper to buy a compatible or necessary product. Examples of cross-selling include:

- A sales representative at an electronics retailer suggests that the customer purchasing a digital camera also buy a memory card.
- The cashier at a fast-food restaurant asks a customer, "Would you like fries with that?"
- The check-out form at an ecommerce site prompts the customer to add a popular-related product or a required accessory not included in the product being purchased.
- A new car dealer suggests the car buyer add a cargo liner or other after-market product when making the initial vehicle purchase.
- A clothing retailer displays a complete outfit so the shopper sees how pieces fit together and buys all the pieces instead of just one.

Cross-selling in the ecommerce environment involves identifying related products and creating appropriate offers, while in-person cross-selling could require training in effective approaches. In both cases, though, the goal is to make more money for the company while creating a satisfied customer.

Best practices for cross-selling success include:

- Recommend the accessory required for proper operation or use of the product purchased, such as a power cord for a computer printer that doesn't include one in the box.
- Bundle related products so the customer doesn't need to look for necessary components or accessory.
- Offer a discounted price on a bundled product offer to encourage immediate purchase with a temporary price savings.
- Demonstrate how the additional products work with the product being purchased.
- Make it easy for the customer to say "yes" by addressing potential customer objections in the cross-sell conversation. For example, a waiter showing diners the dessert tray can overcome "I shouldn't" by suggesting that diners share a dessert.

Figure 12.2 shows the cross-selling example in the retail industry. The company adds additional products, which could be desirable for the customer during the order process. In their own web shop, every online retailer has the opportunity to offer products in cross-selling. Some shop systems such as Magento, Shopware, OXID or WooCommerce also offer the option of automating cross-references to products.

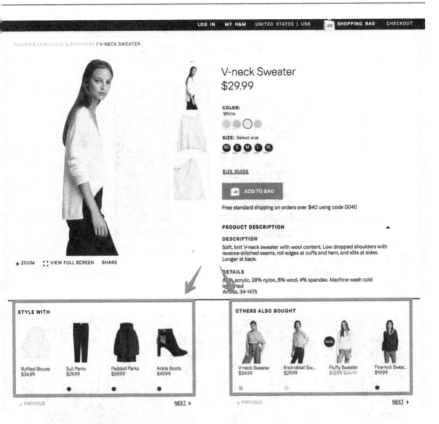

Fig. 12.2. Cross-selling example. (Source: SellerSmith Blog (2017). All knowledge and tips related to sales-boosting for Shopify merchants. Retrieved May 13, 2022. https://www.sellersmith.com/blogs/shopify/cross-sell-3-things-you-should-never-forget-1)

The articles already viewed by the user within a customer journey usually serve as the basis for this. In addition, pretty much every shop platform also offers the option of manually linking articles. The retailer needs a little sure instinct here, because the "wrong" products can even hinder the user in the purchasing process. For example, if a cross-linked product is currently not available ("out of stock"), this can lead to the purchase being abandoned.

12.4 Upselling

Upselling is a sales strategy that involves encouraging customers to buy a higher-end version of a product than what they originally intended to purchase. Figure 12.3 shows the example for a mobile phone with the offer of a technically higher version.

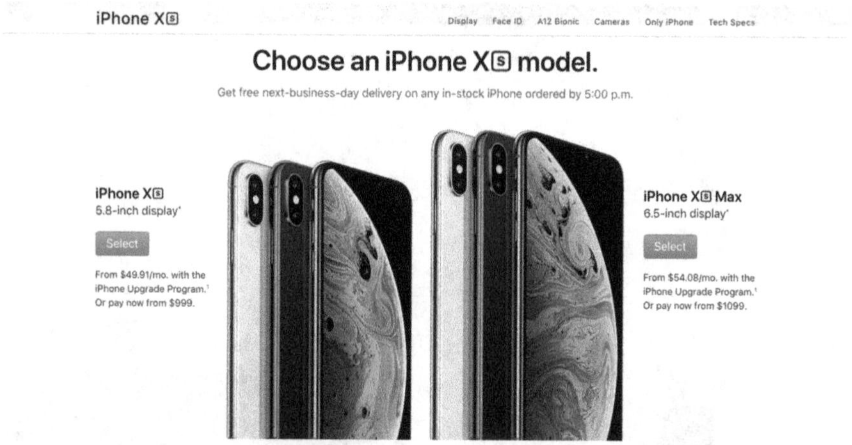

Fig. 12.3 Upselling. (Source: Personizely (2019). How to sell more – sales techniques from apple. Retrieved May 13, 2022. https://www.personizely.net/blog/how-to-sell-more-sales-techniques-from-apple/)

Fig. 12.4 Deep selling. (Source: St. Albertßs Place (2011). When buying the large size doesn't pay. Retrieved May 13, 2022. http://mybirdie.ca/files/d74f5b28a0b51fe00c2559612b681776-13963.php)

12.5   Deep Selling

Deep selling is an alternative approach focused on discovering the needs and circumstances of individual consumers, educating them about alternatives and making recommendations to improve their financial well-being. With deep selling, a company will sell more of the same product or service to the customer. So instead of one product, the company will aim to sell two, three or more (Fig. 12.4).

2.6 Consultative Selling

Consultative selling is a sales method in which the actual customer needs are analysed more precisely and the solution offered fully meets the customer's needs. Consultative selling is a sales approach that prioritizes relationships and open dialogue to identify and provide solutions to the real requirements and problems of the customers. It is hyper focused on the customer, rather than the product being sold. This technique helps sales professionals better understand the challenges faced by customers so they can position their solutions in a more compelling and effective way.

12.7 Virtual Selling

Virtual selling or remote selling is the collection of processes and technologies by which salespeople engage with customer remotely with both synchronous and asynchronous communications. These communications are often replacing in-person, face-to-face sales conversations and have become increasingly prevalent in response to the COVID-19 pandemic. Often, companies and sales organizations combine virtual selling with physical selling. Virtual selling is the adaptation in sales processes, because ultimately the place where the conversation takes place changes. However, this creates great opportunities that one should know how to take advantage of:

- Shortened average sales cycle (the period from the first point of contact to completion): appointments can be planned remotely at significantly shorter notice, as long journeys are saved. In addition, shorter consultation intervals can be implemented in this way.
- Customizable and evaluable sales process: Every customer is different. By using remote selling or virtual selling tools, you have the opportunity to respond to individual needs and evaluate their success. In this way, you get to know more about your customers and can tailor your activities to their individual needs.
- More intensive customer care possible: The time of any travel activities can be invested in the customer project. This is how you use your resources efficiently and focus on your customers.
- More resources for looking after potential customers: Sales employees can also use the time they have saved to look after more customers. This saves human resources without reducing the quality of advice.
- Improved work-life balance for sales staff: Professions that involve traveling lead to challenges in families and in leisure time. Your sales staff gains freedom and flexibility thanks to their location independence, an essential factor when it comes to the attractiveness of the employer brand.

12.8 Visual Selling

Visual selling focuses on the relationship between the customers, the context it is placed in and its relevant image.

Visual perception is the ability to interpret the surrounding environment through colour vision, scotopic vision and mesopic vision, using light in the visible spectrum reflected by the objects in the environment. Visual selling is affecting placement of products, signage, display materials, ambiance and employee staffing.

12.9 Case Study: Activities in Amazon to Boost Cross-Selling Activities

Amazon constantly analyses user behaviour on its website and offers customers products practically "live" that match their buying and surfing behaviour. Cross-selling by Amazon happens on the home page digitally (e.g. by "Inspired by your shopping trends") and on the product detail page (e.g. by "Customers who bought this item also bought" or "Customer who bought this item" Have viewed articles, have also viewed "). Through so-called retargeting, products are automatically displayed that the user has viewed but not bought, for example. Cross-selling on Amazon works particularly well on the product detail page, because this is where the purchase probability is highest. In addition to placing cross-references, Amazon also offers cross-selling and upselling in product comparison tables. Vendors also have the option of linking their products with one another using self-created A + content. Largely automated cross-selling on Amazon also works via email in after-sales. After purchasing an item on the platform, the user will receive matching/ additional offers a few days later. For example, if you buy a reflex camera from Amazon, you will automatically receive the matching lenses, camera bags, memory cards or tripods as cross-selling offers.

References

Czinkota, M. R., et al. (2021). *Marketing management: Past, present and future*. Springer.

Homburg, C., Schäfer, H., & Schneider, J. (2012). *Sales excellence: Systematic sales management*. Springer.

Borthwick, D. (2020). *Inside the mind of sales: How to understand the mind & sell anything*. Derek Borthwick.

Zentes, J., Morschett, D., & Schramm-Klein, H. (2019). *Strategic retail management: Text and international cases*. Springer.

13

> *Most people think "selling" is the same as "talking". But the most effective salespeople know that listening is the most important part of their job.*
>
> Roy Bartell

13.1 Introduction to Pricing Strategies

Pricing management is *the process of integrating all perspectives and information necessary to consistently arrive at optimal pricing decisions.* It can be defined as the analysis, planning, determination, enforcement and monitoring of prices and conditions (conditions system). Price management should contribute to the achievement of the marketing and sales strategy and ultimately corporate goals (e.g. profit maximization) by setting (profit) optimal prices and conditions. The tasks of the price management are either taken over by special revenue managers, price managers or are partial tasks of the marketing managers. The central component is the price process. Therefore, strong price management capabilities result in effective management of financial risk and revenue (Simon & Fassnacht, 2019). Pricing management is the process of integrating all perspectives and information necessary to consistently arrive at optimal pricing decisions. The process incorporates the price strategy, price setting and price implementation as shown in Fig. 13.1. Sophisticated price management capabilities result in effective management of financial risk and revenue (Helmold, 2020).

13.2 Price and Value Considerations

For setting the right price, it is important to create, deliver and communicate value in order to extract revenues (value extraction) as shown in Fig. 13.2. If a business becomes complacent and does not look to create new value for their customers, it is likely that their competitors will begin to find ways to fill those needs. Eventually, the company who does not continually innovate and provide for the needs of their customers will become stale. Their failure to continue to add value for their client base

M. Helmold, *Performance Excellence in Marketing, Sales and Pricing*, Management for Professionals, https://doi.org/10.1007/978-3-031-10097-0_13

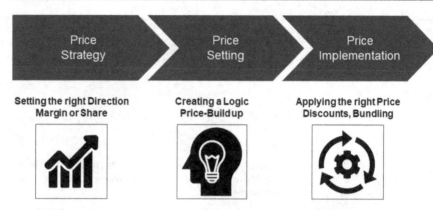

Fig. 13.1 Price strategy, price setting and price implementation. (Source: Author's source)

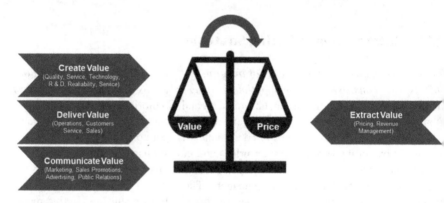

Fig. 13.2 Value considerations. (Source: Author's source)

will allow other companies to better fill those needs and acquire more of the market share. Therefore, a company must always be looking to add value to their customers, or they will go out of business. Projects, therefore, become the lifeline of a viable business. Value creation involves including only those elements in a product or service that a fully informed customer should be willing to pay for value. The term "should be" is used because what customers will actually pay depends upon how the product is marketed and is usually somewhat short of the full value. A great new product or service that promises huge benefits is only a promise. For example, willingness to pay will fall short of value but will move much closer to value if the product comes with a money-back performance guarantee. After creation of value propositions, it is important to deliver the value to the customers. Customers must perceive any type of value. Value delivery can contain several elements:

- Providing multiple industrial product options to customers.
- Fulfilling personalized business needs of customers.
- Helping customers compare different options based on reviews.
- Offering expert consultation at every stage of the buying funnel.

Value Communication involves communicating credibly the differentiating bene-
its of your product. The goal, particularly for a higher-priced product, is to establish
or the customer the "value" identified during the value creation stage. Without that,
you run the risk that the purchasing department does not know the value of your differentiating benefits to their company or that they will not acknowledge the value,
even if they do know what it is. Once you have established the economic value, or at
least have opened a discussion about what it is, you no longer need to justify your
price premium relative to the competition. Instead, you can sell or promote your discount relative to the added value that you deliver. Or, to describe value communication
in the negative, you can show that your lower-priced competitors are nonetheless
overpriced because the savings from buying their products are insufficient to compensate for the value lost by not buying your product!

13.3 Pricing Strategies and Concepts

13.3.1 Introduction and Definition of Pricing Strategies

The price policy (also price management) is part of the marketing mix of a company and
deals with the analysis, determination and monitoring of prices and conditions of production or services. The aim of the pricing policy is to set optimal prices for the company in
relation to the company's goals (e.g. profit maximization, customer satisfaction, growth).
An important decision problem is the lower price limit. The upper price limit, on the other
hand, is determined by demand. Basically, it lies where the price perceived by the customer agrees with his appreciation of the product (Boomerang Commerce, 2015).
However, pricing policy is also used as a purchase price policy for procurement policy
goals. The predominance of the manufacturer's point of view in marketing theory, which
usually understands the consumer as the buyer of the product, means that both the (sales)
pricing policy aimed at commercial customers and the strategies and tactics relating to
purchasing or procurement pricing can easily be overlooked. As a rule, buyers of industrial products are initially entrepreneurs and not consumers. The (sales) price policy of the
retail trade is primarily aimed at the latter. Trade marketing is dedicated to this, as is the
(purchasing) pricing policy aimed at commercial suppliers. Figure 13.1 shows 16 different pricing strategies and concepts. The pricing policy includes all measures for:

- Formation and change of prices.
- Pricing and differentiation of prices.
- Determination of sales conditions (conditions management).
- Development of customer services.

Market-oriented pricing is based both on the prices of competing companies
and on the behaviour of customers. It usually has the goal of maximizing profit.
There are exceptions if, for example, a competitor is to be forced out of the market
or a new product is to be introduced. In order to determine the maximum profit
price, the type of market (monopoly, limited monopoly, etc.) must be taken into

Fig. 13.3 Pricing strategies and concepts. (Source: Author's source)

account, the behaviour of competitors must be analysed and intensive sales research must be carried out. This can lead to very different pricing strategies depending on the market. An important tool here is the price elasticity of demand and supply. In general, it can be said that the (low) price forms a "false" preference (preference) among customers. If the price rises and a competitor is cheaper, the customer switches to the cheaper provider. The price elasticity of demand can be used to determine the extent to which customers react to different price changes. If the elasticity is low, the prices can be varied relatively widely without the customers overly reacting in their sales behaviour. Hardly any customers leave when prices rise. In this case, there is a "real" preference which prompts the customer to remain loyal to the provider in question despite the increased price. The existence of preferences also nullifies the uniformity of the market price. Buyers who prefer a certain brand are willing to pay a higher price than for comparable competitive services. The resulting leeway in terms of price policy (monopoly area) is characteristic of imperfect markets.

In the context of market-oriented pricing policy, measuring the willingness of consumers to pay plays an important role in pricing (Fig. 13.3).

13.3.2 Value-Based Pricing

Value-based pricing is a strategy of setting prices primarily based on a consumer's perceived value of a product or service. Value pricing is customer-focused pricing, meaning companies base their pricing on how much the customer believes a product is worth.

3.3.3 Cost-Based Pricing

Cost-based pricing strategies uses production costs as its basis for pricing, and, to this base cost, a profit level must be added in order to come up with the product price. Cost-based pricing companies use their costs to find a price floor and a price ceiling. The floor and the ceiling are the minimum and maximum prices for a specific product or service – the price range. The ideal thing to do would be setting a price in between the floor and the ceiling. Many companies mass-producing goods such as textiles, food and building materials use this pricing technique.

Advantages:
• Calculations to determine price are simple.
• During price setting, unknowns are taken into account.
• Pricing ensures total profits for the business.

Disadvantages:
• Ignores how customer demand affects price.
• It doesn't take into account actions by competition.
• Price setting cannot be solely based on costs.

13.3.4 Break-Even Pricing

Break-even pricing is the practice of setting a price point at which a business will earn zero profits on a sale. The intention is to use low prices as a tool to gain market share and drive competitors from the marketplace. By doing so, a company may be able to increase its production volumes to such an extent that it can reduce costs and then earn a profit at what had previously been the break-even price. Alternatively, once it has driven out competitors, the company can raise its prices sufficiently to earn a profit, but not so high that the increased price is tempting for new market entrants. The concept is also useful for establishing the lowest acceptable price, below which the seller will begin to lose money on a sale. This information is useful when responding to a customer that is demanding the lowest possible price.

13.3.5 Dynamic Pricing

A dynamic pricing tool analyses historical and market data to provide tailored, automated pricing recommendations. Dynamic pricing tools can contribute incremental revenue by optimizing your nightly rates – and they'll take time off your plate by automating the rate-setting process.

Loss leader pricing examples

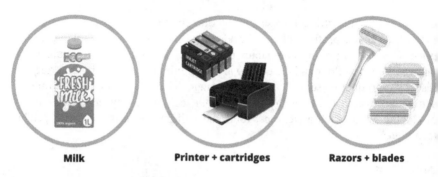

Milk   Printer + cartridges   Razors + blades

Fig. 13.4 Loss leader pricing concept

13.3.6 Loss Leader-Based Pricing

A loss leader is a product intentionally sold at a loss in order to encourage customers into a store or to a particular area of a store. A company offers discounts or temporarily sells a product below list price as a special event, sometimes even selling below cost as a loss leader (Fig. 13.4).

13.3.7 Competition-Based Pricing

Competition-based pricing involves setting prices based on competitors' strategies, costs, prices and market offerings. In highly competitive markets, consumers will base their judgements of a product's value on the prices that competitors charge for similar products. For instance, in the gasoline industry, competition-based pricing is applied (Hamilton & Chernev, 2013).

13.3.8 Premium-Based Pricing

Premium pricing (also called image pricing or prestige pricing) is the practice of keeping the price of one of the products or service artificially high in order to encourage favourable perceptions among buyers, based solely on the price. Premium refers to a segment of a company's brands, products or services that carry tangible or imaginary surplus value in the upper mid- to high price range. The practice is intended to exploit the tendency for buyers to assume that expensive items enjoy an exceptional reputation or represent exceptional quality and distinction. A premium pricing strategy involves setting the price of a product higher than similar products. This strategy is sometimes also called skim pricing because it is an attempt to "skim the cream" off the top of the market. It is used to maximize profit in areas where customers are happy to pay more, where there are no substitutes for the product, where there are barriers to entering the market or when the seller cannot save on costs by producing at a high volume.

Luxury has a psychological association with premium pricing. The implication for marketing is that consumers are willing to pay more for certain goods and not for others. To the marketer, it means creating a brand equity or value for which the consumer is willing to pay extra. Marketers view luxury as the main factor differentiating a brand in a product category.

3.3.9 Target Pricing

Target pricing is a pricing strategy in which the selling price of the product or service is determined first, and then the cost is calculated by reducing the profit margin. The price which is used as starting target price is based on the highest competitive price in the market which customer might want to pay for that product or service. As the name suggests, first the target of selling price is set, and then from there the rest of the calculations are done.

3.3.10 Everyday Low Pricing (EDLP)

Everyday Low Price (EDLP) is a pricing strategy promising consumers a low price without the need to wait for sale price events or comparison shopping. EDLP saves retail stores the effort and expense needed to mark down prices in the store during sale events and is also believed to generate shopper loyalty. It was noted in 1994 that the Walmart retail chain in the United States, which follows an EDLP strategy, would buy "feature advertisements" in newspapers on a monthly basis, while its competitors would advertise weekly (Keller et al., 2019). EDLP strategies generally result in lower fixed costs, since they require less advertising for promotional prices, less labour to execute price changes and simpler pricing and inventory management systems with lower overhead. EDLP can also result in more predictable consumer demand and therefore fewer stocking and supply-chain problems. High-low pricing strategies generally result in lower variable costs, since promotional retailers can sell more products by offering discounts. They are able to take advantage of surplus at the wholesale level and also eliminate excess inventory at the retail level (Fassnacht & El Husseini, 2013). This is particularly useful in markets for perishable goods, such as groceries. In North America, Walmart is widely associated with EDLP, since it incorporated the concept into its slogan. Walmart opened its first store in 1962 in a market where Kmart had been the dominant player using a high-low pricing strategy. Kmart's signature "blue light special" is an example of in-store advertising used to promote a temporary discount as part of the high-low pricing strategy. Walmart's success in EDLP and the decline of other retailers have followed the long-term trend in this market and in consumer buying habits. The growth of Walmart Supercenters in the 1990s was expected to drive the same trend in grocery stores. Despite Walmart's success with the Supercenter concept, high-low pricing

Fig. 13.5 EDLP at Walmart. (Source: Author)

has not been entirely replaced by EDLP in the grocery market. Figure 13.5 shows an example of Walmart with the advertising of the EDLP.

13.3.11 Good Value Pricing

A good value pricing strategy focuses on features, not value. The goal is to make consumers believe they are getting a good product at a fair price. When creating marketing campaigns for these types of products, marketers don't need to focus on building a lot of additional value.

13.3.12 Freemium Pricing

Freemium, a portmanteau of the words "free" and "premium", is a pricing strategy by which a basic product or service is provided free of charge, but money (a premium) is charged for additional features, services or virtual (online) or physical (offline) goods that expand the functionality of the free version of the software. This business model has been used in the software industry since the 1980s. A subset of this model used by the video game industry is called free-to-play.

13.3.13 Seasonal Pricing

Seasonal pricing can be defined as charging different prices for products and services depending on whether it's high season or low season. The idea is to smooth demand by enticing customers with low prices during the slow period, while maximizing revenues with higher prices when demand is strong.

13.3.14 Penetration Pricing

Penetration pricing is a pricing strategy used by businesses to attract customers to a new product or service by offering a lower price during its initial offering. The lower price helps a new product or service penetrate the market and attract customers away from competitors. Market penetration pricing relies on the strategy of using low prices initially to make a wide number of customers aware of a new product. The goal of a price penetration strategy is to entice customers to try a new product and build market share with the hope of keeping the new customers once prices rise back to normal levels. Penetration pricing examples include an online news website offering 1 month free for a subscription-based service or a bank offering a free checking account for 6 months.

- Penetration pricing is a strategy used by businesses to attract customers to a new product or service by offering a lower price initially.
- The lower price helps a new product or service penetrate the market and attract customers away from competitors.
- Penetration pricing comes with the risk that new customers may choose the brand initially, but once prices increase, switch to a competitor.

13.3.15 Skimming Pricing

Price skimming is a product pricing strategy by which a firm charges the highest initial price that customers will pay and then lowers it over time. As the demand of the first customers is satisfied and competition enters the market, the firm lowers the price to attract another, more price-sensitive segment of the population. The skimming strategy gets its name from "skimming" successive layers of cream, or customer segments, as prices are lowered over time.

- Price skimming is a product pricing strategy by which a firm charges the highest initial price that customers will pay and then lowers it over time.
- As the demand of the first customers is satisfied and competition enters the market, the firm lowers the price to attract another, more price-sensitive segment of the population.
- This approach contrasts with the penetration pricing model, which focuses on pentrating a new market.

13.3.16 Price Bundling

Price bundling (product bundling or product-bundle pricing) is a marketing strategy that combines two or more products to sell them at a lower price than if the same products were sold individually. The bundle pricing technique is popular in retail and eCommerce as it offers more value for the price. It can also help build customer loyalty and boost product sales. Price bundling can be applied to any type of product, but it works best when there are two or more items in the bundle. For example, say you own an ice cream shop and want to offer customers deals on their favourite flavours. You could offer a bundle of three ice cream cones for 4 Euro instead of selling them at 1 Euro each (Zentes et al., 2019).

13.3.17 High-Low Pricing

High-low pricing (or hi-low pricing) is a type of pricing strategy adopted by companies, usually small and medium-sized retail firms, where a firm initially charges a high price for a product and later, when it has become less desirable, sells it at a discount or through clearance sales. Prospective customers may be unaware of a product's typical market price or have a strong belief that "discount" is synonymous with "low price" or have strong loyalty to the product, brand or retailer. High-low pricing strategy is effective because of consumer preference and shopping frequency. Consumers with higher income strongly prefer the high-low pricing, and they shop frequently in the brand stores they like.

13.3.18 Markup Pricing

Markup (or price spread) is the difference between the selling price of a good or service and cost. It is often expressed as a percentage over the cost. A markup is added into the total cost incurred by the producer of a good or service in order to cover the costs of doing business and create a profit. The total cost reflects the total amount of both fixed and variable expenses to produce and distribute a product. Markup can be expressed as a fixed amount or as a percentage of the total cost or selling price. Retail markup is commonly calculated as the difference between wholesale price and retail price, as a percentage of wholesale. Other methods are also used.

13.4   Important Aspects to Pricing

- Price is only one element of the company's broader marketing strategy; the marketing strategy combines a profound analysis, the evaluation of options and the implementations of feasible strategies.
- Before setting price, the company must decide on its overall marketing strategy for the product or service including the necessary resources and assets needed.

A company's overall strategy can build around its price and value story for a product or service; however, this needs to be accurately evaluated.

If the company has selected its target market and positioning carefully, then its marketing mix strategy, including price, will be fairly straightforward.

Pricing strategy is largely determined by decisions on market positioning and competitive environments.

- Pricing may play an important role in helping to accomplish company objectives at different levels, e.g. to attract new customers or profitably retain existing ones, to prevent competition from entering the market or to set prices at competitors' levels to stabilize the market.
- Price decisions must be coordinated with product design, distribution and promotion decisions to form a consistent and effective integrated marketing mix program.

13.5   Discount Policy

A sales discount is a reduction in the price of a product or service that is offered by the seller, in exchange for early payment by the buyer. A sales discount may be offered when the seller is short of cash, or if it wants to reduce the recorded amount of its receivables outstanding for other reasons. Discounts are very attractive to customers and may not only bring new clients but can also bring back previous customers. Discounting products and services, particularly in-demand ones, is a good way to get attention.

13.6   Case Study: Pricing Strategy in Starbucks

13.6.1   Premium Pricing

Premium pricing involves setting the prices of products higher than comparable products. Businesses usually use it to boost profits in areas where the customer is happy to pay more. Some brands, such as Starbucks, can charge a premium price because their entire brand image is based around luxury. Starbucks sets its prices on a simple idea: high value at moderate cost. When people feel like they are getting a good deal for their money, they are more likely to pay a higher cost. Starbucks appreciates that the mainstream of their customer base is impervious to price. It uses small price rises that everyday customers may not notice to increase margins. The goal is to use the price increases to guide the customer towards your most profitable product. Starbucks' pricing strategy is carefully calculated and based on a combination of the target market, using a premium approach to branding. The strong brand identity drives sales, despite having higher priced products. Additionally, Starbucks' promotion strategy also drives awareness and sales around special events and holidays. Starbucks do not increase the prices of their products with the highest margins. Starbucks raised the price of a tall coffee in order to convince customers to buy a larger coffee size (with slightly higher margins).

13.6.2 Menu at Starbucks

The menu at Starbucks is highly specialized and focused. The menu items are relevant to the pricing strategy, because the pricing strategy demonstrates how the company is able to price high while also achieving optimal margin. The menu is exactly the same at every single store, and the lack of variables means that Starbucks can source product in bulk to drive down the costs. Starbucks also offers a nice selection of options, without overwhelming the customer. For example, food options are a fraction of the offerings at many other shops, and they are pre-made and ready to heat. The company loses on that special touch that you might see at a local cafe, but Starbucks restaurants are extremely efficient.

13.6.3 Starbucks' Branding Strategy

The Starbucks' branding is exceptional, and it falls into a small group of stores that have locations spanning the globe. Starbucks has achieved its large-scale branding via strategic store placements, as well as consistency in the menu and service. Starbucks stores actually spend far less on advertising than do many other brands – and as one of the first major players in the coffee space, the brand association is organic. Although Starbucks uses a premium pricing strategy, it does so below the luxury threshold. Starbucks stores price in a way that brings greater returns without diminishing volume sales. For example, a luxury coffee brand will sell organic imported coffee with an emphasis on exotic at a $7 cup price point, while Starbucks keeps its Grande standard coffee below the $5 threshold. Although many of its specialty drinks break over $5, maintaining a black coffee below that price point means that Starbucks stores are still priced high but that their prices are below an exorbitant price. Although you can find similar coffee at a lower price point, you pay extra for the brand association and the comfort in knowing exactly what you will get for that price. The pricing strategy reflects the consistency and a willing marketplace. In fact, Starbucks has raised prices in the past, when the actual costs of coffee decreased. This shows that Starbucks has priced its offerings based on market demand and on brand association and not on the price of the raw coffee bean.

13.6.4 Starbuck's Promotion Strategy

Starbucks does not rely solely on organic branding to drive business. The company is very promotion heavy, and the strategy is a clear success. Starbucks uses holiday and seasonal promotions along with strategic marketing campaigns to build anticipation for time-limited beverages, such as the Pumpkin Spice Latte. The seasonal promotion strategy enables the company to maintain its infrastructure and existing menu, while adding a twist that incorporates itself naturally into the offerings. Starbucks management already have the machines and the capabilities to make a latte and nothing additional outside of the seasonal pumpkin ingredient, which is

equired to complete the transaction. This means that they avoid supply chain disruptions and have plenty of time to secure the seasonal raw materials that are added
to regular shipments for each store. This style of promotional strategy can work
with a number of different business niches. Essentially, you are bringing a temporary up-sell to the table, while marketing it ahead of the actual release. Figure 13.6
shows the Starbucks' pricing dashboard.

Fig. 13.6   Starbucks shop

References

Boomerang Commerce. (2015). *Introduction to price perception index (PPI): Achieving competitive pricing without racing to the bottom*. Industry Paper.

Fassnacht, M., & El Husseini, S. (2013). EDLP versus hi-lo pricing strategies in retailing – A state of the art article. *Journal of Business Economics, 83*(3), 259–289.

Hamilton, R., & Chernev, A. (2013). Low prices are just the beginning: Price image in retail management. *Journal of Marketing, 77*(6), 1–20.

Helmold, M. (2020). *Total revenue management (TRM). Case studies, best practices and industry insights*. Springer.

Keller, W. I. Y., Deleersnyder, B., & Gedenk, K. (2019). Price promotions and popular events. *Journal of Marketing, 83*(1), 73–88.

Simon, H., & Fassnacht, M. (2019). *Price management: Strategy, analysis, decision, implementation*. Springer.

Zentes, J., Morschett, D., & Schramm-Klein, H. (2019). *Strategic retail management: Text and international cases*. Springer.

Sales Channels and Sales Partners

14

> *I have never worked a day in my life without selling. If I believe in something, I sell it, and I sell it hard.*
>
> Estée Lauder

14.1 Introduction to Sales Channels

A sales channel consists of the people, organizations and activities necessary to transfer the ownership of goods from the point of production to the point of consumption. It is the way products get to the end-user, the consumer, and is also known as a distribution channel. The sales channel a pathway by the way of which the services or the products go from the manufacturer to the customers or to the end users (Helmold, 2021). The flow of services or goods is usually unidirectional, that is, from manufacturer to the customers only. It is a useful tool for management and is crucial to creating an effective and well-planned sales strategy.

14.2 Sales Channels

14.2.1 Zero Levels Channels: Producer-Consumer

The zero level sales channel is the direct connection between the producer and the customer as shown in Fig. 14.1. The producer sells the goods or provides the service directly to the consumer with no involvement with a middle man such as an intermediary, a wholesaler, a retailer, an agent or a reseller. The consumer goes directly to the producer to buy the product without going through any other channel. This type of marketing is most beneficial to farmers who can set the prices of their products without having to go through the Canadian Federation of Agriculture (Esch et al., 2008). Typically, goods that are consumed by a smaller segment of the market have influence over producers, and, therefore, goods that are produced in the response on the order of a few consumers are taken into account (Keith, 1960). Normally, goods and services of this channel are not utilized by large market segments. Moreover, the price of the goods may be subject to significant fluctuations (Helmold, 2020). For example, high

© The Author(s), under exclusive license to Springer Nature Switzerland AG 2022   147
M. Helmold, *Performance Excellence in Marketing, Sales and Pricing*, Management for Professionals, https://doi.org/10.1007/978-3-031-10097-0_14

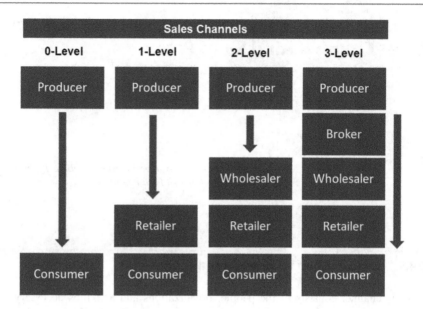

Fig. 14.1 Types of sales channels

demand dictates an increase in the price. In addition, this particular channel has three main ways of direct selling, and these include peddling, mail or sales and trade through manufacturer-owned stores (Kotler et al., 2017). Peddling is an outdated version of trade between two parties, and consignments are often sold in small amounts by sellers who are traveling to different places. For example, sales representative sells New Wave cosmetics to housewives by using a method of peddling. Mail-order sales are usually used to sell catalogues, books, etc., except industrial and bulky goods. For example, a firm sells collectibles through the use of mail-order. This method of selling is normally made without eye contact. In the last method (manufacture-owned stores), the manufacturer itself is surrounded by the stores and directly supplies goods to its stores. For example, Singer sells its sewing machines through its own stores. Due to distance of goods and products between producer and a seller, it takes an advantage to be an effective channel of distribution in its kind, and these advantages include: producers pay close attention with customers and are aware of the thoughts and ideas that are shared with them, there are no intermediaries that could substantially reduce the profit of a company which would then result in significant loss, and delivery time is shortened due to having no obstacles like middleman, etc (Tomczak et al., 2018). Despite these apparent advantages, direct selling has not become a powerful channel. According to an estimate, even less than 3% of total consumers' sales are made in this channel. On the other hand, technological innovations, the aid of the Internet and convenient smartphones are now changing the way that commerce works significantly. The proliferation of Internet-direct channels means that Internet companies will be able to produce and directly trade services and goods with consumers. It can be distributed directly through the Internet, for example, services in the sphere of gambling or software such as antivirus programs.

14.2.2 One Level Channels: Producer-Retailer-Consumer

Retailers, like Walmart and Target, buy the product from the manufacturer and sell them directly to the consumer. This channel works best for manufacturers that produce shopping goods like clothes, shoes, furniture, tableware and toys. Since consumers need more time with these types of items before they decide to purchase them, it is in the best interest of the manufacturer to sell them to an intermediary before it gets into the hands of the consumers. Using an established network that already has brand loyalty is a good strategy to use for producers to get the product to the end-user rapidly. Depending on the form of the retail property, operators can be an independent company, owned by various owners or to engage in the retail network. Intermediaries (retail service) are useful due to their experience, professionalism, ability to offer products to the target market and connections in the industry, as well as advantages in specialization and high quality of work. In other words, manufacturers produce large quantity of goods and products but are limited in its assortment and merchandise. Consumers seek a wider variety in lesser quantities. Therefore, it is highly essential to distribute goods from different manufacturers to suit consumer's needs and wants. When creating a retail store, buyer effort when making a purchase is considered. For example, stores that sell everyday consumer goods are conveniently located in a nearby neighbourhood for residents. The speed and convenience of service for clients' interests are put in high priority. An equally important component of the retail trade is the retail function that plays crucial roles. These include research of products, implementation of storage, setting of pricing policy, arrangements of products and its selection for the creation of different merchandise assortments and exploration of the condition prevailing in the market. This channel is considered to be beneficial if the volume of pre-sale and post-sale is insignificant, the amount of segments of the market is not enormous, and the assortment of goods and products is broad. Ultimately, the significance of intermediaries in distribution business is vital as they help consumers obtain particular goods of a specific brand without unnecessary steps. Thus, mediators play a crucial role in establishing a correspondence between demand and supply.

14.2.3 Two Level Channels: Producer-Wholesaler-Retailer-Consumer

Wholesalers buy the products from the manufacturer and sell them to the consumer. In this channel, consumers can buy products directly from the wholesaler in bulk. By purchasing the items in bulk from the wholesaler, the prices of the goods are reduced. This is because the wholesaler takes away extra costs, such as service costs or sales force costs, that customers usually pay when buying from retail, making the price much cheaper for the consumer. However, the wholesaler does not always sell directly to the consumer. Sometimes, the wholesaler will go through a retailer before the product gets into the hands of the consumer. Each dealer (the manufacturer, the wholesaler and the retailer) will be looking to make a decent profit margin from the product. Hence, each time the buyer purchases the merchandise from another source, the price of the product has to increase, in order to maximize the profit each person will receive. This raises the price of the product for the end-user. Due to the simultaneous and joint work of wholesaler and retailer, a trade can only be beneficial if a market is situated on a large area and the supply of goods is carried out small but urgent consignments (products); it can be cost-effective and profitable by supplying significant consignments (products) to fewer customers. Industrial factories want to utilize the advantages of mass production to produce and sell big lots (batches), while retailers look and prefer purchasing smaller consignments. This method for factories could lead to instant sales, high efficiency and cost-effectiveness. Therefore, particularly in these situations, wholesaler now plays a role where it reconciles these contradictory aspirations. The wholesaler purchases big lots and resells them to retailers in smaller lots. The transportation of products becomes less burdensome because the amount of delivered goods diminishes through the use of this channel (the wholesale). For example, if five manufacturers supply goods directly to a hundred different retail stores, then they will have to have 500 of deliveries (5 times 100). However, if those five manufacturers supply to the same wholesaler, and the wholesaler at this stage provides 100 different retailers, then the total number of deliveries will decrease to 105 (5 plus 100). Another important component to consider in the practice of wholesaling is storage. Storage of goods is another work aspect of a wholesaler. Wholesaler regulates the deliveries of goods, having synchronized the production and consumption of material goods. Moreover, the wholesaler further assumes the financial obligations related to the immobilization of funds invested in the creation of commodity stocks. In the chain of transition of goods, the wholesaler directly communicates and deals with a manufacturer. The contribution of a distributor is highly acknowledged and plays a crucial role in distributing flows of goods before it gets in the hands of wholesalers, retailers and so on (Helmold, 2021). A distributor is the representative of the manufacturer and performs functions on behalf of the manufacturer for the distribution of goods from producer to wholesaler or retailer. A distributor is always on the lookout for orders from different clients and actively promotes producer's products and services. The main tasks of a distributor include studying the market, finding customers, gaining information for new markets, advertising of goods, organizing services for the delivery of goods, stocking up the inventory levels and creating a stable sales network, which includes dealers and other intermediaries, depending on the market situation. Distributors scarcely sell a manufacturer's goods directly to customers.

14.2.4   Three Level Channels: Producer-Agent-Wholesaler-Retailer-Consumer

This distribution channel involves more than one intermediary before the product gets into the hands of the consumer. The middleman, known as the agent, assists with the negotiation between the manufacturer and the seller. Agents come into play when the producers need to get their product into the market as quickly as possible. This happens mostly when the item is perishable and has to get to the market fresh before it starts to rot. At times, the agent will directly go to the retailer with the goods or take an alternate route through the wholesaler who will go to a retailer and then finally to the consumer. A mutual cooperation normally occurs when parties, in particular, the last channel of marketing chain of distribution, meet, due to the fact that producers, agents, retailers/wholesalers and consumers of this channel aid each other and benefit from each other. Their cooperation generates a greater output in terms of further profitability, by discernment and exploring newer markets of sales and building a better business relationship. The participants of distribution channels must have knowledge and experience not only for the effective maintenance of target segments but also to maintain the competitive advantage of the manufacturer. For example, an agent who is able to vary prices for certain products can negotiate and or lower prices. This will assist him in sustaining the comparative advantage, remain on top of its competitors and fulfil market demand. A broker works mainly to bring the seller and the buyer together and to assist in the negotiation process. An intermediary like a broker is usually dependent on the commission of a sold product or production in terms of goods and also is involved in one-off transactions and cannot be an effective channel of distribution. However, he can maintain a competitive advantage over other firms in the form of a particular brand if he has obtained the right to exclusively represent the manufacturer and earn profit. He acts on behalf of the seller (producer or manufacturer) and has no rights to modify prices for products. Besides, having formed a channel of distribution, it is important to remember that the exploitation and utilization of intermediaries in a business (not only wholesalers, retailers but also transport logistics) will lengthen the chain of distribution. A business will then need to consider which channel is more cost-effective and productive in terms of timely delivery, efficiency, pricing policy and where it stands among competitors, for example, overall feedback, higher rating and higher demand from customers. The best use and help of intermediaries can be applied to start-up businesses and perhaps an established business.

14.3 Direct Sales Channels

Direct sales is when a company sells its only products and services "directly" to its client or customer base without an outside party involved. People say that the shortest distance between two points is a straight line, the direct route, and so direct sales is the conventional approach of selling directly to your customer and cutting out the middleman (Düssel, 2006). Direct sales channels involve direct selling through own retail channel members as shown in Fig. 14.2. Direct sales method is used by global brands and smaller entrepreneurial companies to market products and services to consumers. Companies market all types of goods and services, including jewellery, cookware, nutritionals, cosmetics, housewares, energy, insurance and much more. A direct sales channel contains its own sales managers, sales representatives, key account managers, own stores, flagship stores, customer service, call centres, trade

Direct Sales Channels

Own Sales Manager	Customer Service	Sales Driver (in own vans)
Own Sales Reps	Call-Centers	Roadshows
Key Account Manager	Own Trade Fair Stand	Inhouse Sales Events
Door-to-door Sales	Own Webshop	Webinars. Seminars
Own Stores	Home Parties	Telesales (own show/format)
Flagship Stores, Pop-Up Stores	Factory Outlets	Social Media Promotion (e.g. IG Promo Code)

Fig. 14.2 Direct sales channels. (Source: Author's source)

fair stands, webshops, home parties, outlets, sales drivers, roadshows, in-house sales events, webinars, telesales or social media sales. The direct selling channel differs from broader retail in an important way. It isn't only about getting great products and services into consumers' hands. It's also an avenue where entrepreneurial-minded Americans can work independently to build a business with low start-up and overhead costs. Direct selling consultants work on their own but affiliate with a company that uses the channel, retaining the freedom to run a business on their own terms. Consultants forge strong personal relationships with prospective customers, primarily through face-to-face discussions and demonstrations. In this age of social networking, direct selling is a go-to market strategy that, for many companies and product lines, may be more effective than traditional advertising or securing premium shelf space. Millions of Americans from every state, congressional district and community in the United States choose to become involved in direct selling because they enjoy a company's products or services and want to purchase them at a discount. Some decide to market these offerings to friends, family and others and earn commissions from their sales. The most successful consultants may decide to expand their business by building a network of direct sellers. Cutting out the middleman sounds like a good idea at first. Selling directly means that you keep all of the profit; no one is taking a chunk out of your sales. However, on further consideration, this is not always the case. When competently analysed, direct sales are full of hidden (and not so hidden) costs – salaries and overheads. Imagine what it would cost Coca Cola to vend directly to their customers! The costs would eventually prohibit the activity entirely. Instead, Coca Cola chooses to sell its products through third parties, such as shops and supermarkets, and via vending machines. Of course, they still make healthy profits, but they don't incur the cost of having a huge sales operation. That's not to say that Coca Cola Corporation doesn't spend millions on sales and marketing activities, but they don't actually sell directly to their customers. Some companies such as Apple now primarily sells its own products via its website and retail stores, although they have allowed some other companies such as PC World to stock their computers as they've become more popular.

14.4   Channel Sales and Indirect Sales Channels

In order to increase the number of items sold worldwide, with products like the Apple iPod, they have allowed resellers to sell their products too, in order to massively expand where the iPod can be bought. This is known as channel sales (Kotler & Armstrong, 2018). Two-thirds of all computing sales in the world are not direct sales like Apple; instead, they are "channel sales" or "indirect sales". This is where the company employs a third party, a reseller, to sell their products on to their customers. The most obvious example of a company that does this is Microsoft. Microsoft's products are sold through "channel sales" because Microsoft would have to become a retail operation in order to achieve the same level of global sales. This would hugely increase their costs and still not be as effective as channel sales. Both Microsoft and Apple use channel sales because it makes sense. Both companies use channel sales in different ways – Microsoft to reach as far as possible and Apple to expand the sale of their most popular products. Apple has developed a mixed approach, which has allowed it to capture an increasingly large share of the home computer market, while retaining some control over how individual products are sold.

14.5   Indirect Sales Channels

Indirect sales channels involves the sale of a good or service by a third party, such as a partner or affiliate, rather than a company's personnel. Indirect sales may be used in conjunction with a company's direct sales efforts or may be used in lieu of hiring sales staff. Indirect sales are often made through resellers, such as specialty stores and big-box retailers. Indirect sales can allow a company to increase sales quickly without having to hire more sales personnel. Companies often resort to indirect sales when the demand for the product is outpacing the ability of the company to hire competent salespeople or when the price of the product is too low to justify a large sales force (Meffert et al., 2008). Utilizing an indirect sales strategy is also efficient in that it allows the cost associated with a sale to be in proportion to how much success a reseller is. Figure 14.3 shows different ways of indirect sales channels through external retailers, e-Commerce platforms, sales agents, freelance sales representatives, sales promotion agencies, leased sales force, franchise partners, merchants, trade fairs, stands at festivals, stands at external events, external call centres, resellers or external affiliate networks. Indirect sales strategies do have a few downsides, however. For one, added fees can cut into margins. Also, in some

Indirect Sales Channels

Retail	Leased Salesforce	External Call Center
Wholesale	Franchising Partner	Resellers
E-Commerce Plattforms	Merchants	Affiliate Networks
Sales Agents	Trade Fair Partnerships (e.g. Start-Ups)	
Freelance Sales Reps	Stands at Festival	
Sales Promotion Agency	Stands at external Events	

Fig. 14.3 Indirect sales channels. (Source: Author's source)

cases, the use of affiliates or resellers may lead to reduced control of the brand message and compromised customer service. Because companies cannot manage indirect sales teams as easily as if they were in-house, any problems that may arise from the use of third-party sellers can be difficult and costly to remedy. Companies using indirect sales may also have a harder time communicating their goals and objectives to the customer. Advantages of using indirect sales channels are the following:

- Indirect sales involve the use of third parties to market and retail goods or services to end-user consumers.
- Affiliate networks, resellers, independent salespeople and various forms of retail are all examples of indirect sales.
- Because indirect sales involves a middleman, added fees, reduced control over brand image and inconsistent customer service are all risks to the producer.

14.6   Case Study: Direct and Indirect Sales Channels at Apple

Apple is one of the leading technology companies in the world, making everything from phones to computers to earphones. They have really created a full ecosystem to connect all their products and services. Apple has 510 stores like the store in Shanghai (see Fig. 14.4) worldwide but also sells its products through third-party sellers and carrier providers. Apple is able to generate huge amounts of sales through direct and indirect distribution channels worldwide.

Apple designs its products in California, but the rest of the product is process throughout the world. There are many complicated parts to Apple's products, and it would be difficult for one manufacturer to make them all, so Apple has to work with multiple manufacturers throughout the world. Components are made all over the

Fig. 14.4 Apple store in Shanghai

world by specialist of each part and sent to two main assemblers in China to manu-facture the final product, Foxconn and Pegatron. This drastically reduces cost of goods for Apple due to the cheaper labour in China. Products are then sent all over the world to its consumers through different distribution channels.

Apple's direct distribution channel includes their physical stores and their online store. Apple's physical stores allow them to really control their brand image and customer perception of them. All their stores worldwide have the same clean white design with a high employee to customer ratio. This creates a really strong brand image in consumers' minds as they are seeing the same design everywhere they go. They also often open their stores in high traffic locations to get as much exposure as possible. Apple also sells directly through their website. Their website can be accessed from all parts of the world and offers a huge range of languages.

However, even though Apple puts a lot of effort into their physical stores, a large part of their sales and revenue comes from indirect distribution channels. In 2018, Apple reported that 29% of their net sales came from direct channels and 71% came from indirect channels. Consumers can buy Apple products from third-party sellers and carrier providers. This includes stores like BestBuy, Walmart and Target as they are easily accessible and might offer discounts. Apple creates a good brand image through their physical stores and sells their product through third-party companies.

References

Düssel, M. (2006). *Handbuch Marketingpraxis – Von der Analyse zur Strategie, Ausarbeitung de Taktik, Steuerung und Umsetzung in der Praxis*. Cornelsen.

Esch, F. R., et al. (2008). *Eine managementorientierte Einführung* (2nd ed.). Vahlen Verlag.

Helmold, M. (2020). *Total revenue management (TRM) case studies, best practices and industr insights*. Springer.

Helmold, M. (2021). *Successful management strategies and tools: Industry insights, case studie and best practices*. Springer.

Keith, R. J. (1960). The marketing revolution. *Journal of Marketing, 24*(1), 35–38.

Kotler, P., & Armstrong, G. (2018). *Principles of marketing* (17th ed.). Brunel University.

Kotler, P., Kartajaya, H., & Setiawan, A. (2017). *Marketing 4.0: Moving from traditional to digi tal*. Wiley.

Meffert, H., et al. (2008). *Marketing* (10th ed.). Springer.

Tomczak, T., Reinecke, S., & Kuss, A. (2018). *Strategic marketing. Market-oriented corporate an business unit planning*. Springer.

Innovation Management and New Product Launches

15

Innovation distinguishes between a leader and a follower.

Steve Jobs

15.1 Introduction to Innovation Management

New products and innovations are a significant driver and element for the success of an enterprise. If new products and services are not properly launched, companies will not generate revenues, grow or even survive. With today's dynamic economy and the pressures to be more competitive and profitable, solid launch processes are even more critical. "Innovation" comes from the Latin word "innovare" and stands for renewal or reformation. From an economic point of view, innovation is something complex and new that brings economic benefits for an organization and for the company. Innovation management includes elements such as ideas, inventions and diffusions (Müller-Prothmann & Dörr, 2019). Innovations include the generation of ideas and the constant validation and review of these ideas as part of a structured innovation process (Nelke, 2016). Innovation management comprises three levels, as shown in Fig. 15.1. In addition to the operational level, the working level, there are the strategic and normative levels. Innovations are decided on the normative and strategic level and put into practice on the operative level (Helmold & Samara, 2019). Terms that are often used in connection with innovation are ideas, collections of ideas and inventions. An invention must be differentiated to the extent that it has not yet been exploited and used as a creative achievement of a new problem solution compared to innovation. It is the same with the idea, which is a creative thought of something new. In all cases, "new" can always be seen relatively. It can be new for this situation, the company or the world. In particular new developments such as New Work, Industry 4.0 or increasing globalization have an important impact on innovations and innovation management (Granig et al., 2018). Of central

© The Author(s), under exclusive license to Springer Nature Switzerland AG 2022
M. Helmold, *Performance Excellence in Marketing, Sales and Pricing*, Management for Professionals, https://doi.org/10.1007/978-3-031-10097-0_15

Fig. 15.1 Innovation management levels. (Source: Author's source)

importance are the collection of ideas, the selection and the decision which ideas are implemented. This process must be managed by the higher management (Helmold & Samara, 2019).

Management is a term that is used constantly in companies. It stands for the management of a task and for the coordination of activities in order to achieve a defined purpose and goals (Distrelic, 2020; Helmold & Terry, 2016). Accordingly, innovation management is the structured promotion of innovations in companies and includes tasks in the planning, organization, management and control of these innovations. Innovation management deals with all measures to favour innovations in organizations and to generate benefits, for example:

- New products and services to conquer new markets.
- Improved products and services to stand out from the competition.
- Improvement of internal processes in order to strengthen the company.
- Innovations from the inside or to save costs.
- Development of new business models to use new sources of income.
- New Work Styles that enable employees to achieve a better performance.

15.2 Technical Relevance and Attractivity

Innovations are usually complex undertakings with a high expenditure of technology, use resources and therefore usually cause very high costs and investments. It is therefore imperative that the company management sustainably evaluate every innovation with regard to its prospect of success and this with regard to strategic relevance, technology expenditure, benefits and resource intensity. Ideas and

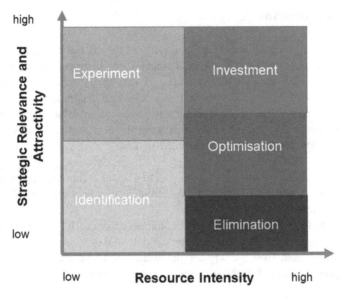

Fig. 15.2 Relationship between innovation management and strategy. (Source: Author's source)

possible innovations always require a strategic and resource-based review (Pfeiffer & Weiß, 1995; Pfeiffer et al., 1991). Figure 15.2 shows the relationship between strategy and resource use.

15.3   Strategic Relevance of Innovation Management

The strategic relevance and attractiveness of the innovation is the sum of all technical and economic advantages that can be gained by exploiting the strategic development opportunities in a technology area. The technology attractiveness depends on the one hand on the technology properties (potential side) and on the other hand on the requirements of (future) users (demand side).

The two sizes of the technology portfolio, technology attractiveness and resource strength, each represent a (highly) aggregated evaluation result in relation to deeper individual factors. Experts envisage the following things to check and determine technology attractiveness (Helmold & Samara, 2019):

- Further development potential: To what extent can technical further development increase performance, raise quality and decrease cost?
- Range of application: How can the number of possible areas of application of the technology and the quantities per area of application be assessed?
- Compatibility: What negative or positive effects can be expected in user and surrounding systems (innovation obstacles, drivers)?

15.4   Resource Intensity

The strength of the resources expresses the extent to which the assessed company has the prerequisites in comparison to its potential competitors to make the considered technological alternative successful, i.e. H, in a timely manner and in the form of marketable products. In other words, it is a measure of a company's technical and economic strength or weakness in relation to a technology relative to its competitors. Experts in tourism propose the following three indicators to determine the strength of resources (Helmold & Samara, 2019):

- Technical-qualitative degree of mastery: How is our technology-specific know-how to be assessed in relation to the competition; is there a lead or lag in development?
- Potentials: To what extent are financial, human and material resources available to exploit the existing further development potential of the technology?
- (Re)action speed: How quickly can the evaluating company exploit the further development potential of the technology compared to the competition?

15.5   Future Potential of Innovations

In addition to the studies described above with regard to strategic relevance and use of resources, innovations must be subjected to a future prognosis in which the future prospects of success are evaluated. Scenario analyses can be used to forecast the development of the user side (Pfeiffer et al., 1991). Pfeiffer and his co-authors also emphasize the great importance of a higher-level system and environment perspective that extends beyond individual technologies. On the one hand, this means that technical peripheral systems are included in the analysis (e.g. the establishment of a methanol or hydrogen supply infrastructure required for the implementation of fuel cell drives for cars). On the other hand, non-technical framework conditions are also decisive for the technology assessment (e.g. the possible tightening of exhaust gas legislation). In the context of the identification of innovations, the necessary resources and strategic relevance are still relatively low. In this phase, ideas are collected, evaluated and selected. In the next step, the strategically relevant ideas must be tested (Fig. 15.2: Experiment). This testing usually takes place through experiments. However, observations, workshops, panels or analysis groups can also be used. With the selection of strategically important innovations, the use of resources in companies automatically increases. Primary materials have to be bought, the products have to be mass-produced, and marketing towards customers requires pro-active marketing. This phase of the investment involves a very high expenditure of resources and thus financial resources (equity or debt). After the investment phase, optimization begins so that fewer resources are required. The optimization takes place through standardization, unification, volume effects or technical innovations. In the last step, if it turns out that the innovation no longer has any strategic relevance, all activities are eliminated and shut down (Helmold & Samara, 2019).

15.6   Fields and Tasks of Innovation Management

Innovation management forms two key pillars. On the one hand, innovation management includes the creation of suitable and structured framework conditions, so that ideas arise everywhere in the company and are implemented into successful innovations. It is very much about organizational development activities (Helmold, 2021). Second is the actual innovation, the active search, development and implementation of ideas. This requires creativity and appropriate project management, for example (Scholz et al., 2015). Innovation management is very versatile and multifaceted. The fields of action of innovation management include the following elements:

- Future management: Identification of trends and future opportunities and risks.
- Development of the innovation strategy and planning of the innovation activities, for example, with an innovation roadmap.
- Organization and distribution of roles in innovation management, such as decision-making structures and process ownership.
- Idea management for finding, developing and evaluating ideas.
- Innovation process for transforming an idea into a successful innovation: concept development, business plan, solution development, prototypes, implementation and marketing.
- Creating an innovation culture that promotes innovation.
- Portfolio management and innovation controlling (e.g. innovation indicators) to control innovation activities.
- Dealing with patents and property rights.
- Open innovation and innovation networks to use external innovation sources and resources.
- Management of change (change management) in the course of innovation projects.

Figure 15.3 depicts innovations in several areas like products, networks, services, processes, communication systems, routines, concepts or activities (Helmold & Terry, 2021).

15.7   Product Launches

A product launch is the initial distribution of a marketable product or service in a market. A product launch refers to a business's planned and coordinated effort to debut a new product to the market and make that product generally available for purchase (Pfohl & Gareis, 2000). A product launch serves many purposes for an organization – giving customers the chance to buy the new product is only one of them. It also helps an organization build anticipation for the product, gather valuable feedback from early users and create momentum and industry recognition for the company.

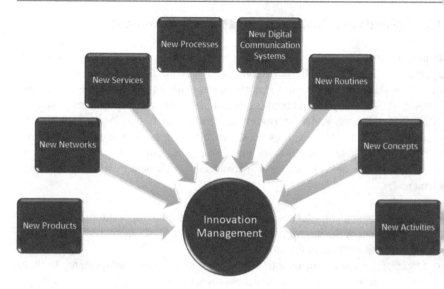

Fig. 15.3 Innovation management elements. (Source. Author's source)

15.8   Product Launch Roadmap and Process

15.8.1 Roadmap

A product launch roadmap is an essential visual with a high-level overview of the customer journey. Launch roadmaps can take a variety of different forms (Cooper & Kleinschmidt, 1987). Some look like mind maps, like this example, while others take on the form of a simple timeline or an infographic. The seven stages of the new product development process include:

1. Idea generation.
2. Idea screening.
3. Concept development and testing.
4. Building a market and sales strategy and logic.
5. Product development.
6. Market testing.
7. Market commercialization.

It takes many departments to launch a product and a sophisticated marketing plan (Czinkota et al., 2021). Some companies assign the task of product launch to a specific functional group within the company; others set up "virtual teams" that come together to implement a launch (Biazo & Fillipini, 2021). Whatever the approach, six key functional groups should be represented on the launch team: marketing, engineering, sales, customer service, public relations (often a vendor) and channel or strategic partners. Sometimes, these functional areas are within the

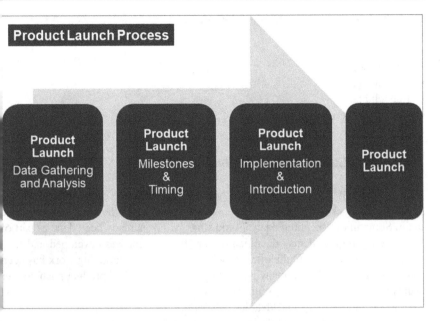

Fig. 15.4   Product launch phases. (Source: Author)

company, and sometimes these functions are represented by outside vendors (channel partners and public relations) (Turayi, 2021). Some of these groups may be
needed throughout the entire launch process; others may be involved only during
the launch planning and implementation phase. Most launches involve marketing
and engineering, but the sales organization is sometimes left out. In fact, the involvement of the sales organization is especially critical during the entire launch process
to provide feedback regarding existing customers and identify the marketing and
sales materials that may be needed for the launch. There are three main phases of
the process (Fig. 15.4), each with several steps:

Data gathering and analysis phase:
- Product definition.
- Strategic objectives.
- The customer.
- Market analysis.
- Competition.
- Distribution plan.
- Market strategy and programs phase:
- Market strategy.
- Message development.
- External marketing.
- PR and advertising.
- Internal marketing.
- Marketing plan.

Launch planning and implementation phase:
- Planning process.
- Launch team.
- Launch schedule.
- Launch budget.
- Launch plan.
- Launch implementation.

15.8.2 Data Gathering and Analysis

The first phase of the launch process is the data gathering and analysis phase, and the first task is to assess what is being launched and how much of the work has been done so far. Sometimes, the initial analysis and strategy have already been done as part of a "marketing requirements" document before the product was developed and may just need to be updated. Quite often, however, none of the marketing work has been done at all because the company may be operating under the "product push" rather than "market pull" philosophy (common in high-tech). Whatever the case, it's imperative to develop a crisp and detailed description of the product or service being launched, and then the rest of the steps can begin: the strategic objectives, analysing and characterizing the customer and market, a thorough competitive analysis and developing a distribution plan. The market strategy and programs phase relies upon the results of the data gathering and analysis phase. From the results of the competitive analysis and the customer characteristics, the overall market strategy, positioning statements and a hierarchy of key messages are developed. The next step is identifying the right marketing programs and venues for reaching the target customer and convincing them to buy the product or service. Marketing programs include external and internal marketing, PR and advertising. All of the results of the first two phases are captured in the marketing plan, along with a narrative that ties everything together and tells a story. This plan is not only useful for the launch team to use as a guide during launch, but it is also a very useful document to share with outside vendors who may be helping with the launch, such as website designers or PR agencies. These first two phases of the launch process are critical because they help the launch team think through the launch before the work is done and the money is spent. The launch plan is the "project management" document for the launch. The first part of this plan consists of allocating the resources (the launch team and other human resources) to the launch deliverables (the marketing programs identified in the marketing plan). This is captured in a spreadsheet called the "resource allocation".

15.8.3 Milestones and Timing

The second major piece of the launch plan are timing and milestones. This consists of two parts. The first is a one-page launch timeline that shows the major launch deliverables (marketing programs) and who will be doing them plotted along a timeline demarcated by weeks before the launch date. The other part is a detailed schedule that shows the due dates for all deliverables, the overlaps and the precise order in which they will be done. The timeline can easily be done in PowerPoint, and the schedule can be done using a simple spreadsheet program like Excel or project management software such as Microsoft Project. The spreadsheet method is easier, and it has the added utility of being able to turn it into a weekly status report by adding columns for owner, status and comments. The third part of the launch plan is the budget displayed in a spreadsheet, with estimates for each deliverable, and arranged by week or by month (usually launches take place over a few weeks, not months, so weeks make more sense).

15.8.4 Implementation and Introduction

The final step is implementation and introduction, which can be chaotic if there are a lot of deliverables being developed at the same time (which is usually the case!). However, if the launch plan is solid and thought through in adequate detail, the plan itself will really help to manage the bustle of activity as the launch date nears. One way to make this last phase easier is to identify the review and approval process for launch deliverables, such as website content, printed materials, etc., ahead of time and build that into the launch schedule, along with time for key people who might travel, go on vacation, etc. These are the situations that can hold up the launch during the implementation step. The first two phases of the launch process can take anywhere from just 2 weeks (if some of the analysis has already been done) to 6 weeks if everything has to be done "from scratch". The launch plan may take 2 or 3 weeks to put together, especially if multiple outside vendors are involved; it takes time to get bids in, choose vendors and get people to commit to a schedule and deliverable. Launch implementation may take several weeks, depending on how many deliverables there are and how long it takes to create them. Websites, for example, will take several weeks, but a simple printed brochure may only take a week or so. If this process is followed consistently, the entire launch can be completed in 8–12 weeks. It is important to follow a consistent process every time. This realistic but simple 3-phase process seems to work very well not only in terms of getting everything done but also in keeping the entire team (and management) informed and in the loop about critical decisions that may need to be made during the launch.

15.9   Case Study: Digital Innovation in a Bakery in Tokyo

Figure 15.5 shows an example of innovation management in a bakery store in Tokyo. The device helps customers and employees to focus on relevant activities, rather than non-adding value processes. The customer can place the selected goods on the scanning device. A camera is identifying the goods purchased and showing the price. The customers can pay easily with cash or credit card. The device helps

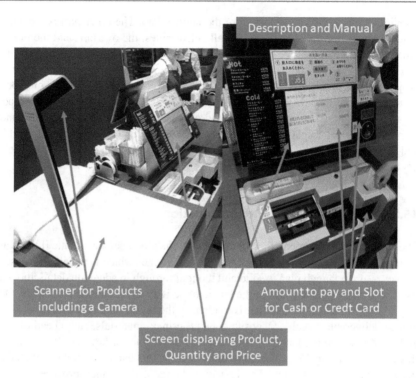

Fig. 15.5 Innovation in a bakery in Tokyo. (Source. Author's source)

employees to focus their activities on giving advice to customers rather than payment execution. Additionally, the process improved the transaction time significantly. There is no waiting time anymore for customers. Thus, an innovation helped to create more added value to customers.

References

Biazo, S., & Filippini, R. (2021). *Product innovation management: Intelligence, discovery, development*. Springer.

Cooper, R., & Kleinschmidt, E. (1987). New products: What separates winners from losers? *Journal of Product Innovation Management, 4*(3), 169.

Czinkota, M. R., et al. (2021). *Marketing management: Past, present and future*. Springer.

Distrelic. (2020). *Nachhaltige innovationen*. Abgerufen am 18 February 2020. https://www.distr-elec.de/current/de/technologien/10-technische-innovationen-fur-eine-nachhaltigere-zukunft/.

Granig, P., Hartlieb, E., & Heiden, B. (2018). *Mit Innovationsmanagement zu Industrie 4.0: Grundlagen, Strategien, Erfolgsfaktoren und Praxisbeispiele*. Springer.

Helmold, M. (2021). *Kaizen, lean management und Digitalisierung. Mit den japanischen Konzepten Wettbewerbsvorteile für das Unternehmen erzielen*. Springer.

Helmold, M., & Samara, W. (2019). *Progress in performance management: Industry insights and case studies on principles, application tools, and practice*. Springer.

Helmold, M., & Terry, B. (2016). *Global sourcing and supply management excellence in China.* Springer.

Helmold, M., & Terry, B. (2021). *Operations and supply management 4.0: Industry insights, case studies and best practices.* Springer.

Müller-Prothmann, T., & Dörr, N. (2019). *Innovationsmanagement: Strategien, methoden und Werkzeuge für systematische Innovationsprozesse.* Hanser Verlag.

Nelke, A. (2016). *Kommunikation und Nachhaltigkeit im Innovationsmanagement von Unternehmen: Grundlagen für die Praxis (Wirtschaftsförderung in Lehre und Praxis).* Springer.

Pfeiffer, W., & Weiß, E. (1995). Methoden zur Analyse und Bewertung technologischer Alternativen. In E. Zahn (Ed.), *Handbuch technologiemanagement* (pp. 663–679). Schäffer-Poeschel.

Pfeiffer, W., Metze, G., Schneider, W., & Amler, R. (1991). *Technologie-Portfolio zum management strategischer Zukunftsgeschäftsfelder* (6th ed.). Springer.

Pfohl, H.-C., & Gareis, K. (2000). Die Rolle der Logistik in der Anlaufphase. *Zeitschrift für Betriebswirtschaft, 11*(70), 1189–1214.

Scholz, U., Pastoors, S., & Becker, J. H. (2015). *Einführung in nachhaltiges innovationsmanagement und die Grundlagen des green marketing.* Tectum.

Turayi, Y. (2021). *The launch: A product marketer's guide: 50 key questions & lessons for a successful launch.* Medium.

International Marketing and Sales

16

The way to get started is to quit talking and begin doing.

Walt Disney

16.1 Market Entry Strategies with High and Low Investments

Nowadays, a progressively more dynamic and global economic environment causes a higher number of enterprises to pick an entry strategy to become international. The choice of a strategy of entry into foreign markets constitutes one of the most relevant decisions for a company, for it impacts on its performance and means it is being ready to cooperate, to a greater or lesser extent, with global supply chains. The present article identifies the determining factors of the strategies of entry into international markets as implemented by Peruvian businessmen, which impact on the integration level into an international market. The companies that participated in this exploratory study have growing exportation levels within the non-traditional sector. The results allow to appreciate exporters employing entry strategies with low levels of integration and predominantly prefer low-risk markets and high resemblance to the Peruvian market, with regard to cultural affinity and business behaviour. An important decision companies make at the moment of becoming international in order to reach greater growth and competitiveness is the choice of an entry strategy, for the choice they make and the way the strategy is implemented can determine the success or failure of their international enterprise. On one hand, a company might decide to become fully integrated and establish a subsidiary in a foreign market. On the other hand, a company might decide to hire independent distributors and be in charge of attracting new clients. In each level of integration, the degree of risk and control varies as well the degree of collaboration (Fig. 16.1).

**Level of Management/
Controlling**

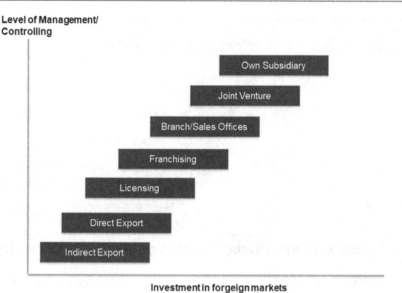

Investment in forgeign markets

Fig. 16.1 International market entry strategies with high and low investments

16.2   International Marketing and Sales Strategies

16.2.1 International Sales Entry Concepts

There are a variety of ways in which a company can enter a foreign market. No one market entry strategy works for all international markets. Direct exporting may be the most appropriate strategy in one market, while in another you may need to set up a joint venture, and in another you may well license your manufacturing. There will be a number of factors that will influence your choice of strategy, including, but not limited to, tariff rates, the degree of adaptation of your product required, marketing and transportation costs. While these factors may well increase your costs, it is expected the increase in sales will offset these costs. The following strategies are the main entry options open to you. If the foreign sales country is easy to enter and if the company is culturally close, it is suitable to create an own subsidiary or a sales office as shown in Fig. 16.2.

16.2.2 Direct and Indirect Exporting

Direct and indirect exporting are two options available to a firm wishing to establish marketing presence in a foreign market. In direct exporting, a firm performs the activities necessary for selling products in a foreign market. A firm becomes an indirect exporter when it performs no special activity for the selling of a product in a foreign market. Indirect exporting is performed through an intermediary. Exporting

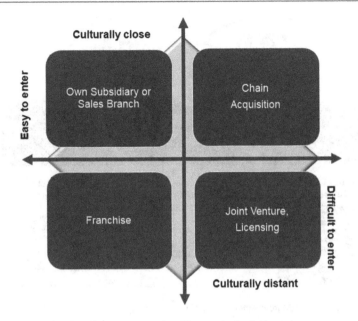

Fig. 16.2 International market entry strategies. (Source: Author's Source)

involves marketing the products you produce in the countries in which you intend to sell them. Some companies use direct exporting, in which they sell the product they manufacture in international markets without third-party involvement. Companies that sell luxury products or have sold their goods in global markets in the past often choose this method. Alternatively, a company may export indirectly by using the services of agents, such as international distributors. Businesses often choose indirect exporting if they're just beginning to distribute internationally. While companies pay agents for their services, indirect exporting often results in a return on investment (ROI) because the agents know what it takes to succeed in the markets in which they work (Nielsen et al., 2021).

16.2.3 Licensing

Licensing occurs when one company transfers the right to use or sell a product to another company. A company may choose this method if it has a product that's in demand and the company to which it plans to license the product has a large market. For example, a movie production company may sell a school supply company the right to use images of movie characters on backpacks, lunchboxes and notebooks (Fig. 16.3).

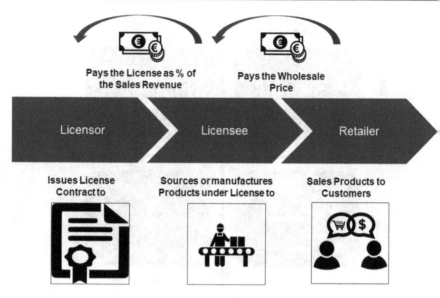

Fig. 16.3 Licensing. (Source: Author's source)

16.2.4 Franchising

A franchise is a chain retail company in which an individual or group buyer pays for the right to manage company branches on the company's behalf. Franchises occur most commonly in North America, but they exist globally and offer businesses the opportunity to expand overseas. Franchising typically requires strong brand recognition, as consumers in your target market should know what you offer and have a desire to purchase it. For well-known brands, franchising offers companies a way to earn a profit while taking an indirect management approach (Boehm, 2021) (Fig. 16.4).

16.2.5 Branches and Sales Offices as Own Subsidiary

Compared to the previously mentioned entry strategies, a wholly owned subsidiary provides greater control over strategic and operational decisions, greater economies of operation and greater potential for identifying with local values and aspirations. With a wholly owned subsidiary, both investment commitment and exposure to risk are the highest (Helmold & Samara, 2019). The selection of a market entry strategy is facilitated by evaluating the following two conditions: those internal to the firm and those existing in foreign markets. In evaluating internal conditions, managers should answer the following: How much risk is the company willing to undertake? How much return does the company expect on its investment? How long is the designated payback period? How much cash flow does the company expect? How much control does it want on decision-making related to manufacturing and marketing? How experienced is the company in international marketing? What are the

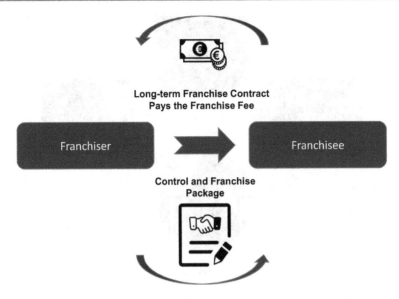

Fig. 16.4 Franchising. (Source: Author's source)

short-term and long-term goals of the company? The answers to these questions help a company select an appropriate entry strategy developed in the context of economic opportunity and political risk present in different country markets.

16.2.6 Joint Venture

Some companies attempt to minimize the risk of entering an international market by creating joint ventures with other companies that plan to sell in the global marketplace. Since joint ventures often function like large, independent companies rather than a combination of two smaller companies, they have the potential to earn more revenue than individual companies. This market entry strategy carries the risk of an imbalance in company involvement, but both parties can work together to establish fair processes and help prevent this issue (Fig. 16.5).

16.2.7 Own Subsidiary

16.3 Strategic Alliances and Partnering

Partnering is almost a necessity when entering foreign markets, and in some parts of the world (e.g. Asia) it may be required (Nielsen et al., 2021). Partnering can take a variety of forms from a simple co-marketing arrangement to a sophisticated strategic alliance for manufacturing. Partnering is a particularly useful strategy in those

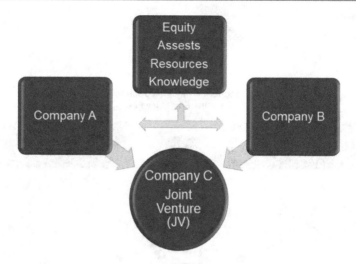

Fig. 16.5 Joint Venture. (Source: Author's source)

markets where the culture, both business and social, is substantively different than your own as local partners bring local market knowledge, contacts and if chosen wisely customers.

16.4   Turnkey Projects

Turnkey projects are particular to companies that provide services such as environmental consulting, architecture, construction and engineering. A turnkey project is where the facility is built from the ground up and turned over to the client ready to go – turn the key and the plant is operational. This is a very good way to enter foreign markets as the client is normally the government, and often the project is being financed by an international financial agency such as the World Bank so the risk of not being paid is eliminated.

16.5   Glocalization Strategies

Glocal marketing and sales as shown in Fig. 16.6 is a term that combines "global" and "local" marketing; it is a strategy employed by global brands to adapt to local needs. Glocal marketing aims to:

- Maintain global brand messaging.
- Adapt to the needs of the local culture.

This allows them to maintain brand consistency all around the world but to adapt their message to different products, services or experiences that better suit

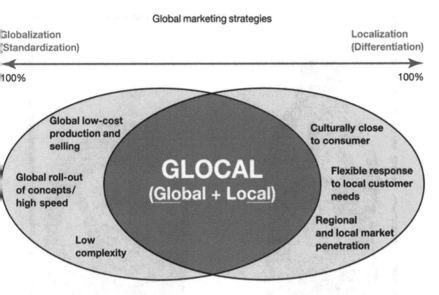

Fig. 16.6 Glocal marketing and sales strategy

the local culture. For example, McDonald's has restaurants in 119 countries. Their goal is to preserve the brand message of simple and affordable fast food. However, they also need a menu that suits the local people's dietary needs. This has led them to use glocal marketing to promote various menus in different countries, such as their no-beef menu in India, that focuses on chicken, vegetarian and local variations.

16.6   Case Study: Glocal Strategy of Persil

Persil is a Anglo-German brand of laundry detergent manufactured and marketed by Henkel around the world except in the United Kingdom, Ireland, France, Latin America (except Mexico), China, Australia and New Zealand, where it is manufactured and marketed by Unilever. Persil was introduced in 1907 by Henkel. It was the first commercially available laundry detergent that combined bleach with the detergent. The name was derived from two of its original ingredients, sodium perborate and sodium silicate. Meanwhile Henkel operates the Persil brand everywhere else, not just Germany and Austria (where it is undisputed market leader) and most of the rest of Europe but also the United States where it was officially launched for the first time in 2015 and is now one of the main challengers to P&G's Tide. Neither company relishes the split ownership, but occasional attempts by either one to buy out the other have regularly led to a polite but firm refusal. At least both are united in their opposition to US giant Procter & Gamble. Henkel declared combined global sales of €1.2bn from the Persil brand in 2015. Persil is executing a glocal sales strategy as shown in Fig. 16.7. Persil Black and Persil Abaya are the same product but different packaging and market communication.

Fig. 16.7 Glocal strategy of Persil

References

Boehm, H. (2021). *Praxiswissen Franchising: So multiplizieren Sie Ihr Geschäftsmodell – Leitfaden und Toolbox für Gründer*. Springer.

Helmold, M., & Samara, W. (2019). *Progress in performance management: Industry insights and case studies on principles, application tools, and practice*. Springer.

Nielsen, C., et al. (2021). *Business models and firm internationalisation (Routledge frontiers in the development of international business, management and marketing)*. Routledge.

Market Research

17

> *A sales rep's time is just as important as the manager's, and a*
> *great sales manager always respects that fact.*
>
> Adam Honig

17.1 Market Research Process

Marketing research is a systematic process of analysing data that involves conducting research to support marketing activities and the statistical interpretation of data into information. This information is then used by managers to plan marketing activities, gauge the nature of a firm's marketing environment and attain information from suppliers (Berghoff et al., 2012). A distinction should be made between marketing research and market research. Market research involves gathering information about a particular target market (Homburg et al., 2022). As an example, a firm may conduct research in a target market, after selecting a suitable market segment (Czinkota et al., 2021). In contrast, marketing research relates to all research conducted within marketing. Market research is a subset of marketing research. (Avoiding the word consumer, which shows up in both, market research is about distribution, while marketing research encompasses distribution, advertising effectiveness and salesforce effectiveness). Marketing researchers use statistical methods (such as quantitative research, qualitative research, hypothesis tests, Chi-square tests, linear regression, correlation coefficients, frequency distributions, Poisson and binomial distributions, etc.) to interpret their findings and convert data into information. The stages of research in Fig. 17.1 include:

- Define the problem and decide market research.
- Gain primary and secondary data.
- Analyse data and research.
- Interpret data and write report.
- Implement findings and actions.

© The Author(s), under exclusive license to Springer Nature Switzerland AG 2022   177
M. Helmold, *Performance Excellence in Marketing, Sales and Pricing*, Management
for Professionals, https://doi.org/10.1007/978-3-031-10097-0_17

Fig. 17.1 Marketing research process

17.2   Market Research Methodologies

Marketing research is often partitioned into two sets of categorical pairs, either by target market:

- Consumer marketing research, (B2C).
- Business-to-business (B2B) marketing research.

or, alternatively, by methodological approach:

- Qualitative marketing research.
- Quantitative marketing research.

Consumer marketing research is a form of applied sociology that concentrates on understanding the preferences, attitudes and behaviours of consumers in a market-based economy, and it aims to understand the effects and comparative success of marketing campaigns (Homburg et al., 2012). Thus, marketing research may also be described as the systematic and objective identification, collection, analysis and dissemination of information for the purpose of assisting management in decision-making related to the identification and solution of problems and opportunities in marketing (Malhotra, 2002). The goal of market research is to obtain and provide management with viable information about the market (e.g. competitors), consumers, the product/service itself, etc.

17.3   Primary Research

17.3.1 Surveys

Market surveys as shown in Fig. 17.2 in marketing involve analysing a given market in order to gain insight into the buying potential and attributes of the target audience for a product or service. The main goal and objective of a market survey is to collect data surrounding a target market such as competitor analysis, pricing trends and customer expectations. Whether you are leading a start-up company or a tenured business, it is important to understand the needs of your customers. Executing professional market research requires good planning (Mooi & Sarstedt, 2011).

- What do they want out of a product/service?
- How much would they pay for the product/service?

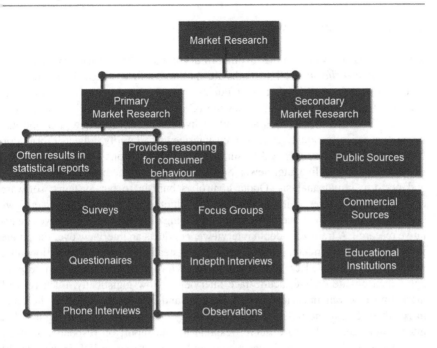

Fig. 17.2 Market research tools. (Source: Author's source)

- Where would they most likely shop to find the product/service?
- A market survey helps answer these questions directly from target consumers.

In turn, this information can help build an effective marketing and advertising strategy as well as contribute to enhancing the features of a new concept before entering the product or service into the market. Surveys are usually carried out with the help of statistical methods, e.g. regression, correlation or factor analysis (Mooi & Sarstedt, 2011). Statistics provide demographic information such as the number of potential customers in a geographical area, their ages, income levels and consumer preferences. Used as part of competitor analysis, statistics can identify the major competitors, their market share and trends in the longevity of their products.

17.3.2 Questionnaires

The questionnaire is a type of survey that consists of a series of questions, often designed for statistical analysis of the feedback. Questionnaire as a research instrument is a tried and true method historically; it was invented already in 1838 by the Statistical Society in London. The great advantages with questionnaires, as opposed to telephone surveys or face-to-face interviews, are that they are cheap to conduct, and they do not require staff to call or approach people.

17.3.3 Phone Interviews

Telephone interviews are similar to other forms of market research interview *but are carried out over the phone*. Teledepths are similar to a face to face depth interview, with the researcher utilizing a topic guide as opposed to a structured questionnaire. Computer-assisted telephone interviewing (CATI) is primarily a quantitative data collection method, which uses a blend of live telephone interview and optional interactive voice response (IVR) survey interviews to rapidly collect information from your targeted sample. CATI surveys often contain one or two open-ended questions asked by a live interviewer. Software systems immediately process results and perform initial analysis. Quota control is built-in to our systems: software actively tracks progress without the time lag which often occurs when interviews occur in the field. Telephone In-Depth Interviewing (Telephone IDI) involves qualitative research. A trained in-depth interviewer conducts an interview over the phone with a targeted respondent, using a topic guide instead of a structured questionnaire. Telephone IDIs enable Research America's interviewing team to reach more respondents than on-site or live face-to-face interviews allow logistically. Each type of marketing research interview has its benefits and drawbacks. CATI is fast, but impersonal. Telephone IDIs can reach more respondents across wider regions, but interviewers are unable to observe, respond to and report on respondents' body language and other nonverbal cues which are helpful during an IDI. In any type of telephone interview, it's harder to develop rapport with the respondent, which is helpful when study topic involves sensitive, or very personal, questions.

17.3.4 Focus Groups

Market research focus groups are controlled interviews of a target audience that are led by facilitators. Participants in a focus group are selected based on a set of predetermined criteria, such as location, age, socioeconomic status, race and more. Focus groups are designed to identify consumers' feelings, perceptions and thoughts about a particular product, service or solution. The first step to having an effective focus group is to clearly define the purpose of the group. You need to know what you want the discussion to accomplish and what demographic best helps you achieve that. With a goal clearly defined, it's much easier to choose participants that are qualified to partake in the focus group. Focus group discussions should be held in an environment that is non-threatening and receptive. Unlike interviews, which usually occur with an individual, a focus group allows members to interact and influence each other during the discussion and consideration of ideas. The line of questioning used in focus groups – known as the questioning route, interview guide or protocol – is predetermined and follows a logical sequence intended to mimic a natural exchange. The purpose of a focus group is not to arrive at a consensus, some level of agreement, or to decide what to do about something. Focus groups are valuable because they allow alternative ways of obtaining information from consumers without using surveys, which tend to be viewed as scientific and only produce quantitative data. Focus groups utilize qualitative data collection methods. Just as in the dynamics of real life, the participants are able to interact, influence and be influenced – giving actionable insight into customers' knowledge of their brands, products or services. Focus groups have a distinct advantage over other types of market research because they are flexible by design. You can listen to someone's tone and view their body language when talking to better understand how they feel about a particular subject. A good moderator who prepares well for a focus group will act as a proxy for the decision-makers and capitalize on the ability to talk to customers directly.

17.3.5 In-Depth or Depth Interviews

Depth or in-depth interview is *a qualitative research technique* which is used to conduct intensive individual interviews where numbers of respondents are less and research is focused on a specific product, technique, situation or objective. How is in-depth interview used in market research?

In-depth interviews are a qualitative data collection method that *involves direct, one-on-one engagement with individual participants*. In-depth interviewing can take place face-to-face or – in some cases – over the phone.

In-Depth Interview Advantages
- Interviewers can establish rapport with participants to make them feel more comfortable, which can generate more insightful responses – especially regarding sensitive topics.
- Interviewers have greater opportunity to ask follow-up questions, probe for additional information and circle back to key questions later on in the interview to generate a rich understanding of attitudes, perceptions, motivations, etc.
- Interviewers can monitor changes in tone and word choice to gain a deeper understanding. (Note that if the in-depth interview is face-to-face, researchers can also focus on body language.)
- There is a higher quality of sampling compared to some other data collection methods.
- Researchers need fewer participants to glean useful and relevant insights.
- There is none of the potential distractions or peer-pressure dynamics that can sometimes emerge in focus groups.
- Because in-depth interviews can potentially be so insightful, it is possible to identify highly valuable findings quickly.

In-Depth Interview Disadvantages
- In-depth interviews are quite time consuming, as interviews must be transcribed, organized, analysed and reported.
- If the interviewer is not highly skilled and experienced, the entire process can be undermined.

- The process can be relatively costly compared to other methods. (However, telephone in-depth interviews vs. in-person can significantly reduce the costs.)
- Participants must be carefully chosen to avoid bias, and this can result in a longer vetting process.
- Participants typically expect an incentive to participate, and this must be carefully selected to avoid bias.

17.3.6 Observations

Through direct observation of people, marketing specialists are able to identify actions and watch how subjects respond to various stimuli. For a small business, observational marketing research is one of the simplest ways that one can find out many things about their customers and clients.

Marketing observation can be confusing to both large-scale and small-scale business owners. Many of them don't have the accurate information as far as observation is concerned. In this post, we will clearly distinguish between accurate and misleading information when talking about market observation. Observation is a market research technique in which highly trained researchers generally watch how people or consumers behave and interact in the market under natural conditions. It is designed to give precisely detailed and actual information on what consumers do as they interact in a given market niche.

17.4   Secondary Research

Common examples of secondary research include *textbooks, encyclopaedias, news articles, review articles and meta-analyses*. When conducting secondary research, authors may draw data from public case study: market research. There are three sources for secondary data: public sources, commercial or educational institutions. Figure 17.3 shows the three sources for secondary research.

17.5   Case Study: Market Research Toyota Prius in North America

In 2007, a team of psychologists interviewed Californian early adopters of hybrid vehicles (Copeland, 2019). They discovered most had "only a basic understanding of environmental issues or the ecological benefits of hybrid electric vehicles", but they "bought a symbol of preserving the environment that they could incorporate into a narrative of who they are or who they wish to be". In the same year as this research took place, Toyota shifted 181,000 units of its Prius hybrid in the USA. That is a staggering amount of cars, especially when you consider its nearest rival from Honda racked up 32,575. The strange thing is that on paper both cars were

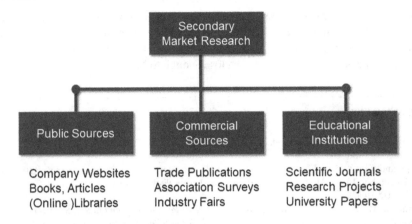

Fig. 17.3   Sources for secondary market research

equal – built by reputable Japanese manufactures, equals in heritage and brand equality. They matched on the usual attributes that would factor into a buying decision (price, running costs, reliability, size, etc.) and, most important of all, on their green credentials. So why did the Prius outsell the Honda Civic Hybrid six to one? In 2011, this was the question two economists pondered in their paper entitled "Conspicuous Conservation: The Prius Effect and Willingness to Pay for Environmental Bona Fides". The paper explores an evolved concept of conspicuous consumption – the theory of acquisition of luxury goods and services as public displays of economic power. The authors believe this same effect applied to a more recent trend of acquiring goods with green credentials and doing so as public displays of doing our bit for the planet. It turns out Honda made a whopping mistake with the Civic Hybrid that only became apparent in hindsight; it looked like a normal Honda Civic. This would have made sound commercial sense, you would think – using an existing body and design that was already well received and selling well, with added green credentials, so you'd be doing your bit for the planet without aesthetic compromise. The problem, however, is that people want other people to know they are doing their bit for the planet. If your car looks like a normal Honda, your neighbours and the other parents parking outside the school will think it's a normal Honda, and that's doing nothing to build your image as an eco-warrior. The Prius, on the other hand, was distinct from a mile away. You would see it cruising down the motorway (in the inside lane of course) and think "there is one of those green cars". Its distinct shape was certainly no accident – Toyota executives instructed designers to develop something unique, regardless of the quality of the styling – it's final utilitarian form sacrificing aesthetics for aerodynamics. A common mistake brands make is they focus too much on where the customer is now and fail to see where they are trying to get to. If you can create products, services, brands and narratives that speak to and can be woven into these aspirations, you can connect with people on a completely different level. Research found that 57% of Prius buyers stated their main reason for choosing the Prius was because "it makes a statement about me" – not because of its price, its reliability or even its green credentials. This just shows the power of distinctiveness and creating products or services that shout out a desired narrative to those close enough to hear.

References

Berghoff, H., Scranton, P., & Spiekermann, U. (2012). *The rise of marketing and market research.* Palgrave Malcom.

Copeland, G. (2019). *Hoew Toyota sold six times as many cars as its hybrid rival.* Retrieved December 15, 2021, from. https://www.marketingweek.com/toyota-prius-sold-six-times-hybrid-rival.

Czinkota, M. R., et al. (2021). *Marketing management: Past, present and future.* Springer.

Homburg, C., Schäfer, H., & Schneider, J. (2012). *Sales excellence: Systematic sales management.* Springer.

Homburg, C., Klarmann, M., & Vomberg, A. (2022). *Handbook of market research.* Springer.

Malhotra, N. K. (2002). *Basic marketing research: A decision-making approach.* Prentice Hall.

Mooi, E., & Sarstedt, M. (2011). *A concise guide to market research: The process, data, and methods using IBM SPSS statistics.* Springer.

Supply Chain Management and Distribution Channels

18

> *Progress cannot be generated when we are satisfied with existing situations.*
>
> Taiichi Ohno

18.1 Upstream and Downstream Supply Chain Management (SCM)

Supply chain management (SCM) can be described as the process of planning managing, executing and improving the key business process that ensure effective delivery of products and services from suppliers through to the end customer as shown in Fig. 18.1 (Helmold & Terry, 2021). Sales and distribution channels can be described as downstream activities of organizations. Distribution (or place) is one of the four elements of the marketing mix. Distribution is the process of making a product or service available for the consumer or business user who needs it. This can be done directly by the producer or service provider or using indirect channels with distributors or intermediaries. The other three elements of the marketing mix are product, pricing and promotion. Decisions about distribution need to be taken in line with a company's overall strategic vision and mission. Developing a coherent distribution plan is a central component of strategic planning. At the strategic level, there are three broad approaches to distribution, namely, mass, selective and exclusive distribution. The number and type of intermediaries selected largely depend on the strategic approach. The overall distribution channel should add value to the consumer. SCM involves the process of enabling the effective flow of information, materials and services from suppliers from upstream supply chain with raw materials and materials to operation and to finally deliver products and services to end customer or the downstream supply chain. SCM allows the simultaneous integration of customer specifications which is an important aspect that helps in enhancing better performance of the internal process, which ultimately influences greater upstream supplier performance (Werner, 2020). Based on these definitions, it is evident that the common feature of SCM is to enhance end-to-end coordination as a

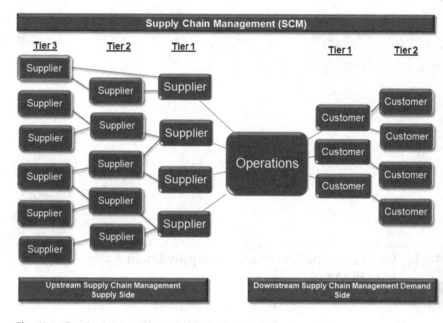

Fig. 18.1 Supply chain management (SCM). (Source: Author's source)

result of effective integrating of both internal and external processes in the supply chain in order to deliver value to the end customer. Therefore, it can be argued to suggest that the potential benefits of an enhanced SCM can be considered to provide higher quality of products or services, effective cost savings, shorter and more reliable delivery times, fewer disruptions and risk reduction. Customer satisfaction and effective service delivery can be seen to be the key factors that enable a business to survive in the highly competitive market (Bozarth & Handfield, 2013). Effective supply chain management (SCM) practices have become valuable in enhancing competitive advantage by reducing waste and increasing efficiency, therefore improving the overall organizational performance and its strategy.

By concentrating on core competencies and shifting services to supplier networks that are in competition with one another, new models, strategies and processes emerge, which lead supplier management into a central role in every company. For a long time now, the focus in the future has not only been on increasing company-internal cost advantages but much more on the exchange of information and the exploitation of global cross-company potential. Scope of added value can no longer be handled by the manufacturer alone but must rely on innovative, efficient and flexible supplier structures. Increasing competition, global trends, the COVID-19 pandemic, sustainability elements, technological change and shortened product life cycles place ever higher demands on companies and their suppliers in numerous industries. The increasing variety of products, shorter innovation cycles and cross-sector business models with digital business processes also increase the complexity of future control of value networks. However, the planning, control and

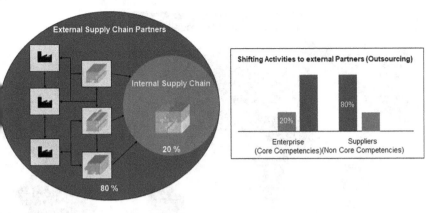

Fig. 18.2 Shifting activities to the upstream supply chain management. (Source: Author's source)

monitoring of the upstream value creation networks, i.e. the supplier networks, become more difficult, so that these tasks have to be covered by holistic, standardized and innovative supplier management. However, modern supplier structures are becoming increasingly volatile. The control of the external value-added networks must therefore also adapt to the new requirements. Risk prevention in the supply chain is therefore of central importance to every company, but only 17% of companies operate preventive supplier management with early and standardized involvement of their suppliers, and more than two-thirds only assess a selection of suppliers (Dust, 2016). These alarming figures emerge from the study "Total Supplier Management – Strategic Competitive Advantages through Risk Prevention in Supplier Management". The representative survey of 221 companies from different sectors from industry, trade and services was carried out by the Technical University of Berlin in cooperation with the BME region Berlin-Brandenburg (Dust, 2016). Figure 1.2 shows the proportion of peripheral competencies being transferred to external suppliers to more than 80% (outsourcing). In contrast, own core competencies, i.e. processes and skills from which competitive advantages are developed for your own company, are around 20% (Fig. 18.2).

18.2   Globalization and Global Supply Networks

Global supply chains and supply chains cause problems due to their complexity and growing challenges. However, it should also be emphasized that increasing requirements, response times and risk protection contribute to the differentiation of companies and value-added networks (Dust, 2019). Not only the own company but also its supplier networks are in constant competition in order to gain the favour of the customer. Value networks are competitive, global and customer-relevant. They enable companies to provide services that are coordinated across the company, in which the individual partners focus on their core competencies, as Fig. 8.1 shows (Fig. 18.3).

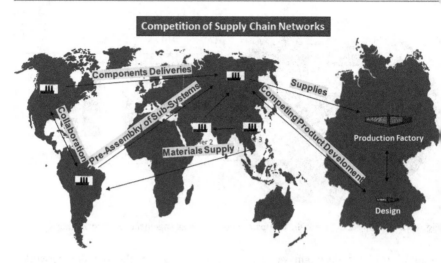

Fig. 18.3 Globalized supply and value chains. (Source: Marc Helmold)

The aim of a value-added network in supplier management (supplier network) is usually the realization of collaborative competitive advantages and the possibility of own specialization. Because each partner involved brings their specific core competencies into the network, the conflict of goals between a high degree of specialization on the one hand and a broader, more diverse range of services on the other can be resolved. In the network, the advantages of more flexible task distribution and capacity utilization at network level can be combined with specialization advantages at the level of the value-added units (economies of scale and economies of scope). This works all the better, the more the individual skills complement each other. Examples of a successful implementation of this idea are, e.g. production networks, procurement networks or knowledge and competence networks. The hybridity of the network in comparison to the market and hierarchy is particularly evident from the forms of coordination used. In general, a distinction is made between price, instruction and trust, which are assigned to the institutions market, hierarchy and network according to their focus of application. Figure 8.2 shows global competition and the international orientation of supplier networks. In this real example of the automotive industry, the spatially separate development and production take place in Germany. The development requires cooperation between the two locations in southern and northern Germany. In this constellation, there are tier 1, 2 and 3 suppliers who each produce raw materials, components or systems in their own production and provide them to the downstream level (tier 3 and tier 2 and tier 1). Raw material (e.g. steel) is supplied to the component supplier (tier 2) from China. The tier 2 suppliers are located in the Arabian Peninsula and South America, from where components are sent to the tier 1 system supplier. This

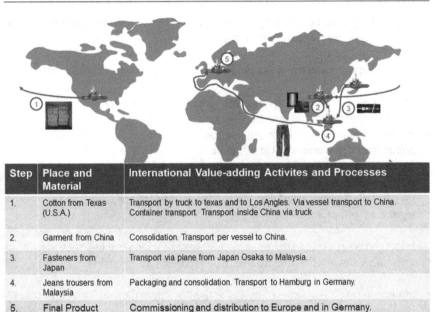

Step	Place and Material	International Value-adding Activites and Processes
1.	Cotton from Texas (U.S.A.)	Transport by truck to texas and to Los Angles. Via vessel transport to China. Container transport. Transport inside China via truck
2.	Garment from China	Consolidation. Transport per vessel to China.
3.	Fasteners from Japan	Transport via plane from Japan Osaka to Malaysia.
4.	Jeans trousers from Malaysia	Packaging and consolidation. Transport to Hamburg in Germany.
5.	Final Product	Commissioning and distribution to Europe and in Germany.

Fig. 18.4 Example of international trade and supply chains. (Source: Author's source)

supplier is located in Russia and delivers the systems to the German end customer. The system check and homologation take place at the supplier's premises before the delivery. The supplier also has employees at the end customer who ensure a smooth process and the synchronization of the supply chain. Development and tier 1 supplier collaborate in the product creation process of development (competitive development). This is how a global value chain works (Helmold & Terry, 2021) (Fig. 18.4).

18.3 Risks in the Supply Chain

Supply chain disruptions on your business by identifying the risks within your supply chain and developing ways to mitigate them. You should document this process in a risk management plan, which is part of your overall business continuity plan. There are two major types of risk to include in your risk management plan:

- External risks – those that are outside of your control.
- Internal risks – those that are within your control.

External risks can be driven by events either upstream or downstream in the supply chain. There are five main types of external risks:

- Demand risks – caused by unpredictable or misunderstood customer or end-customer demand.
- Supply risks – caused by any interruptions to the flow of product, whether raw material or parts, within your supply chain.
- Environmental risks – from outside the supply chain; usually related to economic, social, governmental and climate factors, including the threat of terrorism.
- Business risks – caused by factors such as a supplier's financial or management stability or purchase and sale of supplier companies.
- Physical plant risks – caused by the condition of a supplier's physical facility and regulatory compliance.

Internal risks provide better opportunities for mitigation because they are within your business's control. There are five main types of internal risks:

- Manufacturing risks – caused by disruptions of internal operations or processes.
- Business risks – caused by changes in key personnel, management, reporting structures or business processes, such as the way purchasers communicate to suppliers and customers.
- Planning and control risks – caused by inadequate assessment and planning, which amount to ineffective management.
- Mitigation and contingency risks – caused by not putting contingencies (or alternative solutions) in place in case something goes wrong.
- Cultural risks – caused by a business's cultural tendency to hide or delay negative information. Such businesses are generally slower to react when impacted by unexpected events.

18.4   Supply Risk Prevention and Mitigation

Supply disruptions are defined as "unplanned and unanticipated events that disrupt the normal flow of goods and materials within the supply chain". They distinguish between coordination risks and disruption risks. Supply chain complexity is described by Adenso-Diaz et al. as "the sum of the total number of nodes and the total number of forward, backward and within-tier material flows" in the upstream supply chain network. Such complexity has a huge impact on supply chain reliability and supply chain stability. The overall recommendation made in several papers is to reduce the number of suppliers, since supply chain complexity increases the risk of disruption. Adenso-Diaz et al. highlighted the definitions of various authors, using a variety of criteria: (1) function, (2) type of risk (Ellram & Liu, 2002), (3) drivers of risks and (4) likelihood of occurrence. While the literature on supply management and risk management is growing, there is no organized

.tructure regarding the sources of causal factors for supply chain risks and supply disruptions. Several papers show that supply disruptions can lead to high monetary recovery cost, waste and sharp decreases in sales as pointed out in one of the previous sections by Haslett, Jing and Grant as well as findings in other literature sources such as field research, internal reports and interview displays, which supply disruptions have severe impacts on companies in the analysed European transportation industry. Supply disruptions and their associated risks have been classified in the literature using a variety of criteria, e.g. function (Christopher & Peck, 2004), type of risk and drivers of risk. Hendricks and Singhal (2005) pointed out that enterprises without operational slack and redundancies in their supply chains experience negative stock effects. They also revealed the tremendous impacts of supply chain disruptions on stock price performance and shareholder value. Causal factors for supply disruptions are automatically associated with risks in the supply network, as stated by Zsidisin, Tomlin and Wieland and Wallenberg. Several authors outline incidents in which supply disruptions caused production standstill or temporary stops in manufacturing companies in the European industry. Other authors refer to capacity management in terms of supply disruptions as being a crucial risk factor for supply chain discrepancies. Due to such risks, specific measures are necessary in terms of overcoming potential supply disruptions caused by supplier capacity shortages (Hittle & Leonard, 2011). Mitigations and preventive measures can take the form of diverse capacity management, back-up equipment or alternative manufacturing locations, as recommended by Hittle and Leonard (2011) (Fig. 18.5).

It is useful to compare the supply chain strategies of companies and their resulting ability to cope with some of the abovementioned disruptions. Zsidisin, Rao and Goldsby created models which can be used by managers to measure and assess the vulnerability of their company and supply chain in relation to the associated risks. Typology may also provide avenues for future research and thus guide practitioners in the management of their supply chain risk portfolio. Such a classification is a useful tool for supply chain managers in differentiating between independent and

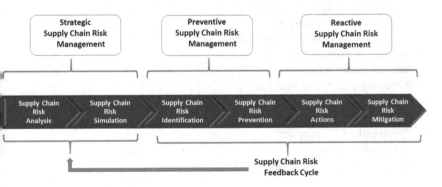

Fig. 18.5 Risks in supply chains. (Source: Author's source)

dependent variables and the mutual relationships which would help them to focus on those key variables that are most important for effective risk minimization in a supply chain. Zsidisin typologized causal factors for supply disruptions into different categories – high, medium and low risk – based on managerial perception. Other authors besides Zsidisin have built on this typology and outlined causal factors for supply disruptions as follows, which comprise the:

- Capacity shortages.
- New product launches.
- Disaster issues (e.g. earthquake, flood).
- Lack of supply chain transparency.
- Labour-related issues (e.g. strike).
- Constraints on market capacity.
- Pricing instabilities.
- Quality discrepancies.
- Transport issues.
- Product transfers to sites or plants.
- Inflexible production capacities.

18.5   Method of Global Risk Evaluation

Once a company has decided what it is going to evaluate, the next step is to establish how it will evaluate the performance of the supplier. There are many ways to do this, and some are more costly, time consuming and resource intensive than others. By quantifying the level of risk and the projected benefit of a method of evaluation, company personnel can determine the most appropriate method or combination of methods that should be used. Some methods that companies commonly use to evaluate and measure supplier performance include:

- Site visits by cross-functional teams.
- Supplier audits (process, special process or product audits).
- Paper supplier questionnaires.
- Web-based supplier questionnaires.
- Organizing existing data.
- Internal questionnaires.
- Requiring external certifications.
- Developing own certifications.
- Third-party reviews.
- Phone call with a supplier.
- Independent ratings.
- Contacts with other supplier customers.

18.6   Fair Trade

Fair trade is a controlled trade in which the producers receive a minimum price for their products, which is determined by a fair-trade organization. This is intended to enable producers to earn a higher and more reliable income than in conventional retail even at lower market prices. The amount of a fair price has been a topic of business ethics that has been discussed for decades. In addition, this form of trade tries to build long-term "partnership" relationships between traders and producers. In production, international environmental and social standards as well as those prescribed by the organizations should also be complied with. The very heterogeneous fair trade movement mainly focuses on goods that are exported from developing countries to industrialized countries. Fair trade encompasses agricultural products as well as products from traditional handicrafts and industry and is increasingly expanding into new areas such as tourism under the name "fair travel". Fairly traded products are offered in natural food and world shops as well as in supermarkets and restaurants. According to the umbrella organization Fairtrade International, over 1.5 million farmers took part in such programs in 2015.

18.7   Glocal Supply Chains

With rapid advances in communications and information technologies, manufacturers are now able to truly operate globally, source their raw materials where it is cheapest and most practical and expand their customer base internationally (Cousins et al., 2008). However, manufacturers must also adapt their offerings to local trends, predict which items will be in greater demand in a particular region and adjust their stocks accordingly. In today's connectivity and information technology world, political, economic and social relationships naturally tend to be global, interwoven and interdependent. That is exactly the fundamental characteristic of globalization. This term was first used in the 1980s in an economic context and since then has spread more and more and in other contexts.

Globalization has brought numerous advantages for the manufacturing industry, such as the possibility of easy access to technical knowledge or the opportunity to learn from countries that are pioneers in areas such as automation and digitization. In addition, in a globalized world, it is easier to communicate with business partners in real time, no matter where they are. This is a clear advantage for business transactions and helps to build trust between business partners.

However, one of the most controversial aspects of globalization is the risk of homogenization. In a globalized society, the same goods are often produced and sold in vastly different markets, with little attention paid to the preferences and habits of the different end customers. In the long run, this can have a negative impact on sales and prevent companies from really gaining a foothold in a particular region.

That is why a new term has recently been circulating that shows that companies can act globally and still target the specifics of regional markets – welcome to the age of glocalization. The transition from globalization to glocalization was driven by several factors. First of all, the recent past has shown more and more clearly that failure to observe local market conditions can have a negative impact on business and lead to problems in ongoing operations and in the supply chain. The second reason for this transformation is the increased public awareness of the need to support the national and regional economies through the local procurement of raw materials, which can also help optimize the supply chain and reduce transport costs.

However, in fact glocalization is not really a new concept, because international corporations have always been forced to adapt their production to local demand. Automobile manufacturers have always had to adhere to specific regulations when diversifying their product range depending on the sales market – an obvious example of this is the side on which the steering wheel is installed and whether the speedometer shows miles or kilometres per hour.

What is new is the influence that glocal business models have on supply chain management, as manufacturers strive to establish a supply chain that operates globally and yet adapts to local demand.

18.8   Incoterms 2020

Foreign trade between exporters and importers can only function smoothly if the exports and imports include standardized and generally recognized trade clauses in their delivery and payment conditions that regulate the transfer of risk and place of delivery, transport costs and transport risk, the obligation to take out transport insurance and the destination. The Incoterms regulate which of the duties the seller or buyer is responsible for. If the Incoterms are the basis, only a certain abbreviation needs to be used without having to describe the distribution of costs and risks in detail.

The Incoterms are clauses that enable the contracting parties to make extensive, standardized regulations on the place of performance, other performance obligations and the transfer of risk within the framework of a sales contract.

Incoterms, a widely used terms of sale, are a set of 11 internationally recognized rules which define the responsibilities of sellers and buyers. Incoterms specifies who is responsible for paying for and managing the shipment, insurance, documentation, customs clearance and other logistical activities. There are certain terms that have special meaning within Incoterms, and some of the more important ones are defined below:

- Delivery: The point in the transaction where the risk of loss or damage to the goods is transferred from the seller to the buyer.
- Arrival: The point named in the Incoterm to which carriage has been paid.
- Free: Seller's obligation to deliver the goods to a named place for transfer to a carrier.

Incoterm 2020	Loading at origin	Export customs declaration	Carriage to port of export	Unloading of truck in port of export	Loading on vessel/airplane in port of export	Carriage (sea/air) to port of import	Insurance	Unloading in port of import	Loading on truck in port of import	Carriage to place of destination	Import customs clearance	Import duties and taxes	Unloading at destination
EXW Ex Works	Buyer	Buyer	Buyer	Buyer	Buyer	Buyer	Buyer	Buyer	Buyer	Buyer	Buyer	Buyer	Buyer
FCA Fre Carrier	Seller	Seller	Buyer/Seller	Buyer	Buyer	Buyer	Buyer	Buyer	Buyer	Buyer	Buyer	Buyer	Buyer
FAS Free Alongside Ship	Seller	Seller	Seller	Seller	Buyer	Buyer	Buyer	Buyer	Buyer	Buyer	Buyer	Buyer	Buyer
FOB Free On Board	Seller	Seller	Seller	Seller	Seller	Buyer	Buyer	Buyer	Buyer	Buyer	Buyer	Buyer	Buyer
CPT Cost,	Seller	Seller	Seller	Seller	Seller	Seller	Buyer	Buyer/Seller	Buyer/Seller	Seller	Buyer	Buyer	Buyer
CFR Cost Freight,	Seller	Seller	Seller	Seller	Seller	Seller	Buyer	Buyer	Buyer	Buyer	Buyer	Buyer	Buyer
CIF	Seller	Seller	Seller	Seller	Seller	Seller	Seller	Buyer	Buyer	Buyer	Buyer	Buyer	Buyer
CIP	Seller	Seller	Seller	Seller	Seller	Seller	Seller	Buyer/Seller	Buyer/Seller	Seller	Buyer	Buyer	Buyer
DPU	Seller	Seller	Seller	Seller	Seller	Seller	Seller	Seller	Seller	Seller	Buyer	Buyer	Seller
DAP	Seller	Seller	Seller	Seller	Seller	Seller	Seller	Seller	Seller	Seller	Buyer	Buyer	Buyer
DDP	Seller	Seller	Seller	Seller	Seller	Seller	Seller	Seller	Seller	Seller	Seller	Seller	Buyer

Fig. 18.6 Incoterms 2020

- Carrier: Any person who, in a contract of carriage, undertakes to perform or to procure the performance of transport by rail, road, air, sea, inland waterway or a combination of such modes.
- Freight forwarder: A firm that makes or assists in the making of shipping arrangements.
- Terminal: Any place, whether covered or not, such as a dock, warehouse, container yard or road, rail or air cargo terminal.
- To clear for export: To file Shipper's Export Declaration and get export permit (Fig. 18.6).

18.9   Distribution Channels

18.9.1 Sales and Physical Distribution Channels (Fig. 18.7)

18.9.2 Channel Members Adding Value (Fig. 18.8)

18.10   Case Study: Lidl's Glocal Supply and Distribution Strategy

18.10.1 Lidl's Glocal Supply Strategy

As part of the Schwarz group of companies based in Neckarsulm, the Lidl retail company is one of the leading companies in the food retail sector in Germany and Europe. Lidl is currently present in 32 countries and operates around 10,800 branches in 29 countries worldwide. In Germany, around 83,000 employees in around 3200 branches ensure customer satisfaction every day. Dynamic in daily implementation, high performance in the result and fairness in dealing with one

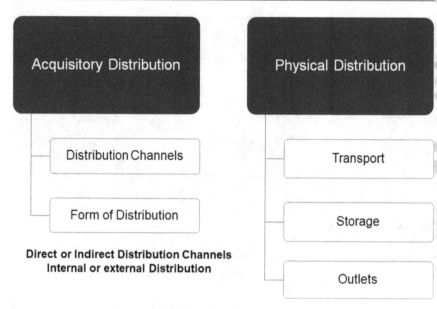

Fig. 18.7 Acquisitory and physical distribution channels

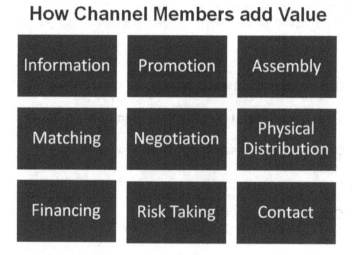

Fig. 18.8 Channel members adding value

another characterizes the work at Lidl. Since 2008 the Lidl online shop offers non-food products to various categories, wines and spirits as well as travel and other services. The range of the Lidl online shop is constantly expanding and currently comprises around 30,000 items. As a discounter, Lidl attaches great importance to an optimal price-performance ratio for its customers. Simplicity and process orientation determine daily actions. Lidl takes responsibility for society and the environment and focuses on five areas of activity in the area of sustainability: product range, employees, environment, society and business partners. Lidl generated sales of EUR 81.2 billion in the 2018 financial year, of which EUR 22.7 billion from Lidl Germany were achieved. Lidl Germany is one of the first grocery retailers to publish a list of the main suppliers for its food and non-food private label range on its website. The company is thus making a relevant contribution to greater transparency in its global supply chains. It lists independent manufacturers that Lidl commissions to manufacture its own brand products such as baked goods, beverages, cosmetics, cleaning agents or hardware such as toys, sports equipment or garden furniture. The list is updated regularly and supplements the main production sites in the supply chain published in 2017 for the textile and shoe range of Lidl's own brands. "In our own brand range, we can work directly with the manufacturers to promote a more responsible production method. In order to know where and how our products are made, it is important to know our business partners as well as possible. At the same time, our customers want to learn more about how our products are made. We want to meet this wish, combined with our demand for more transparency", says Jan Bock, Purchasing Manager at Lidl Germany.

18.10.2 Glocal Distribution Through Network

As one of the large grocery retailers, Lidl sources its goods from suppliers in the region and all over the world. The basis of every business relationship is the "Code of Conduct" prescribed by Lidl, which guarantees basic rights for employees along the supply chain. Lidl also places a special focus on the implementation of recognized minimum standards: Independent and local experts regularly check all production sites for Lidl non-food products in accordance with the recognized amfori Business Social Compliance Initiative (BSCI) or the international standards for social accountability (SA 8000) and systematically examine potential for improvement.

References

Bozarth, C. C., & Handfield, R. B. (2013). *Introduction to operations and supply chain management* (3rd ed.). Harlow Pearson.

Christopher, M., & Peck, H. (2004). Building the resilient chain. *International Journal of Logistics Management*, 15(2), 1–5.

Cousins, P., Lawson, L. B., & Squire, B. (2008). *Strategic supply management: Principles*. Theories and Practice.

Dust, R. (2016). *Lieferanten–/Risikomanagement. Bislang wenig Risikoprävention in der supply chain*. In BME. Abgerufen am 28.9.2020. https://www.bme.de/bislang-wenig-risikopraevention-in-der-supply-chain-1468/

Dust, R. (2019). Total Supplier Management. *Hanserverlag München*.

Dust, R., Goldschmit, J. P., & Gürtler, B. (2011). Total Supplier Risk Monitoring - Datenqualität als zwingende Grundlage einer effektiven Lieferantenbewertung. *Qualität und Umweltmanagement, 10*(2011), 10–11.

Ellram, L. M., & Liu, B. (2002). The financial impact of supply management. *Supply Chain Management Review, 6*(6), 30–36.

Evans, B., & Mason, R. (2015). *The lean supply chain: Managing the challenge at Tesco.* Kogan Page.

Fayezi, S., & Zomorrodi, M. (2016). *Supply chain management: Developments, theories and models. In handbook of research on global supply chain management* (pp. 313–340). IGI Global.

Helmold, M. (2021). *Innovatives Lieferantenmanagement.* Wertschöpfung in globalen Lieferketten. Springer.

Helmold, M., & Terry, B. (2021). *Operations and supply management 4.0. Industry insights, case studies and best practices.* Springer.

Hendricks, K. B., & Singhal, V. R. (2005). An empirical analysis of the effect of supply chain disruptions on long-run stock price performance and equity risk of the firm. *Production Operations Management, 21*(5), 501–522.

Hittle, B., & Leonard, K. M. (2011). Decision making in advance of a supply chain crisis. *Management Decision, 49*(7), 1182–1193.

Johnson, G., et al. (2017). *Exploring strategy* (11th ed.). FT Prentice Hall.

Khojasteh, Y. (2018). *Supply chain risk management. Advanced tools, models, and developments.* Springer.

Kim, C., & Mauborgne, R. A. (2015). *Blue Ocean strategy, expanded edition: How to create uncontested market space and make the competition irrelevant.* Harvard Business Press.

Lidl. (2021). www.lidl.co

Werner, H. (2020). *Supply chain management.* Springer.

Where there is no Standard, there can be no Kaizen.

Taiichi Ohno

19.1 Introduction to Promotion and Advertising

Promotion is a set of activities with the main aim of persuading the customer to buy a product, service or brand through highlighting the advantages. Advertising is known to be an impersonal promotion that is typically used to draw the attention of customers towards products or service through a selected paid media. It is one of the core elements of the marketing mix, and it is suitable for creating awareness, attracting and inducing customers to initiate a purchase. Discount coupons, value-added services, trial offer, free distribution of samples, offers on festive seasons and rebate are amongst ways how promotion is done. Promotions help the company to increase sales since the goods or services are offered at a low price. Direct marketing, advertising, personal selling and public relations are activities involved in promotions. Advertising is a form of communication that is used to convey a single message to a large population within a short time. The main aim of advertising is to persuade, inform and create awareness of a product or service to a customer. Figure 19.1 shows the different features of promotion and advertising.

19.2 Promotion

19.2.1 Objectives of Promotion

In marketing, promotion refers to any type of marketing communication used to inform target audiences of the relative merits of a product, service, brand or issue, most of the time persuasive in nature. It helps marketers to create a distinctive place in customers' mind; it can be either a cognitive or emotional route. The aim of promotion is to increase awareness, create interest, generate sales or create

Basic Terms	Advertising	Promotions
Meaning	It is a method of driving customers' attention towards products or services through paid media	It is a set of activities that inform, persuade and create awareness about a product, service or brand
What is it	Subset	Superset
Core Objective	Building a brand image and boosting sales	A short term technique of pushing sales
Strategy	Promotional	Marketing
Impact	Long-term effect	Short-term effect
Result	Gradual and slow but can be seen after sometime	Tend to be fast but short-lived

Fig. 19.1 Promotion and advertising characteristics. (Source: Author's source)

brand loyalty. It is one of the basic elements of the market mix, which includes the four Ps, i.e. product, price, place and promotion. Promotion is also one of the elements in the promotional mix or promotional plan. These are personal selling, advertising, sales promotion, direct marketing publicity and word of mouth and may also include event marketing, exhibitions and trade shows. A promotional plan specifies how much attention to pay to each of the elements in the promotional mix and what proportion of the budget should be allocated to each element. Promotion covers the methods of communication that a marketer uses to provide information about its product. Information can be both verbal and visual. The term promotion derives from the Old French, *promocion* meaning to "move forward", "push onward" or "advance in rank or position" which, in turn, comes from the Latin *promotionem* meaning "a moving forward". The word entered the English language in the fourteenth century. The use of the term promotion to refer to "advertising or publicity" is very modern and is first recorded in 1925. It may be a contraction of a related term, sales promotion, which is one element in the larger set of tools used in marketing communications. The terms, promotion and marketing communications can be used synonymously, but, in practice, the latter is more widely used. Here are three objectives of promotion: First is to encourage and present information (mostly products/services) to consumers (both old and new) and others. Second, the objectives of promotion are to increase demand and to differentiate a product. Lastly, another purpose of a promotion and its promotional plan can have a wide range, including: sales increases, new product acceptance, creation of brand equity, positioning, competitive retaliations or creation of a corporate image (Helmold, 2022) (Fig. 19.2).

Fig. 19.2 Promotion and advertising strategies. (Source: Author's source)

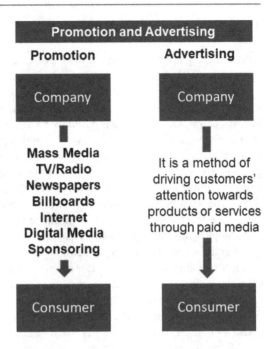

19.2.2 Promotions in a Physical Environment

Promotions can be held in physical environments at special events such as concerts, festivals, trade shows and in the field, such as in grocery or department stores. Interactions in the field allow immediate purchases. The purchase of a product can be incentive with discounts (i.e. coupons), free items or a contest (Bennett, 2009). This method is used to increase the sales of a given product. Interactions between the brand and the customer are performed by a brand ambassador or promotional model who represents the product in physical environments. Brand ambassadors or promotional models are hired by a marketing company, which in turn is booked by the brand to represent the product or service. Person-to-person interaction, as opposed to media-to-person involvement, establishes connections that add another dimension to promotion (Kotler et al., 2019). Building a community through promoting goods and services can lead to brand loyalty.

19.2.3 Promotions in Media

Examples of traditional media include print media such as newspapers and magazines, electronic media such as radio and television and outdoor media such as banner or billboard advertisements. Each of these platforms provides ways for brands to reach consumers with advertisements.

19.2.4 Promotions in Digital Media

At present, digital media is one of the biggest ways of promotion; it includes all the digital channels especially the Internet and social networking websites/apps. This is a proven and modern way for brands to interact with consumers as it releases news, information and advertising from the technological limits of print and broadcast infrastructures. Digital media is currently the most effective way for brands to reach their consumers on a daily basis. Over 2.7 billion people are online globally, which is about 40% of the world's population. Sixty-seven per cent of all Internet users globally use social media. Mass communication has led to modern marketing strategies to continue focusing on brand awareness, large distributions and heavy promotions. The fast-paced environment of digital media presents new methods for promotion to utilize new tools now available through technology. With the rise of technological advances, promotions can be done outside of local contexts and across geographic borders to reach a greater number of potential consumers. The goal of a promotion is then to reach the most people possible in a time-efficient and a cost-efficient manner. Social media, as a modern marketing tool, offers opportunities to reach larger audiences in an interactive way. These interactions allow for conversation rather than simply educating the customer. Facebook, Snapchat, Instagram, Twitter, Pinterest, Tumblr as well as alternate audio and media sites like SoundCloud and Mixcloud allow users to interact and promote music online with little to no cost. You can purchase and buy ad space as well as potential customer interactions stores as likes, followers and clicks to your page with the use of third parties. As a participatory media culture, social media platforms or social networking sites are forms of mass communication that, through media technologies, allow large amounts of product and distribution of content to reach the largest audience possible. However, there are downsides to virtual promotions as servers, systems and websites may crash, fail or become overloaded with information (Marquardt, 2021). You also can stand risk of losing uploaded information and storage and at a use can also be affected by a number of outside variables. Brands can explore different strategies to keep consumers engaged. One popular tool is branded entertainment or creating some sort of social game for the user. The benefits of such a platform include submersing the user in the brand's content. Users will be more likely to absorb and not grow tired of advertisements if they are, for example, embedded in the game as opposed to a bothersome pop-up ad. Personalizing advertisements is another strategy that can work well for brands, as it can increase the likelihood that the brand will be anthropomorphized by the consumer. Personalization increases click-through intentions when data has been collected about the consumer. Brands must navigate the line between effectively promoting their content to consumers on social media and becoming too invasive in consumers' lives. Vivid Internet ads that include devices such as animation might increase a user's initial attention to the ad. However, this may be seen as a distraction to the user if they are trying to absorb a different part of the site such as reading text. Additionally, when brands make the effort of overtly collecting data about their consumers and then personalizing their ads to them, the consumer's relationship with the advertisements, following this data collection, is frequently positive. However, when data is covertly collected, consumers can quickly feel like the company betrayed their trust. It is important for brands to utilize personalization in their ads, without making the consumer feel vulnerable or that their privacy has been betrayed.

19.2.5 Promotions through Sponsoring

Sponsorship generally involves supplying resources (such as money) to a group or an event in exchange for advertising or publicity. Company will often help fund athletes, teams or events in exchange for having their logo prominently visible.

19.3 Advertising Tools

19.3.1 Print Advertising

Once a huge driver of sales, print is taking a back seat to the many digital forms of advertising now available to marketers. However, if there is one thing that's certain about advertising, it's that being different is good, and when consumers tire of digital ads, a return to printed pieces and the tactile feeling and permanence they provide is definitely in the cards. Typically, print can be split into three subcategories:

19.3.1.1 Periodical Advertising

If it's in a magazine, a newspaper or anything else that comes out at regular intervals, then it's periodical advertising (a.k.a. a print ad). For decades, print ads were the gold standard for advertisers and their clients. To grab the centre spread of a big magazine or the back cover of a newspaper meant millions of people saw the message.

19.3.1.2 Brochures, Leaflets, Flyers, Handouts and Point-of-Sale Advertising

Although some of these media can be placed within the pages of newspapers and magazines, they are treated as a separate entity, usually because they have less chance of being seen. From something that sits on a counter or customer service desk to a glossy car brochure, small print media offer a more intimate and long-form way of engaging the consumer. Use this approach when you have more information than you can cram into a print ad.

19.3.1.3 Direct Mail Advertising

Either of the techniques mentioned above can be incorporated into direct mail. It simply means that your printed pieces are mailed directly to the consumer. This is a technique that has been, and continues to be, abused by inferior marketing agencies that have turned the craft into junk mail. If it is creative and intelligently conceived and executed, direct mail can be a fantastic way to engage the customer. Do not count it out.

19.3.2 Digital Ads

If you see an advertisement via the Internet, then it is classified as online advertising. In fact, there are ads on this very page, and most other websites you visit, as they are the primary revenue driver for the Internet. Another avenue of online advertising is native advertising, which is the digital variation of the old print advertorials and sponsored content. There are many digital marketing strategies including placing ads on popular websites and social media sites.

19.3.2.1 Google Ads

Google Ads allows companies to bid on the placement of an ad on Google's search engine results page. By using keywords or common search terms, searches that are related to the business and their products and services appear in the search results. For example, a company that advertises insurance will show up in any search queries for insurance products. The business pays Google if the ad is clicked on, which is why it's called a cost per click basis. Google AdSense allows a company to host ads on their website from Google to generate revenue for the site. For businesses looking to advertise, they can enrol in AdSense, and Google, through its algorithms, will match the ad to various websites with related content or search parameters. As a result, companies can reach larger audiences through Google's placement of advertisements. Google places advertisements on other websites to produce clicks and website traffic.

19.3.2.2 LinkedIn Advertising

Companies can create a business page and post content, videos and product offerings on their page as a way of reaching the millions of LinkedIn users. A LinkedIn page can be an extension of a company's website and drive traffic to the site through links in the content. Also, employees of the company can establish LinkedIn pages with similar content that contain links to the company's website and product offerings. Companies can also place ads on LinkedIn that can be targeted to particular traits or demographics of LinkedIn users. For example, if a business wanted to advertise to people that worked in the field of accounting, an ad can be placed that only targets LinkedIn users that work in the accounting industry or have an accounting degree. With LinkedIn, many members belong to groups. Ads can be targeted to a specific group like a cryptocurrency group or a technology group.

Other social media sites, such as Facebook and Twitter, offer similar programs like the ones outlined from Google and LinkedIn. With digital advertising, it's important to research and target the specific audience that'll likely buy a company's product or service before placing an ad.

19.3.3 Telephone Advertising

A dominating force in digital advertising is through mobile devices such as cell phones, iPads, Kindles and other portable electronic devices with Internet connectivity. Current trends in mobile advertising involve major use of social media such as Twitter, Instagram, Snapchat, LinkedIn and Facebook. Mobile advertising is similar to online advertising and is increasingly gaining importance as a method of reaching new customers.

19.3.4 Product Placement Advertising

Product placement is the promotion of branded goods and services within the context of a show or movie, rather than as an explicit advertisement. If you have ever seen a movie and wondered, "Wow, they sure are driving a lot of Fords in this scene" or "Does everyone in this TV show drink Pepsi?", then you are noticing product placement. It's a way that these films and shows get funding and is a great way for advertisers to reach a targeted demographic.

19.3.5 Guerilla Advertising

Also known as ambient media, guerrilla advertising (or marketing) has become prominent over the last 20 years. It is a broadly used term for anything unconventional and usually invites the consumer to participate or interact with the piece in some way. Location is important, as is timing. The driving forces behind guerrilla advertising or marketing are creative ideas and innovation, not a large budget. Quite often, you will ask for forgiveness rather than permission with these campaigns, and they will spread via word of mouth and social media.

19.3.6 Broadcast Advertising

A mass-market form of communication including television and radio, broadcast advertising has, until recently, been the most dominant way to reach a large number of consumers. Broadcast advertising has suffered from the popularity of DVRs and "ad-skipping" technology. However, it is still an effective way to reach millions of people, especially when the Super Bowl comes around.

19.3.7 Outdoor Advertising

Also known as out-of-home (OOH) advertising, this is a broad term that describes any type of advertising that reaches consumers when they are away from home. Think of billboards, bus shelter posters, fly posters and even those big digital boards in Times Square.

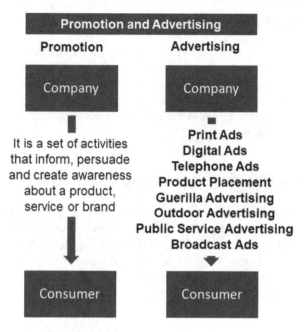

Fig. 19.3 Advertising tools. (Source: Author's source)

19.3.8 Public Service Advertising

Unlike traditional commercials, Public Service Advertisements (PSA) are primarily designed to inform and educate rather than sell a product or service. PSAs traditionally appear on TV and radio but are also heavily promoted online (Fig. 19.3).

19.4 Case Study: Promotion and Advertising Strategy of Rolex

19.4.1 Marketing Strategy of Rolex

Found in 1905, Rolex is a world brand dealing in designing, manufacturing and sale of luxurious watches. It is ranked amongst the top by Forbes amongst the world's most powerful global brands. The company has more than 4000 employees globally. It mainly serves the niche segment of the consumers. Rolex company has the capability of producing about 2000 luxurious watches per day. Marketing Strategy of Rolex analyses the brand with the marketing mix framework which covers the 4Ps (product, price, place, promotion). There are several marketing strategies like product innovation, pricing approach, promotion planning, etc. These business strategies, based on Rolex marketing mix, help the brand succeed. Rolex's marketing strategy helps the brand/company to position itself competitively in the market and achieve its business goals and objectives. Let us start with the Rolex Marketing Strategy and Mix to understand its product, pricing, advertising and distribution strategies:

19.4.2 Rolex Product Strategy

Rolex has been first in the industry in introducing many breakthroughs. Rolex were the first company to introduce waterproof wristwatches, first to introduce wristwatches where the date and time on the dial changed automatically, first to introduce wristwatches that showed two time zones together and the first company that earned chronometer certification. Their products are known for its accuracy, and the watch movement is very accurate. Thus, the watches are the products in the marketing mix of Rolex. The company also offers watches under the brand name Tudor, which is slightly less expensive than Rolex watches. The prices of watches range from $5000 and go beyond millions. Basically, the prices of the products are based on the model and the cost of the materials used. The marketing mix pricing strategy of Rolex is based on quality, type and competition. Additionally, labour cost is also high as highly skilled workers are required to make these masterpieces. Rolex wrist watches are perceived as an exclusive product made for wealthy class of people. Rolex is a price setter in the market and hence does not set its prices for the products based on its competitors; rather, it sets the price for its own products. Also it never offers any kind of discount or sales offer to the customers. Hence, it can be said that Rolex follows high-end exclusive pricing strategy.

19.4.3 Rolex Promotion and Advertising Activities

Rolex company is known for aggressively promoting its watches. The promotional strategy in its marketing mix strategy is comprehensive and uses all media. The logo of Rolex is quite simple and contains a crown. It shows that the crown is precious and only lucky ones get to wear this crown. It depicts its product as a symbol of prosperity, success and luxurious brand. It also adds to the social status of the user. Rolex promotes itself by sponsoring with high-profile events such as car races, Australian open, Wimbledon and many golf tournaments. Rolex tries to advertise itself through its special connection with tennis wherein Rolex is an official time keeper. It has always marketed its product as personalized watch for each and every high-end customer. It does not choose channels of large marketing such as advertisements on national channels along with bytes on radios. The brand has been associated with global celebrities for endorsements like tennis superstar Roger Federer. Hence, this concludes the marketing mix of Rolex.

References

Bennett, G. A. (2009). *The big book of marketing: Lessons and best practices from the World's greatest companies*. McGrawHill.

Helmold, M. (2022). *Strategic performance management. Achieving long-term competitive advantage through performance excellence*. Springer.

Kotler, P et al. (2019). *Grundlagen des Marketing: Jetzt mit eLearning #besser lernen* (Pearson Studium - Economic BWL). Pearson Deutschland Halbergmoos.

Marquardt, A. (2021). *#1 AUF SOCIAL MEDIA: Die Social Media Marketing Anleitung für mehr Reichweite, Kunden und Umsatz* (auf Facebook, Instagram, LinkedIn, TikTok & Co.). AS Rottenburg.

*Quality needs to be constantly improved, but it is just as
necessary to make sure that quality never deteriorates.*

Shigeru Mizuno

20.1 Lean Production System

20.1.1 Introduction to the Lean Production System

The Toyota Production System (TPS), the Just-in-Time Production System or Lean Production System can be described as the ideal combination of four principles (Imai, 1986). These principles are the zero defect principle, the pull principle, the tact principle and the flow principle as displayed in Fig. 20.1 (Helmold & Samara, 2019).

20.1.2 Pull System

The pull system is one of the lean manufacturing principles and is used to reduce waste in the production process. In this type of system, components used in the manufacturing process are only replaced once they have been consumed, so companies only make enough products to meet customer demand (Pascual, 2013). The opposite principle is the push system, in which as many products as possible are generated to be sold via marketing activities. The principles aim to avoid overproduction and stockpiling, thereby saving working capital, by letting demand dictates the rate at which goods or services are delivered. In this way, the customer, or the next step in the chain, "pulls" value through the process.

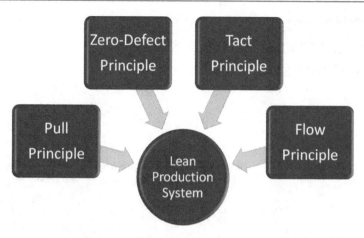

Fig. 20.1 Four Lean Production Principles

20.1.3 Zero Defect Principle

The starting point in Toyota's success story, zero defects is all about identifying errors or defects as closely as possible to where they occur. By so doing, and by neither accepting nor passing on defects, issues are resolved quickly and efficiently, avoiding subsequent rework and quality issues. The zero-defect principle is a concept of the Toyota Production System and is aimed at the reduction of defects through error prevention (Ohno, 1990). It is directed at motivating people to prevent mistakes by developing a constant, conscious desire to do their job right the first time. In reality, zero defects are not possible; however, the concept ensures that there is no waste existing in a project (Helmold & Terry, 2016). Waste refers to all unproductive processes, tools, employees and so on. Anything that is unproductive and does not add value to a project should be eliminated, called the process of elimination of waste. Eliminating waste creates a process of improvement and correspondingly lowers costs. Common with the zero defects theory is the concept of "doing it right the first time" to avoid costly and time-consuming fixes later in the project management process (Belekoukias et al., 2014). The concept of zero defects is grounded on four major elements for implementation in real projects:

- Quality is a state of assurance to requirements. Therefore, zero defects in a project means fulfilling requirements at that point in time.
- Right the first time. Quality should be integrated into the process from the beginning, rather than solving problems at a later stage.
- Quality is measured in financial terms. One needs to judge waste, production and revenue in terms of budgetary impact.
- Performance should be judged by the accepted standards, as close to perfection as possible.

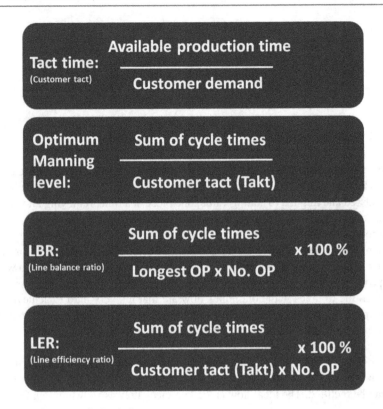

Fig. 20.2 Takt time and other ratios

20.1.4 Production in Line with Customer Tact

The tact refers to the rhythm at which goods or services are produced to meet customer demand. With a consistent, continuous rhythm providing a heartbeat for your production processes, it is far easier to regulate, responding flexibly and effortlessly as demand rises or falls. Takt time is defined as the average time available (time available minus breaks, maintenance or set-up) divided by the customer requested quantity as shown in Fig. 20.2.

Thecycle average time between the start of production of the first unit and the start of production of the next unit (and so on), when these production starts, is set to match the rate of customer demand. For example, if a customer wants 15 units with the available time of 9 minutes and the steady flow through the production line, the average time between production starts should be 36 seconds for one part or unit (9 minutes multiplied by 60 s = 540 s; 540 s divided by 15 unites requested by the customer = 36 s per part). In fact, the takt time simply reflects the rate of production needed to match the demand. In the previous example, whether it takes 4 minutes or 4 years to produce the product, the tact time is based on customer demand. If a process or a production line is unable to produce at takt time, either demand levelling, additional resources or process re-engineering is needed to correct the issue (Helmold & Terry, 2016).

- Directly tie production efficiencies to fiscal reporting.
- Reduce investigation time for root cause analysis.
- Shorten equipment ROI through increased utilization.
- Decrease costs through waste elimination.
- Increase customer satisfaction through quality improvement.

20.1.5 Flow Principle

Value should be added in a smooth, uninterrupted flow, from the start to the end of the production process. The ultimate effect of this principle is that all process steps are focussed and aligned to adding value, one piece at a time, removing all wasteful and unnecessary activities from the process. The advantage of a continuous flow in operations is that it features stability, continuity and balance and doesn't waste time (the non-renewable resource). No time wasted on waiting between steps means time is being maximized for its capabilities. Operations are not able to introduce a waste-less process without the continuous flow, as it is the truly ideal process state. However, the troubles with continuous flow are that it's very hard to achieve, process steps aren't generally balanced, and all process contains inherent waste activities. When one starts out to achieve continuous flow, many process problems will appear and come to the surface. Most individuals think this is bad – it's actually a good thing. The optimal process features continuous flow, and any problems that stand in your way from achieving continuous flow are problems that are now visible and can be rectified. The ideal flow is the one-piece flow as shown in Fig. 20.3.

20.1.6 Andon System for Superior Quality

Andon (Jap.: アンドン or あんどん or 行灯) is a lean manufacturing tool referring to a system to notify management, maintenance and other workers of a quality or process problem. The centrepiece is a device incorporating signal lights to indicate

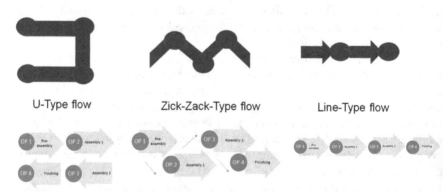

Fig. 20.3 Types of flows in operations. (Source: Marc Helmold)

which workstation has the problem. The alert can be activated manually by a worker using a pull cord or button or may be activated automatically by the production equipment itself. The system may include a means to stop production so the issue can be corrected. Some modern alert systems incorporate audio alarms, text or other displays. An Andon system is one of the principal elements of the Jidoka method pioneered by Toyota as part of the TPS and therefore now part of the lean concept. It gives the worker the ability, and moreover the empowerment, to stop production when a defect is found and immediately calls for assistance. Common reasons for manual activation of the Andon are part shortage, defect created or found, tool malfunction or the existence of a safety problem. Work is stopped until a solution has been found. The alerts may be logged to a database so that they can be studied as part of a continuous improvement program. The system typically indicates where the alert was generated and may also provide a description of the trouble. Modern Andon systems can include text, graphics or audio elements. Audio alerts may be done with coded tones, music with different tunes corresponding to the various alerts or pre-recorded verbal messages. Usage of the word originated within Japanese manufacturing companies and in English is a loanword from a Japanese word for a paper lantern (Imai, 1986). Figure 20.4 shows an Andon example at Alstom in China. The red light means the disruption of production in the respective production operation.

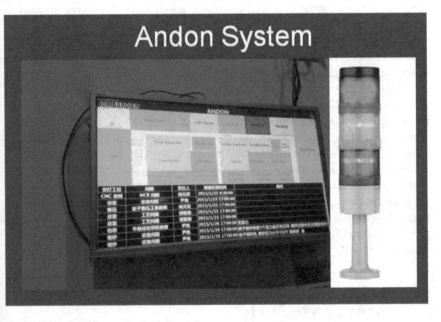

Fig. 20.4 Andon. (Source: Author's source)

20.1.7 Poka-Yoke

Poka-yoke is a Japanese term that means "mistake proofing". A poka-yoke is any mechanism in a lean concept, a process that helps an equipment operator avoid (*yokeru*) mistakes (*poka*). Its purpose is to eliminate product defects by preventing, correcting or drawing attention to human or other errors as they occur. The concept was formalized, and the term adopted, by Shigeo Shingo as part of the TPS. It was originally described as baka-*yoke*, but as this means "fool proofing" (or "idiot proofing") the name was changed to the milder *poka-yoke*.

20.1.8 Gemba and Shop Floor Management

Gemba is also a Japanese term meaning the real or right place. A production environment considers the shop floor as the most important place and the employees in the operation and support functions as the most important human capital for adding value (Pascual, 2013).

20.2   Shadow Boards

Shadow boards are specific boards for parts, tools, equipment in operations, manufacturing or service areas to reduce waste and waiting time. The aim of the shadow board is to achieve an organized workplace where tools, supplies and equipment are stored in appropriate locations close to the work area or work stations. It provides the basis for standardization in the work place. They are a simple and inexpensive tool which provides tangible efficiencies and cost savings as well as intangible benefits. Figure 20.5 shows a shadow board for screws in Mitsubishi Japan. The appropriate storage, allocation and preparation of screws avoid waiting time and the possibility of errors. The advantages of using shadow boards include avoiding waste, such as time looking for the appropriate tool or even having to buy a new one, wasted time in looking for supplies and interchanging tools between tasks. Shadow boards also provide the ability to quickly gauge the location of tools and equipment or if they are missing. Shadow boards are used in the sort and set in order stages of the implementation and operation of a 5S system in a workplace and kaizen initiatives. Shadow boards can be different sizes and located in many different areas of a process or plant. The key is that they are appropriately located and hold all the necessary tools for the area or work station.

20.2.1 Customers Want to Buy from Companies with Health Standards

Health, safety and environment (HSE) is the concept and paradigm that implements and secures practical aspects of environmental protection and safety at work. From a health and safety standpoint, it involves creating organized efforts and procedures

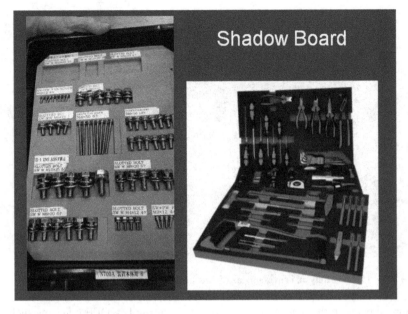

Fig. 20.5 Shadow board. (Source: Helmold. Shadow board. Mitsubishi Shinkanzen Production n Osaka)

for identifying workplace hazards and reducing accidents and exposure to harmful situations and substances. It also includes training of personnel in accident prevention, accident response, emergency preparedness and use of protective clothing and equipment. From an environmental standpoint, it involves creating a systematic approach to complying with environmental regulations, such as managing waste or air emissions all the way to helping operations' departments reduce the company's carbon footprint. Successful HSE programs also include measures to address ergonomics, air quality and other aspects of workplace safety that could affect the health and well-being of employees and the overall community. Figure 20.6 displays HSE requirements in a Chinese operations environment.

20.2.2 Overall Equipment Effectiveness (OEE)

Manufacturing a product is a complex process. Without metrics and guidelines, it is very easy to lose control. The OEE is a tool that combines multiple manufacturing issues and data points to provide information about the process. By analysing and calculating data, it also functions as a framework for root cause analysis. Through a documented process of combining the underlying data OEE provides specific process information. All members of the manufacturing team, from assembly technicians to financial personnel, can use the data to understand the current state of the manufacturing process. By having a predetermined framework of the impact of machine availability, performance and quality, OEE provides a framework to track underlying issues and root causes. OEE also provides a framework for

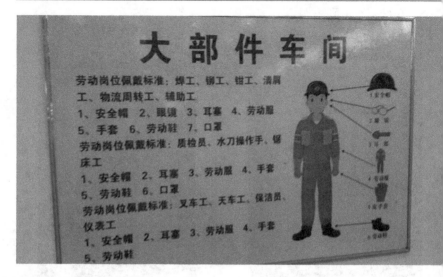

Fig. 20.6 Health, safety and environment. (Source: Author's source)

improvements in the manufacturing process. By using key OEE concepts such as the Six Big Losses, waste exposed by tracking OEE can be understood, and efficiencies can be improved. The components of this framework are the following:

- Availability.
- Performance.
- Quality.

OEE is a very simple metric to immediately indicate the current status of a manufacturing process and also a complex tool allowing you to understand the effect of the various issues in the manufacturing process and how they affect the entire process (OEE = availability × performance × quality). Availability refers to the machine or cell being available for production when scheduled. At the most basic level, when a process is running, it is creating value for the end user. When a process is stopped, it's creating a cost with no associated value. Whether it's due to mechanical failure, raw materials or operator issues, the cell or machine is either producing or not producing. By comparing scheduled run time to actual run time, the availability component of OEE allows for a determination of lost production due to down time. Performance is determined by how much waste is created through running at less than optimal speed. By comparing the actual cycle times against ideal cycle times, OEE allows for a determination of how much production was lost by cycles that did not meet the ideal cycle time. Quality focuses on identifying time that was wasted by producing a product that does not meet quality standards. By comparing the quantity of good to reject parts, the per cent of time actually adding value by producing good product is exposed. By itself, OEE only provides data about your

Fig. 20.7   OEE calculation. (Source: Author's source)

manufacturing process. Companies that use OEE as a metric have found success when combining it with general lean manufacturing programs and also as part of TPM systems. When using OEE with these systems, the benefits become significant: Fig. 20.7 shows an example of the OEE. High-performing companies can achieve an OEE higher than 85 per cent (Helmold & Samara, 2019). In the calculation, the OEE has the elements availability (83.3%), performance (90.0%) and quality (98%). Based on the actual figures, it is now possible to optimize each at the inefficient categories. The availability ratio is below 90% and needs special actions for improvements.

20.2.3   Kanban System

Kanban is a visual system for managing work as it moves through a process. It is a concept related to lean and just-in-time (JIT) production, where it is used as a scheduling system that tells you what to produce, when to produce it and how much to produce. Initially, it arose as a scheduling system for lean manufacturing, originating from the Toyota Production System (TPS).

20.2.4 Supermarkets

Supermarkets ordinarily are located near the supplying process to help that process see customer usage and requirements. Each item in a supermarket has a specific location from which a material handler withdraws products in the precise amounts needed by a downstream process. As an item is removed, a signal to make more (such as a kanban card or an empty bin) is taken by the material handler to the supplying process. Toyota installed its first supermarket in 1953 in the machine shop of its main plant in Toyota City (Ohno, 1990). Toyota executive Taiichi Ohno took the idea for the supermarket from photos of American supermarkets showing goods arrayed on shelves by specific location for withdrawal by customers.

20.3   Case Study: Porsche Production System

Companies such as Porsche have understood that the low value-adding activities of the own organization lead automatically to increasing activities on the supply side (Freitag, 2004). Porsche was also hampered by antiquated production methods. Some 20 per cent of its parts were delivered three or more days too late, for example. In addition, supply disruptions led to severe problems in the value chain and caused recalls (Greiml, 2010). The former head of Porsche, Dr. Wendelin Wiedeking, who had been deeply impressed by what he had seen on visits to Japanese auto firms such as Toyota, Nissan and Honda, believed that only a radical "lean manufacturing" cure would save the company. He flew in teams of the same Japanese consultants who had helped Toyota and gave them free rein. "A cultural revolution from top to bottom" is the way he describes what happened next, as the consultants organized the workforce into teams and one by one eliminated poor practices (Kalkowsky, 2004). Wiedeking made one now-fabled appearance on the assembly line wielding a circular saw, which he used to cut down the roof-high racks of spare parts that towered over the production line. After the lean cure of the own production facilities, Porsche extended the lean concept to suppliers and established the supplier development department in 2006 (the name of the department is FEL, Finance-Purchasing, Supply Management). This department is in charge of extending lean principles to the supply networks and to synchronize production systems. In the following section, the concept of lean supply management will be discussed. Lean principles have:

- To apply lean principles throughout the supply chain.
- To integrate suppliers.
- To be customer oriented.
- To have flat hierarchies.
- To establish competencies to core functions.
- To apply lean principles to shop floor (Gemba).
- To concentrate only on essential success factors.

To reduce waste.
To continuously improve.
To apply a pull system.
To apply a learning organization.

References

Belekoukias, I., Garza-Reyes, J. A., & Kumar, V. (2014). The impact of lean methods and tools on the operational performance of manufacturing organisations. *International Journal of Production Research, 52*(18), 5346–5366.

Freitag, M. (2004). Toyota. *Formel Toyota. Manager Magzin, 12,* 12–14.

Greiml, H. (2010). The Toyota recall crisis. Toyota recalls 1.1m vehicles to fix floor mats. *Automotive News,* 12–15.

Helmold, M., & Samara, W. (2019). *Progress in performance management. Industry insights and case studies on principles, application tools, and practice.* Springer.

Helmold, M., & Terry, B. (2016). *Global sourcing and supply management excellence in China. Procurement guide for supply experts.* Springer.

Imai, M. (1986). *Kaizen. Der Schlüssel zum Erfolg der Japaner im Wettbewerb.* Ullstein.

Kalkowsky, M. (2004). Nur Porsche hat das lean management begriffen: Interview with prof D. Jones. *PRO, 31,* 16.

Ohno, T. (1990). *Toyota Production System. Beyond large Scale Production.* New York: Productivity Press.

Pascual, M. D. (2013). *TOYOTA: UNDERSTANDING THE KEY TO SUCCESS: Principles and strengths of a business model.* Pluma Publishin.

Change Management for Marketing and Sales Activities

21

> *The measure of intelligence is the ability to change.*
>
> Albert Einstein

21.1 Definition of Change Management

The permanent change and transformation of organizations is an important element in order to adapt to the environment. Change management can be defined as the sum of tasks, measures and activities that are intended to bring about a comprehensive, cross-departmental and far-reaching change in an enterprise or organization. Change management includes the implementation of new a mission, vision, strategies, structures, systems, processes and behaviours in an organization. The ultimate goal of change is to obtain a long-term favourable position in the market and to gain a sustainable competitive advantage (Helmold, 2020). Synonyms for change management found in literature are business process re-engineering, turnaround management, transformation management, lean management, innovation management or total quality management (Vahs, 2019). Change is increasingly determining the everyday businesses and activities of companies. In order to manage change in the most optimal way, special change management techniques are required, which can be summarized under the term change management (Lauer, 2019, 2020). The human factor is at the forefront of all considerations, because the implementation of change depends on the active support of employees. Since everyone has their own needs, ideas and experiences, some of which do not conform to the official company organization, there can be no simple recipe for how to successfully manage change. Rather, it is a complex process that has to start at three points: the organization and individuals concerned, the corporate structures and the corporate culture (Lauer, 2019). Another important element in the context is the technological factor including systems, routines, methods and instruments (Helmold, 2020). Figure 21.1 summarizes the elements of change management (Helmold & Terry, 2020).

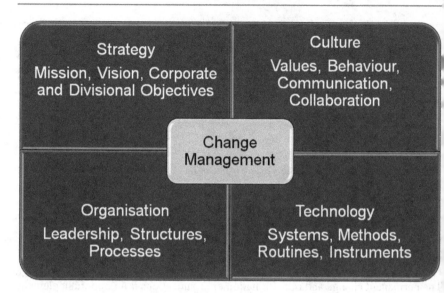

Fig. 21.1 Elements of change management. (Source: Author's source)

21.2   External and Internal Reasons for Change

The need for corporate change can be caused both externally and internally. Externally, companies face an increasingly dynamic environment that requires constant adjustment of their own structures if they want to be successful in sales and also in the preceding procurement markets. The external change is caused by the market environment, politics, technology, ecology, the overall economy or institutions, as well as in the markets themselves, for example, by increasing competition. To explain internal change, the metaphor of human development is used, which – like corporate development – is characterized by a succession of growth, crisis and higher maturity. There are so-called life cycle models for entrepreneurial change that exemplify the typical development phases. Change is often necessary, however, because companies are successful in exaggerating the offensive spirit of their efforts. Here, too, the connection to the human psyche is established, and this phenomenon is analogously referred to as "burnout". Figure 21.2 outlines triggers for change from outside (exogenous triggers) and inside of the organization (endogenous triggers). Exogenous triggers can be described as governmental requirements, new laws, regulations, economic impacts, competitive reasons, market developments, innovations or the advice from consultants. Endogenous triggers are caused by internal stakeholders, such as managers, employees, shareholders, banks, investors or customers.

Exogeneous Triggers for Change	Endogeneous Triggers for Change
• Governmental Reasons • Laws and Regulations • Economic Impacts • Competition • Market Developments • Innovations • Trends • Consultants	• Management • Employees • Banks and Investors • Suppliers • Customers • Other Stakeholders • Production and Service Requirements

Fig. 21.2 Triggers for change. (Source: Author's source)

Fig. 21.3 Elements of Kurt Lewin's change management model. (Source: Author's source)

21.3   Change Management Concepts

21.3.1   Change Management Concept of Kurt Lewin

The Kurt Lewin's model (unfreezing, changing and refreezing) is widely accepted in psychology for implementing change. The implementation of change involves the current state of organization that has to be changed into a desired state, but this will not occur quickly but simultaneously. Kurt Lewin's three stages model or the planned approach to organization is one of the cornerstone models which is still relevant in the present scenario. Lewin, a social scientist and a physicist, during the early 1950s, propounded a simple framework for understanding the process of organizational change known as the Three-Stage Theory which he referred as unfreeze, change (transition) and freeze (refreeze). According to Lewin, change for any individual or an organization is a complicated journey which may not be very simple and mostly involves several stages of transitions or misunderstandings before attaining the stage of equilibrium or stability. For explaining the process of organizational change, he used the analogy of how an ice block changes its shape to transform into a cone of ice through the process of unfreezing. Lewin's model is shown in Fig. 21.3.

Stage 1 – Unfreezing: This is the first stage of transition and one of the most critical stages in the entire process of change management. It involves improving the readiness as well as the willingness of people to change by fostering a realization by moving from the existing comfort zone to a transformed situation. It involves making people aware of the need for change and improving their motivation fo accepting the new ways of working for better results. During this stage, effectiv communication plays a vital role in getting the desired support and involvemen of the people in the change process.

Stage 2 – Changing: This stage can also be regarded as the stage of transition or the stage of actual implementation of change. It involves the acceptance of the new ways of doing things. This is the stage in which the people are unfrozen, and the actual change is implemented. During this stage, careful planning, effective com munication and encouraging the involvement of individuals for endorsing the change are necessary. It is believed that this stage of transition is not that easy due to the uncertainties or that people are fearful of the consequences of adopting a change process.

Stage 3 – Freezing: During this stage, the people move from the stage of transition (change) to a much more stable state which we can regard as the state of equilib rium. The stage of refreezing is the ultimate stage in which people accept o internalize the new ways of working or change, accept it as a part of their life and establish new relationships. For strengthening and reinforcing the new behaviour or changes in the way of working, the employees should be rewarded, recognized and provided positive reinforcements, supporting policies or structures that car help in reinforcing the transformed ways of working.

21.3.2 Change Management Curve of Elisabeth Kürbler-Ross

In 1969 Kürbler-Ross described five stages of grief in her book *On Death and Dying*. These stages represent the normal range of feelings people experience when dealing with change in their lives or in the workplace. All change involves loss at some level. The "five stages" model is used to understand how people react to change at different times (Kessler & Kürbler-Ross, 2005). The stages were first observed as a human response to learning about terminal illness. They have also been used to understand our individual responses to all kinds of change. The five stages of grief Kübler-Ross observed and wrote about are denial, anger, confusion, crisis and acceptance. The model has been extended by several scientists and change management experts with reorientation and integration (Helmold 2020) as shown in Fig. 21.4. The Change Curve is a popular and powerful model used to understand the stages of personal transition and organizational change. It helps you predict how people will react to change, so that you can help them make their own personal transitions and make sure that they have the help and support they need.

Step 1 – Denial and Shock: It is said that every change at the beginning is difficult. Change is a shock to people, as they have to get rid of standard and beloved hab its and behaviours. Transformation and changes scare many employees, who ask questions like:
- What's new for me?
- Where is my path going?
- Will I keep my job?

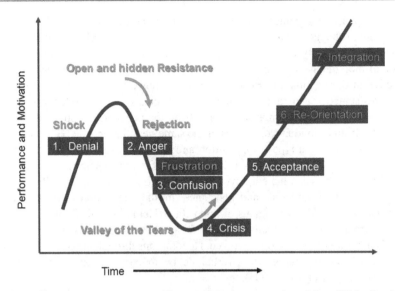

Fig. 21.4 Change management curve. (Source: Author's source, adopted from Kübler-Ross)

- Why do we need a change at all?
- Are there alternatives?
- What is the goal of the change?
- What does this change bring to me (the person concerned)?
- What does this change mean for me and my career?
- What do I need for this change?
- How and where will I be supported in this change and get help?

Many questions come to mind of those affected. It is particularly important here for the company, undergoing a transition and transformation process, to have a clear and appropriate communication strategy. Fears and shock not only block productivity and creativity; in the worst, case they can paralyse an entire company. Open, honest and transparent communication via various channels can minimize anxiety and shock. Communication here is in no way limited to the intranet. Managers also have to pick up their employees and colleagues; in groups and one-on-one discussions, barriers can be reduced or prevented immediately before they arise.

Step 2 – Anger: If there was good communication, open and transparent reporting right at the start of the change, the anger and rejection factor will be optimally lower. However, the shock is transitioning to anger. In this phase, change managers hear repeatedly:
- We have never done this before.
- I don't want this.
- I don't need it.
- It does not make sense.
- It is not good for me.

In this phase, companies often have a strong wind of rejection and resistance According to change management experts, resistance can take place actively as well as passively, verbally or non-verbally. Resistance refers to the activities and the action of individuals or groups who oppose something that should be agreed as an objective in the negotiation. Resistance can be shown in a visible and open way (open resistance) or in a more subtle and disclosed way (hidden resistance). Resistance in negotiations normally come from the negotiation opponents but can also come from individuals or groups of the same negotiation side (Helmold et al., 2020). Resistance is a type of opposition and can be broken through analytically applying emotions or warning tactics. The most difficult problem is to identify signals of resistance, when the employees or people do not openly, formally or informally convey their concerns and resistance. In such case, non-verbal analytical techniques help to identify signals of opposition (Helmold et al. 2019). Resistance occurs verbally or non-verbally in negotiations in various forms, which in most cases is unaware of the persons involved. Negotiations through language (verbal) or gestures or facial expressions (non-verbal, i.e. behaviour or facial expression) must be negotiated (Hilsenbeck, 2004).

Open Resistance
Open resistance is characterized by the fact that it is deliberately exercised by opponents of the opposition and thus also connects a goal. Recognizing open resistance is relatively simple, as expressions and behaviours are openly visible:

- Open contradiction (examples: "I disagree ...")
- Open rejection (example: "I cannot agree with your proposal ...")
- Open intervention (example: "I cannot accept your proposal, so I suggest that ...")
- Rejection by obvious shaking of the head.
- Rejection by gestures with the poor or index fingers.

Normally, the reasons for open resistance have a rational cause, which can be discussed with those affected and whose overcoming all interested parties have an interest (Hilsenbeck, 2004). This form of resistance is usually constructive, so that dealing with open resistance is possible. To break resistance or to refute and mitigate it with a fact-based argumentation can be a suitable strategy here. In this way, the energy which the resisting persons have invested in their resistance can be channelled in the sense of reaching the goals of the transformation, or in simple terms.

Hidden Resistance
Much more difficult is dealing with covert or hidden resistance. In this context, people, who are resisting, usually have no interest in being recognized (Hilsenbeck, 2004). For personal or tactical reasons, they act out of the hidden or the second row. Their interests are mostly destructive, that is, they want to prevent something without being recognized as the causer. Paradoxically, in many cases, resisting parties are not even aware of their resistance. This makes the handling of this form of

esistance even more difficult (Volk, 2018). If the covert resistance is not recognized
n time, the entire outcome of the transformation and change may be at stake.
Signals for hidden resistance in transformation processes can be:

Comments and statements with limitations (example: "I understand your point of
view, but ...")
The absence of important decision-makers (alpha types) or influencing persons
(beta types).
The late appearance in change management meetings of important decision-
makers (alpha types) or influencing persons (beta types).
The permanent postponement and of meeting and delay of tasks due to alleged
scheduling difficulties.
Non-verbal signals of resistance such as mental absence or disinterest. The
demand for perfect solutions.
The demand that we move as a negotiator first.
The extensive and long consideration and discussion of relatively unimportant
special cases.
The general agreement with simultaneous registration of reservations, which
should be clarified later.

Handling Resistance

Resistance must be recognized in transformational processes, and it is important that
managers determine and identify the motives of the resistance. With open and rational resistance, counterarguments and the reformulation of one's own goals can lead
to the refutation of the resistance and the achievement of a result. For questions that
do not play a key role in the transition, managers can also ignore the resistance and
respond to the employee's demands or tackle them later. If the ram state is not resolv-
able, and this is at the core of the transition, there will probably be no bargaining
success. Unconscious or hidden resistance is very difficult to recognize. The process
of identyfying and mitigating resistance should include the following sequence:
detect resistance, understand the resistance, weigh the resistance and finally break
resistance. It is advisable to listen to the resistance of the other side and to understand
the motives (Volk, 2018). A change agent can help by listening to the fear and concerns of the employees. For those employees, who are eventually not willing to follow the change, it is important to break resistance. Breaking resistance can be done
via certain patterns like warning, making concessions, rationality, conviction by
arguments, rational emotions or appeal to mutual benefits. Warning means to have a
facts-based signal (verbally or non-verbally) that the change and transformation will
be pursued for the sake of the company. Without that change, the company may not
succeed in the long term. A warning is factual and objective and should be phrased
with good argumentation and clear message. In ultimate cases, it can be the dismissal
of employees. Another way could be the granting of small and individual minor concessions to the negotiation opponent. When understanding the motives of employees,

Table 21.1 Recommendations to handle resistance

No.	Description
1.	Breaking resistance with factual and objective arguments
2.	Breaking resistance with clear warnings, not threats
3.	Breaking resistance by utilizing pioneers and supporters
4.	Breaking resistance by making concessions for irrelevant issues
5.	Breaking resistance with reflectional discussions of consequences without change
6.	Breaking resistance by understanding the fears and concerns of the people

Source: Author's source

it could be possible to identify areas to give in that area of importance for employee Deflection might also a be a way to break such resistance (Helmold et al., 2019) Table 21.1 gives recommendations how to handle resistance successfully.

Step 3 – Confusion and Frustration: The change curve is now going down dramati-cally steeply. After the rejection, those affected experience severe frustration and confusion. It descends rapidly downhill towards a state of a crisis, **the valley of tears**.

At this point, many employees come to the point of rational acceptance. Employees resign to the situation but still argue against it. Regardless of the change, a correspond-ing position from the management should be available in this stage. This should openly allow problems, fears or simply frustration to be unloaded. A change agent can help employees to cope with the fears. In this way, the confusion and frustration can be bun-dled and quick solutions offered. In any organisation and company should be a trained change manager, a change expert or systemic change consultant, who has the qualifica-tion and competencies to initiate changes and to train other people. This creates a change management culture by using talents and experts throughout the organisation.

Step 4 – Crisis, Valley of the Tears: From a purely rational perspective, employees already know and understand at this stage that there is no way of return. The path the enterprise has taken is irreversible. At this stage, affected employees affected reach an emotional low. They gave everything, climbed the inner walls, were annoyed and fought so hard against the change, but they did not succeed. We all know the feeling when the knot opens and the light at the end of the tunnel becomes visible. Employees can now finally and emotionally accept the change in order to proceed with the transformation.

Step 5 – Acceptance and Try It Out: After the valley of tears, those employees affected are fresh and free. The mind is cleansed; the mindset opens for some-thing new. The person concerned actively wants to see how and what is possible, what happens and where the journey is going. The first hesitant statements can be:

- Maybe there is something good.
- My everyday life could improve.

- It's not as difficult as I thought!
- It does not look as bad as I thought.
- I understand now the need for change.

In this stage, the management should offer support to those affected in this phase through change agents and frequent meetings. It is now important to keep the employees encouraged in trying out, testing and playing with the new tools or systems. The more help is offered through all phases, the better, smoother and faster the transition will proceed.

Step 6 – Reorientation: After many test runs, trying out and reviewing the documents, those affected increasingly come to realize that it is time for a new start. Added value is actively recognized; the light at the end of the tunnel shows the first outline of the landscape. In this stage, managers can now go to the full integration.

Step 7 – Integration: In the last stage, the change has been integrated into the company. New tools, methodologies or processes are a matter of course in everyday life. The question of "why" no longer arises. Those affected live and communicate added value openly. Formerly affected people become ambassadors and helpers for colleagues who are still in the midst of the change curve. These positive influences support the process and the working atmosphere.

21.3.3 Change Management Phase Model of Kotter

Kotter analysed that 70% of all change projects fail, most of them in the initial phase. This is the research result of John P. Kotter, an expert in the field of change management. Two factors are responsible for the low success rate: Not the technology, but the human being is the greatest obstacle to change (Helmold & Samara, 2019). Based on this knowledge, Kotter developed the 8-step model in 1996. The theory shows eight phases of change management and gives managers tips on how to successfully drive change. The focus of the model is communication – from person to person. The 8-step model by John P. Kotter is a further development of the popular 3-phase model by Kurt Lewin. According to the theory, changes in companies can only be successful if they go through all eight stages of change and are intensively accompanied by managers (Kotter, 2012). The eight steps are outlined in Fig. 21.5.

1. **Show Urgency.**
   Raise awareness of the urgency of change among both managers and employees. For example, develop scenarios that could occur if there is no change. Discuss with your managers and employees and make strong arguments.
2. **Build Leadership Coalition.**
   Build a good leadership team by getting trend-setting people for your idea and bringing them together under the flag of change. Make sure you have a good mix of people from different departments and with different skills.

Fig. 21.5 Change management model by Cotter. (Source: Author's source)

3. **Develop Mission, Vision and Strategy.**
   Wrap up a strong vision and concrete strategies with which you want to achieve the goal. Communicate this in a well-prepared and strong speech. An overarching goal for the company helps to implement change.
4. **Communicate the Mission, Vision and Strategies.**
   Constant drip hollows the stone: Do not be afraid to communicate the vision to the managers and employees again and again. This creates trust and increases motivation.
5. **Clear Obstacles.**
   Are there structures in your company that slow down change? Take a close look at the status quo and get rid of unfavourable organizational structures, work processes and routines.
6. **Make Short-Term Successes Visible.**
   Do not set goals that are too time-consuming and costly to begin with but also define intermediate goals that can be reached quickly. Employees who achieve these goals should be rewarded.
7. **Continue Driving Change.**
   After each goal is achieved, analyse what went well and what could have gone better. Always develop new ideas and goals and bring new employees to your management team.
8. **Anchoring Changes in the Corporate Culture.**
   Anchor the achieved goals firmly in your corporate culture. Only after this has been achieved can Kotter speak of a successful change management process.

Since Kotter's 8-phase model gives specific instructions for successful change management, it can serve you well in practice. Critics complain that Kotter's model does not explain how to act in the event of setbacks and that initiatives by employees or so-called "bottom-up" perspectives are ignored. However, like no other change management model, it shows the importance of good communication for sustainable change (Kotter, 2012).

21.3.4 ADKAR Change Management Model

The ADKAR change management model was created by Jeffery Hiatt in 1996. The change management concept is a bottom-up method which focuses on the individuals behind the change (Hiatt, 2006). It's less of a sequential method and more of a set of goals to reach, with each goal making up a letter of the acronym. By focusing on achieving the following five goals, the ADKAR model can be used to effectively plan out change on both an individual and organizational level:

- Awareness (of the need to change).
- Desire (to participate and support the change).
- Knowledge (on how to change).
- Ability (to implement required skills and behaviours).
- Reinforcement (to sustain the change).

Hiatt sees the change of the individual as the basis for sustainable corporate success. The transformation of an entire company can only succeed through individual changes. Thus, the transformation can be understood as the sum of many small changes. A change is only successful when employees adopt new tools, techniques and processes, fully implement them and maintain them in the long term. Then, the ROI, the "return on investment", can also be clearly displayed. When enterprises and its managers drive individual changes, the organization will also master organizational changes (Hiatt, 2006).

There is no need for complex, time-consuming methods, which are actually a science in themselves! As a change manager and change agent, companies need an easy-to-understand, simple and comprehensive tool or method with which they can quickly identify gaps and barriers in the change process of the respective employee. Only then management will be able to lead and guide the employees through the change in a targeted manner (Hiatt, 2006).

21.3.5 McKinsey 7S Model

McKinsey 7S model is a tool (Fig. 21.6) that analyses firm's organizational design by looking at seven key internal elements: strategy, structure, systems, shared values, style, staff and skills, in order to identify if they are effectively aligned and

Fig. 21.6 Change management communication. (Source: Author's source, adopted from McKinsey)

allow organization to achieve its objectives (McKinsey, 2020). McKinsey 7S model was developed in the 1980s by McKinsey consultants Tom Peters, Robert Waterman and Julien Philips with a help from Richard Pascale and Anthony G. Athos. Since the introduction, the model has been widely used by academics and practitioners and remains one of the most popular strategic planning tools. It sought to present an emphasis on human resources (Soft S), rather than the traditional mass production tangibles of capital, infrastructure and equipment, as a key to higher organizational performance. The goal of the model was to show how seven elements of the company – structure, strategy, skills, staff, style, systems, and shared values – can be aligned together to achieve effectiveness in a company. The key point of the model is that all the seven areas are interconnected and a change in one area requires change in the rest of a firm for it to function effectively. Fig. 3.5 outlines the seven categories in the McKinsey model, which represents the connections between seven areas and divides them into "Soft Ss" and "Hard Ss". The shape of the model emphasizes interconnectedness of the elements (Helmold, 2020).

21.4   Case Study: Change Management in Nissan

The three stages of change management of Kurt Lewin can be aptly explained through the aid of an example of Nissan Motor Company which was on the stage of bankruptcy due to the issues of high debts and dipping market share. During that period, Carlos Ghosn took charge as the head of the Japanese automaker who was faced with the challenge of implementing a radical change and turning around the operations of Nissan, by keeping the resistance to change under control which was inevitable under such circumstances by forming cross-functional teams to recommend a robust plan of change in different functional areas. For facing the business challenges, he developed a change management strategy and involved the employees in the process of change management through effective communication and reinforcement of desired behaviours. For refreezing the behavioural change of the employees, he introduced performance-based pay and implemented an open system of feedback for guiding and facilitating the employees in accepting the new behaviour patterns at work.

References

Helmold, M. (2020). *Lean management and kaizen. Fundamentals from cases and examples in operations and supply chain management.* Springer.

Helmold, M., & Samara, W. (2019). *Progress in performance management. Industry insights and case studies on principles, application tools, and practice.* Springer.

Helmold, M., & Terry, T. (2020). *Operations and supply management 4.0. Industry insights, case studies and best practices.* Springer.

Helmold, M., Dathe, T., & Hummel, F. (2019). *Erfolgreiche Verhandlungen. Best-in-Class Empfehlungen für den Verhandlungsdurchbruch.* Springer.

Helmold, M., Dathe, T., & Hummel, F. (2020). *Successful international negotiations. A practical guide for managing transactions and deals.* Springer.

Hiatt, J. (2006). *DKAR: A model for change in business, government and our community.* Prosci Learning Center Publications.

Hilsenbeck, T. (2004). *Verhandeln.* Handbuch von Dr. Thomas Hilsenbeck. Retrieved 30.5.2018. http://www.thomas-hilsenbeck.de/wp-content/uploads/Dr-Th-Hilsenbeck-Handbuch-Verhandeln-Vers-5_0.pdf.

Kotter, J. P. (2012). *Leading change.* Harvard Business Press.

Kübler-Ross, E., & Kessler, D. (2005). *On grief and grieving: Finding the meaning of grief through the five stages of loss.* Scribner.

Lauer, T. (2019). *Change management. Der Weg zum Ziel.* Springer.

Lauer, T. (2020). *Change management. Fundamentals and success factors.* Springer.

McKinsey. (2020). *7-S-Framework.* Retrieved 21 Aug 2020. https://www.mckinsey.com/business-functions/strategy-and-corporate-finance/our-insights/enduring-ideas-the-7-s-framework.

Vahs, D. (2019). *Organisation: Ein Lehr- und Managementbuch.* Schäfer Poeschel Stuttgart.

Volk, H. (2018). Emotionale Dynamik eines Gespräches verstehen. Was den alltäglichen Wortwechsel entgleiten lässt. In: *Beschaffung aktuell.* 06.2018. S. 70-71.

Artificial Intelligence (AI) and Cyber Tools in Marketing and Sales

22

> *Now the playbook is we build AI tools to go find these fake accounts, find coordinated networks of inauthentic activity, and take them down; we make it much harder for anyone to advertise in ways that they shouldn't be.*
>
> Marc Zuckerberg

22.1 AI in Marketing and Sales

22.1.1 Introduction to AI in Marketing and Sales

Of all a company's functions, marketing has perhaps the most to gain from artificial intelligence. Marketing's core activities are understanding customer needs, matching them to products and services and persuading people to buy – capabilities that AI can dramatically enhance (Kreuzer, 2022). No wonder a 2018 McKinsey analysis of more than 400 advanced use cases showed that marketing was the domain where AI would contribute the greatest value. Chief marketing officers are increasingly embracing the technology: An August 2019 survey by the American Marketing Association revealed that implementation of AI had jumped 27% in the previous year and a half. Also, a 2020 Deloitte global survey of early AI adopters showed that three of the top five AI objectives were marketing oriented: enhancing existing products and services, creating new products and services and enhancing relationships with customers.

22.1.2 AI-Powered Marketing and Sales Reprint

While AI has made inroads in marketing, we expect it to take on larger and larger roles across the function in the coming years (Davenport et al., 2021). Given the technology's enormous potential, it's crucial for CMOs to understand the types of marketing AI applications available today and how they may evolve. Drawing on more than a decade of experience studying data analytics, AI and marketing and advising companies across industries about them, we've developed a framework that can help CMOs classify existing AI projects and plan the rollout of future ones. However, before we describe the framework, let's look at the current state of play. Many firms now use AI to handle narrow tasks, such as digital ad placement (also known as "programmatic buying"); assist with broad tasks, like enhancing the accuracy of predictions (think sales forecasts); and augment human efforts in structured tasks, such as customer service. (See the sidebar "Well-Established AI Applications in Marketing" for a list of some common activities AI can support.) Firms also employ AI at every stage of the customer journey. When potential customers are in the "consideration" phase and researching a product, AI will target ads at them and can help guide their search. We see this happening at the online furniture retailer Wayfair, which uses AI to determine which customers are most likely to be persuadable and, on the basis of their browsing histories, choose products to show them. AI-enabled bots from companies such as Vee24 can help marketers understand customers' needs, increase their engagement in a search, nudge them in a desired direction (say, to a specific web page) and, if needed, connect them to a human sales agent by chat, phone, video or even "cobrowsing" – allowing an agent to help the customer navigate a shared screen. AI can streamline the sales process by using extremely detailed data on individuals, including real-time geolocation data, to create highly personalized product or service offers. Later in the journey, AI assists in upselling and cross-selling and can reduce the likelihood that customers will abandon their digital shopping carts. For example, after a customer fills a cart, AI bots can provide a motivating testimonial to help close the sale – such as "Great purchase! James from Vermont bought the same mattress". Such initiatives can increase conversion rates fivefold or more. After the sale, AI-enabled service agents from firms like Amelia (formerly IPsoft) and Interactions are available 24/7 to triage customers' requests – and are able to deal with fluctuating volumes of service requests better than human agents are. They can handle simple queries about, say, delivery time or scheduling an appointment and can escalate more complex issues to a human agent. In some cases, AI assists human reps by analysing customers' tone and suggesting differential responses, coaching agents about how best to satisfy customers' needs or suggesting intervention by a supervisor. Marketing AI can be categorized according to two dimensions: intelligence level and whether it's standalone or part of a broader platform. Some technologies, such as chatbots or recommendation engines, can fall into any of the categories; it's how they're implemented within a specific application that determines their classification.

22.1.3 Task Automation in Marketing and Sales

These applications perform repetitive, structured tasks that require relatively low levels of intelligence. They're designed to follow a set of rules or execute a predetermined sequence of operations based on a given input, but they can't handle complex problems such as nuanced customer requests. An example would be a system that automatically sends a welcome email to each new customer. Simpler chatbots, such as those available through Facebook Messenger and other social media providers, also fall into this category. They can provide some help to customers during basic interactions, taking customers down a defined decision tree, but they can't discern customers' intent, offer customized responses or learn from interactions over time.

22.1.4 Machine Learning in Marketing and Sales

These algorithms are trained using large quantities of data to make relatively complex predictions and decisions. Such models can recognize images, decipher text, segment customers and anticipate how customers will respond to various initiatives, such as promotions. Machine learning already drives programmatic buying in online advertising, e-commerce recommendation engines and sales propensity models in customer relationship management (CRM) systems. It and its more sophisticated variant, deep learning, are the hottest technologies in AI and are rapidly becoming powerful tools in marketing. That said, it's important to clarify that existing machine-learning applications still just perform narrow tasks and need to be trained using voluminous amounts of data.

22.1.5 Stand-Alone Solution in Marketing and Sales

Stand-alone applications. These are best understood as clearly demarcated, or isolated, AI programs. They're separate from the primary channels through which customers learn about, buy or get support for using a company's offerings, or the channels employees use to market, sell or service those offerings. Put simply, customers or employees have to make a special trip beyond those channels to use the AI. Consider the colour-discovery app created by Behr, the paint company. Using IBM Watson's natural language processing and Tone Analyzer capabilities (which detect emotions in text), the application delivers several personalized Behr paint-colour recommendations that are based on the mood consumers desire for their space. Customers use the app to shortlist two or three colours for the room they intend to paint. The actual sale of paint is then executed outside the app, although it does allow a connection to order from Home Depot.

22.1.6 Integrated Solutions in Marketing and Sales

Integrated solutions in Marketing and sales are AI applications, that support Marketing, Sales and Pricing with the help of IT. These digital solutions are AI applications, that help customers to make their purchasing decisions. Netflix's integrated machine learning has offered customers video recommendations for more than a decade; its selections simply appear in the menu of offerings viewers see when they go to the site. If the recommendation engine were stand-alone, they would need to go to a dedicated app and request suggestions. Makers of CRM systems increasingly build machine-learning capabilities into their products. At Salesforce, the Sales Cloud Einstein suite has several capabilities, including an AI-based lead-scoring system that automatically ranks B2B customer leads by the likelihood of purchase. Vendors like Cogito, which sells AI that coaches call centre salespeople, also integrate their applications with Salesforce's CRM system (Fig. 22.1).

Combining the two types of intelligence and two types of structure yields the four quadrants of our framework: stand-alone machine-learning apps, integrated machine-learning apps, stand-alone task-automation apps and integrated task-automation apps. Understanding which quadrant applications fall into can help marketers plan and sequence the introduction of new uses.

A Stepped Approach

AI companies believe that marketers will ultimately see the greatest value by pursuing integrated machine-learning applications, though simple rule-based and task-automation systems can enhance highly structured processes and offer reasonable potential for commercial returns. Note, however, that nowadays task automation is increasingly combined with machine learning, to extract key data from messages, make more-complex decisions and personalize communications, a hybrid that straddles quadrants. Stand-alone applications continue to have their place where integration is difficult or impossible, though there are limits to their benefits. Therefore, we advise marketers to move over time towards integrating AI within current marketing systems rather than continue with stand-alone applications.

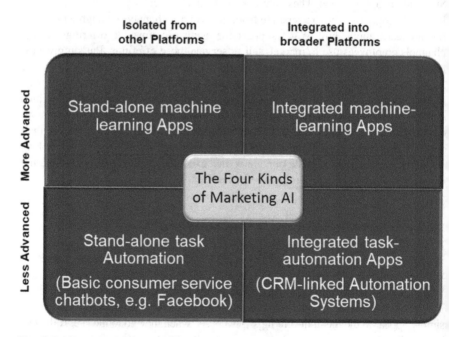

Fig. 22.1   Four elements of marketing AI. (Source: Author's source)

ndeed, many companies are heading in that overall direction; in the 2020 Deloitte survey, 74% of global AI executives agreed that "AI will be integrated into all enterprise applications within three years".

Getting Started

For firms with limited AI experience, a good way to begin is by building or buying simple rule-based applications. Many firms pursue a "crawl-walk-run" approach, starting with a stand-alone non-customer-facing task-automation app, such as one that guides human service agents who engage with customers. Once companies acquire basic AI skills and an abundance of customer and market data, they can start moving from task automation to machine learning. A good example of the latter is Stitch Fix's clothing-selection AI, which helps its stylists curate offers for customers and is based on their self-reported style preferences, the items they keep and return and their feedback. These models became even more effective when the company began to ask customers to choose among Style Shuffle photos, creating a valuable source of new data. New sources of data, such as internal transactions, outside suppliers and even potential acquisitions, are something marketers should look for constantly, since most AI applications, particularly machine learning, require vast amounts of high-quality data. Consider the machine-learning-based pricing model that the charter jet firm XO used to increase its EBITDA by 5%: The key was to tap external sources for data on the supply of private jets and on factors that affect demand, such as major events, the macroeconomy, seasonal activity and the weather. The data XO uses is publicly available, but it's a good idea to also seek proprietary sources whenever possible, because models using public data can be copied by competitors.

22.2   Artificial Intelligence (AI) Tools

22.2.1   AI Tools Will Lead to a Competitive Advantage

In the field of computer science, artificial intelligence (AI), sometimes called machine intelligence, is intelligence demonstrated by machines, in contrast to the natural intelligence displayed by humans and other animals. Figure 22.2 depicts nine elements of artificial intelligence which can lead to a competitive advantage across the value chain.

22.2.2   Autonomous Robots

An autonomous robot is a robot that performs behaviours or tasks with a high degree of autonomy (without external influence). Autonomous robotics is usually considered to be a subfield of artificial intelligence, robotics and information engineering.

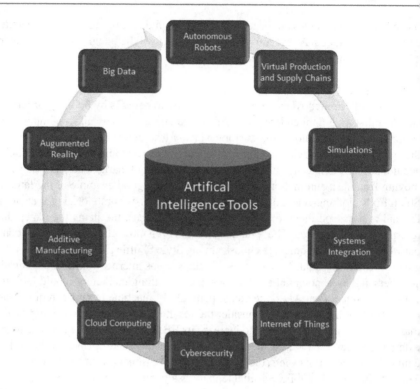

Fig. 22.2 Artificial intelligence tools. (Source: Author's source)

22.2.3 Virtual Production and Supply Chains

Virtual production tends to be used to help visualize complex scenes or scenes that simply cannot be filmed for real. In general, though, virtual production can really refer to any techniques that allow filmmakers to plan, imagine or complete some kind of filmic element, typically with the aid of digital tools.

22.2.4 Virtual and Lean Simulations

Lean simulations include a set of hands-on experiments to teach employees about systems and process improvement in all areas of the value chain. Lean simulations can focus on design, manufacturing, capacity planning or supply chain design. The purpose of simulations is to understand the implications of input variables and alternations of the value chain elements.

22.2.5 Systems Integration

Lean integration is a continuous improvement methodology for bringing disparate data and software systems together. The goal is to maximize customer value. Lean integration is a management system that emphasizes eliminating waste as a sustainable data integration and system integration practice.

22.2.6 Internet of Things

The Internet of Things (IoT) is a system of interrelated computing devices, mechanical and digital machines, objects, animals or people that are provided with unique identifiers (UIDs) and the ability to transfer data over a network without requiring human-to-human or human-to-computer interaction.

22.2.7 Cybersecurity

Cybersecurity is the protection of Internet-connected systems, including hardware, software and data, from cyberattacks. In a computing context, security comprises cybersecurity and physical security – both are used by enterprises to protect against unauthorized access to data centres and other computerized systems.

22.2.8 Cloud Computing

Cloud computing is a type of computing that relies on shared computing resources rather than having local servers or personal devices to handle applications. In its most simple description, cloud computing is taking services ("cloud services") and moving them outside an organization's IT system and environment.

22.2.9 Additive Manufacturing

Additive manufacturing (AM) is the industrial production name for 3D printing, a computer-controlled process that creates three-dimensional objects by depositing materials, usually in layers. The official industry standard term is the ASTM F2792 for all applications of the 3D-technology. It is defined as the process of joining materials to make objects from 3D model data, usually layer upon layer, as opposed to subtractive **manufacturing** methodologies.

22.2.10 Augmented Reality

Augmented reality (AR) is an interactive experience of a real-world environmen
where the objects that reside in the real world are enhanced by computer-generatec
perceptual information, sometimes across multiple sensory modalities, including
visual, auditory, haptic, somatosensory and olfactory.

22.2.11 Big Data

Big Data is a phrase used to mean a massive volume of both structured and unstruc-
tured data that is so large it is difficult to process using traditional database and
software techniques. In most enterprise scenarios, the volume of data is too big or it
moves too fast or it exceeds the current processing capacity.

22.3   Industry 4.0 in Lean Management

Production systems are not like they used to be. The twenty-first century will con-
front enterprises and manufacturing companies with completely novel generations
of technologies, services and products based on computer technologies. In order to
meet competition on global markets and to ensure long-term success, the companies
need to adapt to shorter delivery times, increasing product variability and high market volatility, by which enterprises are able to sensitively and timely react to continuous and unexpected changes. One of the major cornerstones to meet these
challenges is the implementation of digital information and communication technologies into production systems, processes and technologies, which allow novel
developments by combining the physical world and fast data access and data processing via the Internet (Industry 4.0) (see Fig. 22.3). Industry 4.0 is a name given
to the current trend of automation and data exchange in manufacturing technologies. It includes cyber-physical systems, the Internet of Things, cloud computing
and cognitive computing. Industry 4.0 is commonly referred to as the fourth industrial revolution. Industry 4.0 fosters what has been called a "smart factory". Within
modular structured smart factories, cyber-physical systems monitor physical processes, create a virtual copy of the physical world and make decentralized decisions.
Over the Internet of Things, cyber-physical systems communicate and cooperate
with each other and with humans in real-time both internally and across organizational services offered and used by participants of the value chain. There are four
design principles in Industry 4.0. These principles support companies in identifying
and implementing Industry 4.0 scenarios:

- Interconnection: The ability of machines, devices, sensors and people to connect
  and communicate with each other via the Internet of Things (IoT) or the Internet
  of People (IoP).

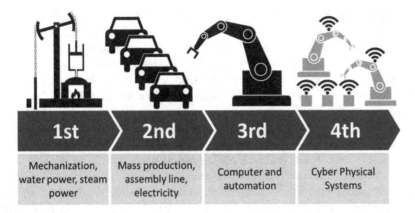

Fig. 22.3 Industry 4.0 evolution. (Source: Adopted from Industry 4.0: The Top 9 Trends for 2018 Liubomyr (El.) Kachur))

- Information transparency: The transparency afforded by Industry 4.0 technology provides operators with vast amounts of useful information needed to make appropriate decisions. Interconnectivity allows operators to collect immense amounts of data and information from all points in the manufacturing process, thus aiding functionality and identifying key areas that can benefit from innovation and improvement.
- Technical assistance: First, the ability of assistance systems to support humans by aggregating and visualizing information comprehensively for making informed decisions and solving urgent problems on short notice. Second, the ability of cyber physical systems to physically support humans by conducting a range of tasks that are unpleasant, too exhausting or unsafe for their human co-workers.
- Decentralized decisions: The ability of cyber physical systems to make decisions on their own and to perform their tasks as autonomously as possible. Only in the case of exceptions, interferences or conflicting goals are tasks delegated to a higher level.

22.4   Case Study: Google's Self-Driving Cars

Research into self-driving cars is not a new phenomenon. In the late 1950s, the first known thoughts on self-driving vehicles were described in Popular Mechanics magazine by a mechanic who argued that altering a roadster to both start itself and back itself into a driveway would be relatively straightforward. Later that year, a GM analyst revealed in Popular Science magazine that the company was already investigating embedding highways with cable and radio-control boxes as a means of developing an infrastructure to support driverless cars. Despite all of the theoretical research into the subject, self-driving cars did not become a reality until 1968. The first physical breakthrough in driverless car technology was the design of a car that used sonar and gyroscopes to drive, steer and stop an automobile. In 1968, the Cornell Aeronautical Laboratory created the "Urbmobile", an electric car that could be driven on the road but could also glide along a subway-style track that utilized roadside guides, magnetometers, magnetic nails and internal computers. The largest breakthrough came years later, however, with the announcement from Google, Inc. of the Google Car in 2010. With the distinctive sensor and camera nub lodged on top of a Toyota Prius, the Google Car quickly became operational and present on roads across the United States. Shortly thereafter, media coverage of the Google Car became increasingly prevalent in addition to promotional commercials demonstrating the benefits of the car. While the benefits demonstrated in the videos seemed to be promising, the Google Car's entrance into the market seemed a far leap away from Google's core business. Google Inc. specializes in Internet-related services and products, with the mission to organize the world's information and make it universally accessible and useful. In 1998, Larry Page and Sergey Brin, two Stanford University computer science graduate students, created a search engine that uses back links, or incoming links, to a website or web page, to determine the importance and therefore rank individual web pages during a web query. Existing competitors, like Yahoo and AOL, on the other hand, were directories of other websites, organized in a hierarchy, as opposed to a searchable index of pages. This allows the Google search process to return more relevant results rather than simply a ranked list of preferred sites. In 1999, Google secured funding from Sequoia Capital and Kleiner Perkins Caufield & Byers, Silicon Valley's two leading venture capital firms. Only one year later, Google became the world's largest search engine with over a billion pages in its index, surpassing industry giants such as Yahoo. Google's dominance of the search market continues today as Google maintains a 67 per cent share of global searches. While Google Inc. began as a company specializing in search, it quickly expanded into other product areas. In 2004, Google launched Gmail, an email client which became the world's largest email provider by 2012 with an estimated 425 million active users. Expanding into the online video domain, Google acquired YouTube in 2006 for $1.65 billion, which reaches over 1 billion unique visitors each month. In 2008, Google launched Chrome, a web browser, and Android, an operating system for mobile devices. In both of these areas as well, Google dominates the market, with a 50 per cent and 68 per cent of the market share, respectively (Miller & Wald, 2013). In 2010, Google announced that the prototype of a driverless car – the Google Car – was completed. According to Google executives at the time, the goal of the Google Car was to "… help prevent traffic accidents, free up people's time and reduce carbon emissions by fundamentally changing car use". With a team assembled consisting of engineers with experience in vehicle technology from the DARPA Challenges, a series of driverless vehicle races sponsored by the US Government, Google was finally able to bring the driverless car phenomenon to reality. The Google Car is a sophisticated system that integrates proprietary hardware and software, using video cameras, radar sensors and a laser range finder to visualize traffic and detailed maps taken from Google Maps to enable navigation between destinations. Google's data centres process the incoming data relayed from the sensors and cameras mounted on the Google Car in order to provide the car with useful information about its environment that is later translated into the physical operation of the vehicle. The key to the Google Car's technological capabilities is the laser range finder nounted on the roof of the modified Toyota Prius, allowing for real-time environmental analysis. In addition, the Google Car is equipped with four radars and a Velodyne 64-beam laser placed strategically around the car to accurately generate a three-dimensional map of its environment. A camera detects traffic lights, while a GPS, wheel encoder and inertial measurement unit control the vehicle's location and log car movement. The software system synthesizes laser measurements produced from the laser beam with high-resolution maps of the world, producing dynamic data models then translated into the physical operation of the vehicle by the car's internal software system. Altogether, the system allows for seamless operation of the vehicle that adjusts to its dynamic environment without the intervention of a driver. In addition to the generic driverless capability, the Google Car's system also adjusts for local traffic laws and environmental obstacles in real-time. For example, if the Google Car approaches a four-way intersection and senses that the driver with the right of way does not move, the Google Car inches forward slightly to indicate to other drivers the intentions of driving through the intersection (Miller & Wald, 2013). Altogether, the technology and adaptation to local conditions not only allows for driverless transportation but also increases safety on the road. Since its introduction, the Google Car has completed 200,000 miles of accident-free computer-led driving, beyond one incident that was arguably caused by another driver. The road test results for the Google Car indicate that the Google Car obeys all of the rules of the road and adjusts to its dynamic environment in real-time with no problems. Thus, with this integrated technology, the car has the capability of being safer than a human driver. The Google Car has the potential to have a profound effect on energy consumption, efficiency and traffic accidents. With subsequent productivity increases, and decreases in costs, the Google Car represents a potentially revolutionizing technology. It is precisely this potential, however, that creates a threat for Google to sustaining a long-term competitive advantage in the driverless car space. As the Google Car may radically shift the structure of affected industries and raises serious privacy concerns, vulnerable industries and consumer groups threaten the viability of the project. Thus, the Google Car faces challenges far greater than competing car manufacturers alone. In squaring off against politically and economically powerful industries that are facing their demise, can the Google Car survive? Can the will to revolutionize driving outweigh the costs of potentially ruined industries and massive unemployment? Who will win the war of the road?

References

Davenport, T. H., Guha, A., & Grewal, D. (2021). *How to design an AI marketing strategy.* Harvard Business Review. Retrieved 22 August, 2022. https://hbsp.harvard.edu/product/S21041-PDF-ENG.

Kreuzer, R. T. (2022). *Künstliche intelligenz im marketing.* Springer.

Miller, C. C. & Wald, M. L. (2013). Self-driving cars for testing are supported by U.S. *New York Times.* Retrieved 10 Dec 2019. https://www.nytimes.com/2013/05/31/technology/self-driving-cars-for-testing-are-supported-by-us.html.

> *The best vision is insight.*
>
> Malcolm Forbes

23.1 Definition of Negotiations

Negotiations are a form of communication, usually in the form of a conversation, about a controversial issue, which are characterized by conflicting needs, interests and motives. Basically, negotiations aim to balance interests by weighing positions and the intensity of needs to reach a conclusion (Obrien, 2016). All people have interests, desires, motives and needs that they want to realize. These needs may be different in nature but have the same characteristics and expressions (Obrien, 2016). Buyers have the desire and need to obtain the lowest purchase price in a transaction, whereas sellers strive for the highest selling price. Both sides aim for the best price for their own side (Obrien, 2016). Intra-company demands for a higher budget are also needs that have to be enforced in intra-company negotiations (Helmold & Terry, 2016). For example, in a company, there may be a desire for additional salespeople to expand into other countries and markets. Job interviews also involve wants and needs of the parties involved, namely, to find the appropriate employee or position. In addition to the actual job, there are numerous elements in job interviews, such as salary, benefits or perks, that are part of the negotiation. Not only in companies but also in personal life, there is a plethora of needs that end up in negotiations. For example, a daughter may want her father to take her to school by car instead of using public transportation, or a family may negotiate where to go on vacation. All of these needs and wants represent negotiations over controversial issues and usually lead to a more or less consensual outcome. Negotiations are interactions between two or more parties about a specific issue with the fundamental interest of the parties to reach an agreement. These are characterized by an envisaged reconciliation of interests and a negotiated outcome (Obrien, 2016). Negotiations are diverse, as all authors describe, and take place in every conceivable area of life (Helmold, 2018; Dathe & Helmold, 2018; Schranner, 2009; Obrien 2016). Examples of negotiations are the following:

- Commercial discussions and agreements between buyers and sellers in commer cial transactions.
- Technical agreements on product performance characteristics between custome and supplier.
- Agreements between supplier and customer on the performance and specifica tion characteristics of services.
- Coalition negotiations between parties to form a government after the last federal elections.
- Online auctions of the purchasing department of a large corporation for the scope of a major project.
- Haggling with the seller at the flea market with the subsequent purchase of an antique piece of furniture.
- Students who have an oral final exam and answer questions from professors.
- Applications and interviews for a position with personnel and technical depart ment and questions about salary.
- Requesting a salary increase from an employee to his supervisor due to good performance.
- Agreement of employee goals within the framework of the annual appraisals by the supervisor and employee.
- Arrangements of freelance consultant about project scope and workload with the commissioning customer.
- Application of an honorary lecturer to a university to lecture to students of economics and business studies.
- Discussion between parents and children about which restaurant the family goes to in the neighbourhood.
- Children asking their parents for sweets at the checkout while shopping in a supermarket.
- Hostage-taking and assertion of the hostage-takers' claims with the police, e.g. getaway car.

The term negotiation originally comes from the Latin stems "Neg" (German: Nein, keine) and "Otsia" (Freizeit), i.e. "no leisure time". Unlike the nobility, the patricians, the citizens of Rome had no leisure time as part of their daily trading and work. In the seventeenth century, the term has been modified in the French language towards the meanings such as "business transaction, agreement, and resolution of a conflict" (Cambridge Dictionary, 2018). Obrien defines negotiation as the process and reaching of an agreement on a particular matter by at least two parties (Obrien, 2016). In this context, all parties aim at balancing interests and eliminating conflict, through common ground (Obrien, 2016; Abdel-Latif, 2015).

Negotiations are therefore characterized by the following attributes and properties:

* At least two or more parties must be involved.
* The objective of the parties must be to reach an agreement.
* The effort of the parties must be to resolve a conflict amicably.
* There must be willingness to give and take from all parties.
* A desired balance of interests must be achieved.
* All parties must take initiatives to find a solution.

If these attributes are only partially fulfilled or not fulfilled at all, one does not speak of negotiations, as Obrien states (Obrien, 2016). In addition to the attributes of negotiations, numerous authors describe that certain success factors are necessary for positive negotiations. Negotiations need to be effective and efficient and take place in the right environment (Obrien, 2016). According to Obrien, the following success factors can be summarized in order to successfully conduct negotiations (Obrien, 2016):

* Effectiveness in negotiations (quality).
* Efficiency in the process of negotiations (time management).
* Climate of negotiations (relations).
* Balance of power of the negotiating partners (equality).
* Agreement on the points of negotiation (communication).
* Shared benefits (fairness).
* Formulation of objectives (clarity).
* Profit orientation (value creation)

23.2   A-6 Concept by Dr. Marc Helmold

Dr. Marc Helmold has held various management positions in the automotive and railway industries since the late 1990s. In these positions, he has conducted negotiations with national and international customers and suppliers in the higher three-digit million range. Within this function and due to the deficits and weaknesses of existing negotiation concepts in the intercultural context, he has developed the A-6 negotiation concept (Helmold, 2018). This concept is interculturally oriented, innovative, up-to-date, sustainable and unique and has already been successfully implemented in various projects. The practical and easy-to-use concept includes six steps from A-1 to A-6, which must be considered in every negotiation to achieve optimal success (Helmold, 2018). In addition to its practical application, cross-cultural specifics are also described in Chap. 4, which come into play in international transactions in countries such as the United States of America, China, France, India or other countries. Although the model is focused on business negotiations, other negotiations, for example, political negotiations, negotiations between private persons, negotiations about alimony, etc., can also be carried out within the framework

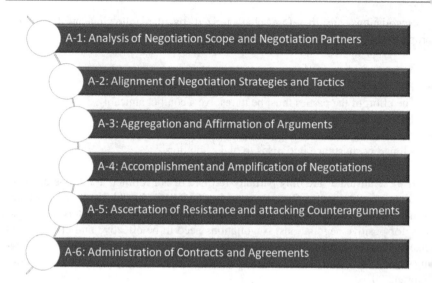

Fig. 23.1 Negotiation A-6 concept

of these six steps. Last, the A-6 concept is an inherently logical construct, which sequentially consists of six steps that build on each other. Figure 23.1 shows the six steps from analysis to respect and compliance with the agreement. After the detailed analysis, a selection of appropriate strategies and tactics takes place. The basis here is the script or manuscript, which is described in the context of this chapter. The strategies and tactics determine the argumentation and the structure of the negotiations (Godeck, 2017). Once one has completed these steps, one can move into the actual negotiation. This is where the radius of action is determined. Within the strategy and argumentation, possible counterarguments of the other side and resistances have been identified as well as tactics to successfully break these resistances without the negotiating partner losing face. As a final step, the shaping of the negotiation outcome and the adherence to the negotiation agreements are crucial (Helmold, 2018).

23.3   The Harvard Negotiation Concept

Negotiations are characterized by an envisaged reconciliation of interests and a negotiated settlement (Obrien, 2016). This is reflected in all existing concepts of negotiation. Probably, the most commonly taught and referred to negotiation concept is the Harvard concept. It is the method of fact-based negotiation. The principle behind it was formulated by the American legal scholar Fisher in 1981 together with Ury in the book "Getting to Yes". In this book, both authors describe how to negotiate constructively and efficiently (Fisher & Ury, 1981). Fisher and Ury state that negotiation is a constant part of our lives. In all situations, agreements need to be reached that are appropriate to the complexity of the situation and the various interests involved. The use of power and leverage usually leads to ineffective and unsatisfactory results. According to the Harvard concept, on the other hand, it is better to seek solutions using a constructive negotiation method (Fisher & Ury, 1981). A good negotiation outcome is transparent, that is, unambiguous in its interpretation, and implementable, that is, the realistic implementation is fair, meaning all parties can accept it. Negotiations should be balanced and benefit all parties in an equal way. Both parties should also aim to add additional value in negotiations and outcomes (Fisher & Ury, 1981). In the Harvard concept, negotiation is not only about factual issues and outcomes but also about the personal relationships between the actors. Similarly, both authors identified that emotional elements such as trust or distrust determine the success or failure of the negotiation (Fisher & Ury, 1981). For a long time, there was a dispute between two "schools" of negotiation on how to conduct negotiations successfully: Some believed that one should negotiate "hard", that is, seek one's own success on the merits at any cost and "defeat" the other side by any means; others recommended negotiating "soft", that is, protect one's good relationship with the other side at all costs and be rather generous on the merits so as not to strain the relationship (Fisher & Ury, 1981).

23.4   The Schranner Negotiation Concept

23.4.1 Concept for Borderline Negotiations

In Schranner's concept "Negotiating on the Edge", a total of seven principles or laws for difficult negotiations are presented (Schranner, 2009). According to his website, Matthias Schranner can demonstrably show successful negotiation techniques that can be directly applied in business life. In various articles, Schranner is seen as the expert in negotiating difficult cases (Schranner, 2015). Schranner's website states that in 95% of all cases, clients are able to negotiate themselves but that in difficult cases, which account for about 5%, his approach can come into play (Schranner, 2015). Schranner identifies three different types of actors in conflict situations (Polwin-Plass, 2016):

1. Escape types.
2. Attack types.
3. Mixed types.

23.4.2 Escape Types

Escape types are described by Schranner as individuals who tend to avoid or not make an appearance in critical situations (Schranner, 2015; Polwin-Plass, 2016). These usually withdraw in critical situations to avoid conflict. While this prevents conflict, the problem remains unresolved. In international negotiations, especially in Asian countries such as China, Japan or South Korea, one will ostensibly encounter escape types who will avoid open conflict (Helmold & Terry, 2016). This will be discussed in detail further on.

23.4.3 Attacker Types

In addition to escape types, there are individuals who are confrontational and direc in their approach to negotiations (Schranner, 2015; Polwin-Plass, 2016). Schranne calls this type "attack type". They go for confrontation and thus solve problems i the short term. They very often destroy relationships in the long term, as they ofte say rash and emotional things (Schranner, 2015; Polwin-Plass, 2016). Especially i critical and dangerous negotiation situations, according to Schranner, attack type talk too much and too rashly, so that they very often betray confidential informatior when not matched (Polwin-Plass, 2016). If attack types interculturally meet escape types or people who act rather reserved and passive, this can lead to a strong loss of face and the final failure of the negotiations (Dathe & Helmold, 2018). In the context of international negotiations, however, it is advisable to wait and let the negotiating adversary talk for the time being (Helmold, 2018).

23.4.4 Mixed Types

According to Schranner, there are individuals who display both characteristics of the first two categories (escape and attack types) to varying degrees (Polwin-Plass, 2016). These are called "mixed types". Depending on the typification of the negotiating opponent, one's own tactics and strategy must be developed in a targeted manner (Polwin-Plass, 2016).

23.4.5 Important Steps in the Schranner Negotiation Concept

Schranner's concept includes seven important rules and focuses on difficult negotiations (Schranner, 2015). Schranner sees the following steps and elements as focal points for negotiations in very difficult cases:

- Never give in.
- Do not compromise.
- Do not play for time and do not postpone.
- Never say no.
- Caution with threats.
- Help the negotiating partner save face.
- If the call is terminated, withdraw the offer.
- Setting the anchor.
- Clarifying the agenda.
- Increase in receivables.
- Creating summaries.

Schranner likes to compare difficult sales negotiations in his seminars with negotiations from his professional life as a police officer and negotiator in criminal cases and explains what can be learned and applied from them for business life.

Example

For example, during a hostage situation, a man threatened a woman with a gun and announced that he would shoot his victim if the police did not leave the room immediately (Polwin-Plass, 2016). This leads to different alternative courses of action according to Schranner. In the first step, there are the following alternative actions based on this real example (Polwin-Plass, 2016):

Give in to the aggressor's wish and leave the room.
Make a threat.
Offer a compromise.
Crack a joke to lighten the situation.
Appeal to the conscience of the hostage-taker.
Say "no".

Negotiations become difficult especially when the negotiating parties are convinced that they are right in one or all aspects of the negotiation (Polwin-Plass, 2016). Even a criminal and hostage-taker has a justification for his act based on his conviction, even though his behaviour does not conform to the law (Polwin-Plass, 2016). When negotiating with a hostage taker as well as in a sales negotiation, it is important according to Schranner not to be irritated or obviously respond to irritation (Polwin-Plass, 2016). Displeasure and anger elicit stress; this stress in turn costs energy, and stressed people become active and thus offensive (Polwin-Plass, 2016). In this regard, Schranner recommends (Polwin-Plass, 2016) to negotiate carefully so as not to jeopardize the conversation. Similarly, his advice is to never give in, especially when strategies and tactics (Sect. 23.4.3) come into play (Polwin-Plass, 2016). According to Schranner, giving in is by far the worst tactic in terms of negotiation. Giving in without reciprocation leads to even higher demands and is a sign of weakness (Polwin-Plass, 2016; Schranner, 2009). Suppose a protracted negotiation is in its final stages, the seller is under quite a bit of pressure, and now the only thing standing in the way of signing is the price. However, the buyer and customer now wants another price reduction in the multi-digit range. An escape type in this situation would try to escape from this situation, as Schranner describes (Polwin-Plass, 2016; Schranner, 2009). This behaviour poses great risks for future negotiations, because the customer would demand an even higher discount in the next negotiation with the successful strategy of exerting pressure. Therefore, Schranner says: "Concessions are allowed, but only with demands in return. You have to weigh up the demands carefully, summarise them several times and then offer cooperation with consideration. This is how goals are achieved and mutual respect is worked out". Especially in price negotiations, you should never compromise. According to Schranner, compromises convey two dangerous risks. Firstly, the buyer would be confirmed in his strategy ("There's still something there".), and secondly, the impression would be created that exerting pressure is a successfully applied strategy ("By exerting pressure, we always succeed".) (Polwin-Plass, 2016) A compromise is a quick way out of a conflict, but it does not lead to a sustainable solution. A conflict must therefore be fought out: "A negotiation is a conflict. To compromise would mean to respond to the middle of the negotiating partner, not to one's own. This leads to the counterpart setting the bar inherently higher next time. You have to be able to withstand pressure in order to be able to raise your own demands. It is important to emphasize common ground" (Schranner, 2009). Schranner therefore recommends making concessions only in return for consideration and not compromising at all. Another recommendation involves ending negotiations with staying power and no adjournments (Polwin-Plass, 2016; Schranner, 2009). Polwin quotes Schranner: "When one plays for time, one hopes to be able to take a more optimal starting position at a later point in time. But if both negotiating partners are playing for time, it becomes problematic, because the possibility of getting into a better position dwindles. As a result, adjourning is no use either, because in the meantime both negotiating partners become even more sure of their case and the next negotiation becomes even more difficult". Furthermore, the identification of the negotiating partner's room for manoeuvre plays a central role, setting a maximum and a minimum price with a pain threshold. According to Schranner, there are always two prices in price negotiations: the obvious price and the invisible price. The invisible one is significantly more important than the visible one, and the seller must approach it carefully. Power and relationships are two important elements in Schranner's concept of negotiation, who recommends the display of power but considers pressure as a critical tool in negotiations (Polwin-Plass, 2016; Schranner, 2009). Pressure and counter-pressure lead to escalation and a mere clarification of power relations without a willingness to cooperate. Negotiation professionals should therefore avoid statements such as "no" or "rejection" in order to continue to flexibly retain all options (Schranner, 2009). A suitable tactic is the introduction of different demands with different prioritizations (Polwin-Plass, 2016; Schranner, 2009). The introduction of demands creates room for manoeuvre for one's own negotiating side. Schranner recommends asking questions in the subjunctive to include demands: "For example, could you imagine buying or doing this or that in addition so that we can accommodate you here and there?" Further, demands should not be communicated through threats. Saving face is an integral part of any negotiation, as the negotiating adversary will need support if they make concessions and deviate from their maximum goal.

The three negotiation concepts described have different characteristics and emphases, as Table 23.1 shows. Harvard's concept is basically developed for all types of negotiations, whereas Schranner's concept focuses on difficult negotiations (Fisher & Ury, 1981; Schranner, 2009). Dr. Helmold's concept targets on negotiations between trading partners in an international context and offers cross-cultural recommendations for action (Helmold & Terry, 2016). All three concepts suggest detailed preparation, with Dr. Helmold's concept targeting the scope of the negotiation, motives, roles and types of people negotiating (Helmold et al., 2022). The

Table 23.1 Comparison of the Dr. Helmold A-6 concept with the Harvard and Schranner concept

Differences between the Harvard, Schranner and Dr. Helmold A-6 negotiation concept

Element	Harvard concept	Dr. Helmold A-6 concept	Schranner concept
Main focus	Basically all negotiations	Customer-supplier negotiations in an intercultural context	Difficult negotiations
Preparation	Analysis of interests, not positions	Scope analysis, Considerations of cultural elements, motives and interests Analysis of persons on the opposite side of the negotiation	Typing of persons on the negotiating counterparty concentration on motifs
Methodology	Focus on interests, not positions Win-win	Systematic, rationally emotionally applied negotiation 6-phase model Win without the other person losing face	7 successful steps to negotiation success Critical negotiations Win
Objective	Consensual outcome, Fair exit	Winning without the negotiating partner losing face	Win
Internationality	No	Important recommendations for action for many countries	Global presence of the Schranner negotiation institute
Intercultural elements	No	Yes	No
Emotionality	No	Yes, but rational emotionality	Yes

Harvard concept recommends a precise preparation with the determination of the best possible alternative (BANTA, Best Alternative to a Negotiated Agreement). Schranner's concept, on the other hand, offers not only a negotiation preparation document, the script, but also a well-founded analysis of the motives and the roles (e.g. decision-maker).

In addition to practical relevance, intercultural issues are also described in international transactions in countries such as the United States of America, China, France, India or other countries. Although the model is aimed at business negotiations, other negotiations, e.g. political negotiations, negotiations amongst private individuals, negotiations on alimony, etc., can be carried out. Lastly, the A-6 concept is a self-contained construct built sequentially in eight steps. This means that after the first step is done, you can go to the second, third up to the sixth and last step (A-6). The following figure shows the six steps from analysis to respecting and following the agreement. After the detailed analysis, a selection of appropriate strategies and tactics will take place. The basis here is the script or manuscript, which is described in the context of this chapter. The strategies and tactics determine the reasoning and the structure of the negotiations. Once you have completed these steps, you can go to the actual trial. Here, the action radius is determined. Within the

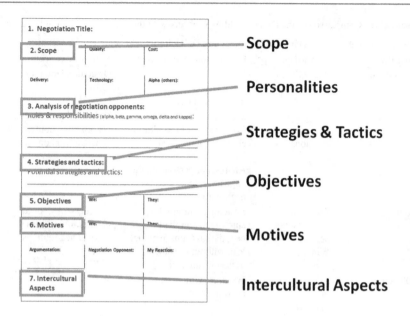

Fig. 23.2 The manuscript of the A-6 concept of Dr. Marc Helmol. (Source: Author's source)

strategy and argumentation, possible counterarguments of the other side and resistances were identified as well as tactics, in order to successfully break these resistances without leaving the negotiating partner the face. As a final step, the design of the results of the negotiations and the observance of the negotiations are of crucial importance. The script or manuscript in Fig. 23.2 plays a central role as a bargaining tool in the A-6 concept. The manuscript is the result of the individual steps, whereby the sequence is dynamic and flexible (not static) (Helmold, 2018). Dynamic in this context means to be very well prepared and to anticipate behavioural patterns of the other side. Dynamism in the negotiations also means reacting agile and flexible to the advances by the negotiating party. In addition to a systematic preparation and analysis, international specialties are at the centre of this model (Helmold, 2018). Similarly, in practice, applied and proven tools are integrated so that the application in practice quickly and well applied is possible.

23.5   Negotiation Personalities

23.5.1 Personalities

Traditional negotiation concepts often outline basic kinds of negotiators, and three have been identified. These types of negotiators are often outlined as soft or collaborative bargainers, hard or competitive bargainers and principled bargainers.

23.5.2 Soft Negotiator

Negotiators with a soft negotiator personality regard the process of negotiations as too close to competition, so they choose a gentle style of bargaining (Helmold et al., 2022). The offers they make are not in their best interests. They may also yield to others' demands and avoid confrontation, and they maintain good relations with fellow negotiators. Their perception of others is one of friendship, and their goal is agreement. They do not separate the people from the problem but are soft on both. They avoid contests of wills and insist on agreement, offering solutions, and are easily trusting others and changing their opinions (Helmold et al., 2022). Soft bargaining, on the other hand, recognizes the potential dangers hard bargaining styles have, particularly for the current and future relationship between the negotiating parties. According to Fisher and Ury, soft negotiators see the other side as friends, and instead of trying to reach victory at all costs, they aim at securing agreement by yielding to the other side and their demands if necessary. Cooperation becomes the leading principle, whereas hard negotiation is based on competition. The result of soft bargaining will often be agreements that are reached quickly but that are not necessarily wise ones, as both sides might fail to reach their legitimate interests in the attempt to be more accommodating than the other side (Fisher & Ury, 1981).

23.5.3 Hard Negotiator

Negotiators who use contentious and competitive strategies to influence are hard or competitive negotiators. This group utilizes phrases such as "this is my final offer" and "take it or leave it". They are direct, make threats, are distrustful of others, insist on their position and apply pressure to negotiate. They see others as adversaries, and their ultimate goal is victory. Additionally, they search for one single answer and insist you agree on it. They do not separate the people from the problem (as with soft bargainers), but they are hard on both the people involved and the problem. Hard bargaining uses all instruments at hand in the pursuit of one-sided advantage. Pressure, threats, bluffing, tricks, etc. are tactics applied in order to outsmart someone or to make him or her do something that is not in his or her interest. Hard bargaining is about pushing through one-sided interests, and it follows the competitive logic of zero-sum games in which one side's losses are the other side's gains (Fisher & Ury, 1981).

23.5.4 Principled Negotiator

Negotiation professionals who bargain this way seek usually integrative solutions and do so by sidestepping commitment to specific positions. They focus on the problem rather than the intentions, motives and needs of the people involved. They separate the people from the problem, explore interests, avoid bottom lines and reach results based on standards independent of personal will. They base their

Table 23.2 Situational negotiator type, SCHLAGFERTIG

Negotiation personality concept: schlagfertig		
S	Situational	Understanding situations for strategies like defence or offence
C	Circumstantial	Considering circumstances of own situation and opponent
H	Holistic	Considering the entire scope in negotiations
L	Logical	Using a structured and systematic way
A	Anticipative	Anticipating demands, strategies and tactics of opponent
G	Gainful	Looking for additional gains and value added
F	Facts based	Grounding negotiations on facts and not goodwill or threats
E	Engaging	Looking actively for negotiation outcomes
R	Reasonable	Making reasonable propositions to opponent
T	Timely	Structuring negotiations in a systematic and timely manner
I	Intercultural	Understanding intercultural specifics
G	Genial	Using the "schlagfertig attributes" for successful negotiations

Developed as part of A-6 concept by Dr. Marc Helmold

choices on objective criteria rather than power, pressure, self-interest or an arbitrary decisional procedure. These criteria may be drawn from moral standards, principles of fairness, professional standards and tradition (Helmold et al., 2022).

23.5.5 Situational Negotiator (Schlagfertig)

Practical examples and field research show that negotiations do not require a static personality or behaviour. Instead of using one of the three personalities, the A-6 negotiation concept by Dr. Marc Helmold uses the competency concept "schlagfertig", which includes several attributes a negotiator should have and apply in negotiations (Helmold et al., 2022). The competencies can be trained and will be outlined in Chap. 8 in detail. Negotiators must have the ability to act situational and circumstantial. Moreover, holistic analyses and logical thinking are key competencies for excellent negotiators (Helmold et al., 2022). Good bargainers need to anticipate situations and must be looking for alternatives or ways to add value in negotiations. That requires a facts-based preparation and execution as well as reasonably made propositions to the negotiation opponent. Time management and intercultural skills round this personality up in order to have the optimum level and most genial personality for negotiations (Helmold et al., 2022). Table 23.2 shows the description of the categories.

23.6   Roles and Responsibilities in Negotiations

Understanding roles and responsibilities of the negotiation opponent are fundamental elements in the preparation phase. Negotiations are determined and led by the negotiation leaders and certain influencers. Roles in negotiations are the alpha (Greek: ἄλφα), the beta (Greek: βῆτα), the gamma (Greek: γάμμα), the omega

Table 23.3 Roles and responsibilities in negotiations

Roles in negotiations		
Type	Greek translation	Description
Alpha	ἄλφα, Α, α	Decision-maker
Beta	βῆτα, Β, β	Influencer
Gamma	Γάμμα, Γ, γ	Co-worker, supporter
Omega	ὦ μέγα, Ω, ω	Critic
Delta	Δέλτα, Δ, δ	Guardian
Kappa	Κάππα, Κ, κ	Double agent

Source: Helmold et al. (2022)

Fig. 23.3   General Manager Dr. Marc Helmold and General Manager Mr. Ge

(Greek: ὦ μέγα), the delta (Greek: δέλτα) and the kappa (Greek: κάππα). Roles must be analysed before any negotiation and can be typologized into these six negotiation categories (Helmold et al., 2022). Table 23.3 summarizes the six categories of important and unimportant roles and responsibilities:

Figure 23.3 shows the General Managers of Alstom, Dr. Helmold, and KTK in China, Mr. Ge. Dr. Helmold negotiated amongst other elements and various frame contracts for Alstom with Mr. Ge.

23.7   Case Study: EU Negotiation Strategy for COVID-19 Vaccines

On 17 June 2021, the European Commission presented a European strategy to accelerate the development, manufacturing and deployment of vaccines against COVID-19. The EU Vaccines Strategy intends to ensure the production in Europe of qualitative, safe and efficacious vaccines and to secure swift access to them for Member States and their populations. Moreover, the strategy reflects the global solidarity effort and ensures equitable access to an affordable vaccine as early as possible. Joint action at EU level is the surest, quickest and most efficient way of achieving these objectives. No Member State on its own has the capacity to secure the investment in developing and producing a sufficient number of vaccines. It is only through swift and unified action by the EU and its Member States that sufficient and speedy supplies of a safe and effective vaccine can be ensured. A common strategy allows better hedging of bets, sharing of risks and pooling investments to achieve economies of scale, scope and speed. The Commission has signed two first contracts to allow the purchase of a vaccine, once proven safe and efficient, with AstraZeneca and Sanofi-GSK. Successful exploratory talks were concluded with Johnson & Johnson on 13 August, CureVac on 18 August, Moderna on 24 August and BioNTech on 9 September. All Member States have endorsed the approach set out by the Vaccines Strategy and signed up to an agreement for its implementation. As a result, all Member States are represented at the Steering Committee which discusses and reviews all aspects of the Advanced Purchase Agreement (APA) contracts before signature. The Committee appoints the members of the Joint Negotiation Team, which negotiates the APAs with the vaccine developers and reports to the Committee. All participants in these instances have been appointed by their governments and have signed declarations of absence of conflict of interest and confidentiality. Before the Advanced Purchase Agreement (APA) is negotiated, the negotiation team holds exploratory talks with the company to find out whether proceeding into detailed contractual negotiations is reasonable. If this is the case and a common understanding is reached on a terms sheet, a tender invitation is sent to the company, which then has to propose an offer. An APA is concluded when both sides have finalized the contractual work. This is discussed and agreed with the Steering Committee. The conclusion of an APA requires the approval of the Commission. If the APA provides for an obligation for the Member States to purchase vaccine doses (even if there might also be additional optional doses in the APA), Member States have 5 working days to notify if they wish to opt out. The contract is only signed if at least four Member States are ready to be bound by it. If the APA provides only for an option for Member States to purchase vaccine doses at a later date, the Commission can approve and sign the APA directly with the company concerned. Member States can decide later whether to exercise the option. It is the Member States that are responsible for purchasing the vaccines when they become available.

References

Abdel-Latif, A. (2015). Nicht verblüffen lassen. Schützen Sie sich vor den zehn dreckigsten Verhandlungsfallen. Abgerufen am 1.4.2018. https://www.focus.de/finanzen/experten/ adel_abdel-latif/nicht-bluffen-lassen-schuetzen-sie-sich-vor-den-zehn-dreckigsten-verhandlungsfallen_id_4772172.html.

Bauer-Jelinek, C. (2007). *Die geheimen Spielregeln der Macht und die Illusionen der Gutmenschen.* Ecowin Verlag.

Brost, M. (2017). Verhandlungen. Tipps für eine erfolgreiche Verhandlungsstrategie. Mehr fordern, als man will. Interview mit M. Schranner. In: Die Zeit. Abgerufen am 11.7.2018. https://www. zeit.de/2017/43/verhandlungen-politik-training-matthias-schranner.

Cambridge Dictionary (2018). *Definition: Negotiation.* Abgerufen am 15.3.2018. https://diction-ary.cambridge.org/de/worterbuch/englisch/negotiation.

Chia, H.-B., Egri, C., Ralston, D., Fu, P. P., Kuo, M. C., & Lee, C. (2007). Four tigers and a dragon: Values differences, similarities, and consensus. *Asia Pacific Journal of Management, S*, 24.

Dathe, T., & Helmold. (2018). *Erfolg im Chinageschäft. Handlungsempfehlungen für kleine und mittlere Unternehmen (KMU)*. Springer.

De Mooij, M., & Hofstede, G. (2010). The Hofstede model. *International Journal of Advertisin, 29*(1), 85–110.

Duden (2018). https://www.duden.de/rechtschreibung/Politik#Bedeutung2. Abgerufen am 15.5.2108.

Fetsch, F. R. (2006). *Verhandeln in Konflikten: Grundlagen – Theorie – Praxis* (German Edition). Verlag für Sozialwissenschaften.

Fisher, R., & Ury, W. (1981). *Getting to yes*. London: Penguin Group.

Geertz, C. (1973). *The interpretation of cultures: Selected essays by Clifford Geertz (1973-10-25)*. Basic Books Group.

Godeck, M. (2017). Die 10 wichtigsten Kennzahlen im Einkauf. In: Technik und Einkauf. Retrieved 1.5.2018. https://www.technik-einkauf.de/ratgeber/die-wichtigsten-kennzahlen-im-einkauf/.

Helmold, M. (2010). *Best-in-Class Lieferantenmanagement in der Automobilindustrie*. Shaker.

Helmold, M. (2018). Erfolgreiche Verhandlungen und Best-in-Class Empfehlungen für den Verhandlungsdurchbruch. Manuskript und Workshopunterlagen im Master- und MBA-Studium.

Helmold, M., & Terry, B. (2016). *Global sourcing and supply management excellence in China*. Springer.

Helmold, M., Dathe, T., & Hummel, F. (2022). *Best-in-class recommendations for breakthrough negotiations*. Springer.

Obrien, J. (2016). *Negotiations for procurement professionals* (2nd ed.). Kogan Page.

Polwin-Plass, L. (2016). Checklisten für den Vertrieb. Verhandlungsstrategie. 22.9.2016. In: Die Vertriebszeitung. Abgerufen am 20.3.2018. https://vertriebszeitung.de/verhandeln-im-grenzbereich-strategien-und-taktiken-im-vertrieb/.

Porter, M. E. (1985). *Competitive advantage. Creating and sustaining superior performance*. Free Press.

Püttier, C. H. and Schnierda, U. (2014). Das überzeugende Vorstellungsgespräch für Führungskräfte: Wie Sie Headhunter, Personalprofis und Top-Manager überzeugen. Campus Frankfurt.

Schranner, M. (2009). Verhandeln im Grenzbereich. Strategien und Taktiken für schwierige Fälle. 8. Auflage. Econ München.

Schranner, M. (2015). 7 Prinzipien für erfolgreiches Verhandeln. BME-Keynote Matthias Schranner gibt sieben Tipps für zielführende Verhandlungen. 15.1.2015. Abgerufen am 20.3.2018. https://www.bme.de/7-prinzipien-fuer-erfolgreiches-verhandeln-888/.

Statistisches Bundesamt (2018). Pressemitteilung Nr. 039 vom 08.02.2018: Deutsche Exporte im Jahr 2017: +6,3% zum Jahr 2016. Exporte und Importe erreichen neue Rekordwerte. Abgerufen am 15.3.2018. https://www.destatis.de/DE/PresseService/Presse/Pressemitteilungen/2018/02/PD18_039_51.html;jsessionid=86A76343A81D3E6B58E2A4A4716DC45E.InternetLive2.

The Telegraph. (2017). http://www.telegraph.co.uk.

Wilkes, K. (2016). Was bewegt Matthias Schranner? Zehn Millionen mehr, bitte! Die Zeit Online. 22.6.2016. Abgerufen am 17.5.2018. https://www.zeit.de/2016/22/matthias-schranner-verhandlungsfuehrer-regierung-geiselnahme.

24

The best ideas have to win.

Steve Jobs

24.1 Future Outlook of Marketing

Marketing, whether direct, digital or measured media, is increasingly fuelled by the power of technology, enabling marketers to realize multiple benefits in both marketing effectiveness and efficiency. Many marketers now find themselves working in more restrictive environments, faced with fewer resources and increased accountability. As such, many are focused on optimizing their return on marketing investment (ROMI) to improve marketing effectiveness, thereby increasing revenue, profit and market share, while maintaining overall marketing spend. These effectiveness objectives are typically a combination of short- and long-term goals, including branding, lead generation and customer relationship management (CRM), which are managed throughout the marketing process from development of strategic intent through campaign execution (Biegel, 2009). Changing consumer behaviour makes marketing effectiveness optimization increasingly challenging, as a result of the various and often unpredictable ways in which the consumer digests and reacts to media. This complexity is further compounded by a multiplicity of other factors:

- Media mix optimization: the allocation of resources across marketing channels, with special attention paid to combinations and sequencing of media selection.
- Product lifecycle compression: the rate at which products are introduced, launched, marketed and replaced.
- Privacy rules and regulations: laws and non-regulated "best practices" that must be applied to direct and digital marketing initiatives in order to protect consumer data and rights.
- Corporate governance: increased requirements for tracking and reporting, driven by internal demands for accountability and external legislation such as Sarbanes-Oxley in the United States.

© The Author(s), under exclusive license to Springer Nature Switzerland AG 2022   263
M. Helmold, *Performance Excellence in Marketing, Sales and Pricing*, Management
for Professionals, https://doi.org/10.1007/978-3-031-10097-0_24

- Resource constraints: heightened economic pressures have hindered the avail ability of internal resources, forcing management to effectively "do more" with the same or fewer resources (primarily staff).
- Globalization: marketing that was predominantly local in practice in the past has become global – facilitated by the Internet and subsequently the ability to inter act in real time – creating the need for standardized marketing messaging and content across geographies, suppliers and marketing channels.

Given these factors, marketers are looking to refine internal processes in order to gain better control, visibility and overall efficiency in marketing opera tions. By operationalizing the marketing process, companies can manage cost through waste reduction and staff optimization, improve speed to market through reduced cycle time and enhance targeting to support the shift from mass to one to-one marketing. These improvements free up resources that can be reinvested in revenue-generating activities, primarily customer acquisition and retention efforts.

24.2   Marketing Trends

24.2.1 Trend 1: Customer Behaviour-Centric Marketing and Sales Activities

A customer-centric way of doing business is focused on providing a positive cus tomer experience before and after the sale in order to drive repeat business, enhance customer loyalty and improve business growth. Customer-centric (also known as client-centric) is a business strategy that's based on putting your customer first and at the core of your business in order to provide a positive experience and build long term relationships.

24.2.2 Trend 2: Increased Importance of Influencers in Marketing

The influencer business has developed rapidly since the social media channel Instagram existed. What once started with moderation and fitness post has now developed into a real online marketing strategy. In this case, the influencers make paid advertising for products and companies and achieve good content thanks to their large reach. However, influencers with a smaller number of followers are also a cheap alternative for your marketing. As a rule, the followers of these so-called nano-influencers are particularly loyal and convinced of the products that are pre sented. So, it is definitely worth doing influencer marketing to increase your com pany's success.

24.2.3 Trend 3: Purpose as Success Factor

Every company already has a purpose, but not every company also uses it for advertising-related purposes. Perhaps you are trying to operate as sustainably as possible and have therefore committed yourself to ecology. You may also get involved socially and support projects that serve the common good – the building of a new hospital or kindergarten, for example – or you proceed in a strictly economic way and above all create jobs (Ried, 2021). For companies, purpose marketing consists of developing these already existing characteristics of your company into a clear, outwardly visible attitude – usually with the support of a specialized purpose agency. A simple example is a grocery store: if this is committed to sustainable management and advertises that only regionally grown food is sold there, this will attract a very specific customer base. In order to reach these people, however, the purpose of your company must first be known, and this is exactly why purpose marketing exists.

24.2.4 Trend 4: Marketing Will Become Green and More Ethical

Green marketing refers to efforts that in the production and marketing of products and services cause less harm to the environment. It is now difficult to open up to local or international markets and to gain competitive advantage over rivals. In this sense, it became necessary to meet the expectations of the consumers and to adapt to the changing world. Today, as environmental problems increase, the consumers' expectations from businesses have changed. Green consumers are generally defined as individuals who adopt environmentally friendly behaviours and/or buy green products among standard alternatives. It is important to create a good image as an environmentalist company in the consciousness of consumers and society, to be environmentalist from the production of the products to putting them on market and to improve recycling. In other words, the creation of the Green Marketing Mix (4P) enables the business process to reach the green goal. Green product refers to the process of environmentally friendly, quality and recycling-oriented processes in the emergence of the product. Green price refers to the expenditures in the manufacturing processes up to the presentation of the product that affect the purchasing behaviour of the consumer. Green distribution refers to the business activities such as logistics carried out required in delivering the product to the market with the least harm to nature. Green promotion is the introduction of a green product and the transfer of environmental information to consumers through the right connections in the field of green product in its corporate activities. Within this process, green strategic marketing is the planning and policy making process by including the green factor in the marketing strategies of the enterprises (Grimm & Malschinger, 2021). Ethical marketing is less of a marketing strategy and more of a philosophy that informs all marketing efforts. It seeks to promote honesty, fairness and responsibility in all advertising. Ethics is a notoriously difficult subject because everyone has subjective judgements about what is "right" and what is "wrong". For this reason, ethical marketing is not a hard and fast list of rules but a general set of guidelines to assist companies as they evaluate new marketing strategies.

24.2.5 Trend 5: Mobile: Authentic and Inclusive Marketing

The marketing function in the future becomes authentically inclusive. Brands reflect the change in our increasingly diverse society and win new customers with a focus on diversity, equality and integration.

24.2.6 Trend 6: Creating an Intelligent and Creative Engine

The new marketing will act as the driver for the "intelligent creative engine" of the enterprise. Unconventional, future-oriented strategies combine both the creative and the analytical skills of marketing talents and thus unleash new potential.

24.2.7 Trend 7: Customers Without Cookies

Picking up customers in a world without cookies leading, high-growth companies show how marketers are rethinking their first-party data strategies and preparing for the elimination of third-party cookies.

24.2.8 Trend 8: Customer-Centric Data Experience

Designing a customer-oriented data experience marketing wins consumers' trust both in handling customer data and in interacting with customers.

24.2.9 Trend 9: Hybrid and Social Customer Experience

Hybrid customer experience brands create dynamic, coherent worlds of experience in both the digital and physical spheres and take a holistic view of the customer when designing.

24.2.10 Trend 10: AI-Optimized Marketing and Advertising

AI-optimized customer service strategies for a real end-to-end customer experience including artificial intelligence and good customer service optimally support consumers throughout the entire customer journey (Fig. 24.1).

Fig. 24.1 Trends in marketing. (Source: Author's source)

24.3 Marketing 4.0

24.3.1 Introduction to Marketing 4.0

Marketing 4.0 includes a number of changes. It used to be vertical, exclusive and individual. Now, it is becoming increasingly horizontal, inclusive and social. In other words, before brands were targeting consumers, the relationship was just "I sell and you buy"; now brands are becoming "friends" of consumers and showing their true values (Kotler et al., 2017). The future of marketing is a cross-dimensional relationship between companies, brands and consumers (Helmold, 2020). The major change from Marketing 3.0 towards 4.0 is the orientation towards a behaviour-oriented and real-time marketing strategy (see Fig. 24.2). With globalization, new technologies and greater ease in communication, enterprises overcome marketing obstacles and borders; be it demographic or geographical, one can unite all thoughts, because everyone can be connected and hence work with everyone. Finally, marketing has also become more social because if before the process of buying it was an individual thing, today the opinion of those in the process is taken

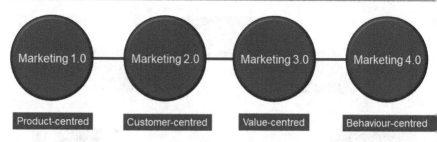

Fig. 24.2   Marketing 4.0 concept. (Source: Author's source)

into account; consumers think ethical brands and products, and that makes marketing a social process. In a society shaped by connection, marketing and its professionals are faced with paradoxes that bring good fruits and challenges at the
same time.

24.3.2 Online Versus Offline

The first question in marketing of the future deals with how customers interact,
whether online or offline. The big paradox is that one cannot function without the
other. Enterprises must therefore understand how to combine these two forms of
interaction.

24.3.3 Informed Versus Distracted Customers

With access to information, customers have gained a lot more knowledge about
brands and products; they are better informed. At the same time, too much information tends to make shoppers buy more popular products.

24.3.4 Negative Versus Positive Defence

With greater connectivity, positive manifestations related to the brand grow, but the
negative manifestations also increase. That's not necessarily bad, because a balance
in the manifestations keeps the discussion about the company going.

24.3.5 Digital Humanization of Marketing Tools

Since we know trends and models, we need to apply Marketing 4.0 in practice, and
that's what we're going to deal with now. Nowadays, however, marketing needs to
develop the human side of brands so that they can build connections and allow customers to identify with them. By developing this first feature and adapting it to the
tools that will follow, your company's marketing is well on its way to becoming 4.0.

4.3.6 Digital Subcultures: Netizens

The latest trend in terms of marketing changes are the subcultures that act as brand agents and support brand representation. These groups are the young, the women and the netizens. While young people adapt to innovations and define trends very quickly, women function as information gatherers, researchers and holistic buyers as they evaluate various aspects before buying. Despite the strange name, the "netizens" can be defined as "citizens of the Internet". They will communicate with other internet users and disseminate information.

4.3.7 Implementing Content Marketing Tools

Content marketing is the format that many companies like to adopt when it comes to advertising. The big question is, why only disclose the phrase of my worth when can also advertise content that will be useful to consumers? The dissemination of content is therefore the new big trend in marketing, and this process consists of eight steps:

1. Goal setting: You need to define what you want to achieve with the campaign and what your growth and development goals are.
2. Public mapping: Understand what your audience is and what kind of person your customer is, and know what their wants are.
3. Content design and planning: Define the main subject of the content, the topics to be covered, the schedule for publishing and the formats to be used.
4. Content creation: Identify who will create the content and when to do so. Create schedules for production.
5. Distribution of content: When you are done with the content, you need to select the channels that will be used for the publication. Among other things, paid channels can be used for this.
6. Extending content: Broadcast your content and expand its breadth so you can build a conversation with consumers and develop that relationship further.
7. Content marketing assessment: Use metrics to assess the effectiveness of your content marketing and determine whether your goals have been achieved.
8. Content marketing improvement: With campaign feedback, it's time to make improvements and learn how to improve on what's already achieved, whether it's new topics, new formats or new sales channels.

By following these steps, you can run a content marketing process in which you track all the steps and thus the likelihood of success of the campaigns.

24.3.8 Engagement Marketing

In order for consumers to reach the excuse phase and become brand ambassadors they have to get involved with the brand, as creating a connection will make th business-customer relationship much closer. Marketing activities will focus o using applications to improve customers' digital experience. Additionally, market ing tools will correspond to the existence of a social CRM, in which a communica tion channel is opened between the two sides and the customers can come int direct contact with the company. Finally, enterprises will concentrate on gamifica tion, in which the consumer receives rewards through their relationship wit the brand.

24.4   Case Study: VR for BMW Customer Experience

BMW is not only heralding a new era of driving pleasure with the BMW iX but i also completely rethinking vehicle development. Traditional engineering tools ar no longer adequate for developing the technological flagship. For that reason, BMW is the first manufacturer in the world to use technology from the gaming industry Since 2015, BMW has been collaborating with video game developer Epic Games A mixed reality system, developed using components from the computer gam industry, is used. This saves a lot of time and effort, particularly in the early stage of development. It is based on Epic Games' Unreal Engine technology, which als powers Fortnite and the racing simulator Assetto Corsa Competizione. Unlike con ventional engineering tools, gaming technologies have such functions as virtua reality and the ability for users to interact. The BMW iX is the first car to have bee developed at BMW using gaming technology. With the help of mixed reality, it i not only possible to quickly visualize vehicle functions and new interior concepts but these tools also give developers a totally new level of flexibility (BMW, 2021) The ability to present vehicle functions and new interior concepts extremely quickly by means of these visual experiences in the virtual reality space opens up variou new avenues – for example, simulation of journeys through cities. Here, it is possi ble to test aspects including visibility over the area around the car and to check how different viewing angles and seating positions affect the view of a display on a screen or how difficult it is to reach. This gives the development engineers the impression of experiencing a real-life road situation inside an actual car.

References

Biegel, B. (2009). The current view and outlook for the future of marketing automation. *Journal o Direct, Data and Digital Marketing Practice, 10*, 201–213.

BMW. (2021). *Innovation and development. A new take on vehicle development.* Retrievec 12.12.2021. https://www.bmw.com/en/events/nextgen/global-collaboration.html.

Grimm, A., & Malschinger, A. (2021). *Green marketing 4.0. Ein Marketing-Guide für Green Davids und Greening Goliaths.* Springer.

Helmold, M. (2020). *Total revenue management (TRM) case studies, best practices and industry insights*. Springer.

Kotler, P., Kartajaya, H., & Setiawan, A. (2017). *Marketing 4.0: Moving from traditional to digital*. Wiley.

Ried, K. (2021). Deloitte-Studie: Die 7 wichtigsten Marketingtrends für 2022. Retrieved 12.12.2021. https://www.wuv.de/wuvplus/die_7_wichtigsten_marketingtrends_fuer_2022.

Top Digital Marketing Trends for 2019 (Marketing Matters) (English Edition) Kindle Ausgabe. New York: Eternal spiral books.

Englisch Ausgabe von Joan Mullally (Autor), Thomas Michaels (Autor), Martin Warner (Autor) Format: Kindle Ausgabe. Teil von: Marketing Matters (32 Bücher).

CPSIA information can be obtained
at www.ICGtesting.com
Printed in the USA
LVHW080220110922
728013LV00004B/61